Migrant Women

Cross-Cultural Perspectives on Women
General Editors: Shirley Ardener and Jackie Waldren
for The Centre for Cross-Cultural Research on Women, Oxford

Vol. 1:   *Persons and Power of Women in Diverse Cultures*
     Edited by Shirley Ardener

Vol. 2:   *Dress and Gender: Making and Meaning*
     Edited by Ruth Barnes and Joanne B. Eicher

Vol. 3:   *The Anthropology of Breast-Feeding: Natural Law or Social Construct*
     Edited by Vanessa A. Maher

Vol. 4:   *Defining Females*
     Edited by Shirley Ardener

Vol. 5:   *Women and Space*
     Edited by Shirley Ardener

Vol. 6:   *Servants and Gentlewomen to the Golden Land: The Emigration of
     Single Women to South Africa, 1820–1939*
      Cecillie Swaisland

Vol. 7:   *Migrant Women*
     Edited by Gina Buijs

Vol. 8:   *Carved Flesh/Cast Selves: Gendered Symbols and Social Practices*
     Edited by Vigdis Broch-Due, Ingrid Rudie and Tony Bleie

Vol. 9:   *Bilingual Women: Anthropological Approaches to Second °Language
     Use*
     Edited by Pauline Burton, Ketaki Kushari Dyson and Shirley Ardener

Vol. 10: Gender, Drink and Drugs
     Edited by Maryon MacDonald

Vol. 11: Women and Missions, Past and Present
     Edited by Fiona Bowie, Deborah Kirkwood and Shirley Ardener

Vol. 12: Women in Muslim Communities: Religious Belief and Social Realities
     Edited by Camillia Fawzi El-Solh and Judy Mabro

Vol. 13: Women and Property, Women as Property
     Edited by Renée Hirschon

Migrant Women

Crossing Boundaries and Changing Identities

Edited by
Gina Buijs

BERG
Oxford • Washington, D.C.

First published in 1993 by
Berg
Editorial offices:
150 Cowley Road, Oxford, OX4 1JJ, UK
22883 Quicksilver Drive, Dulles, VA 20166, USA

Reprinted in 1996

Berg is the imprint of Oxford International Publishers Ltd.

Library of Congress Cataloging-in-Publication Data
Migrant women : crossing boundaries and changing identities / edited by
  Gina Buijs.
      p. cm. — (Cross-cultural perspectives on women)
    Includes bibliographical references and index.
    ISBN 0–85496–729–X. — ISBN 0–85496–869–5 (pbk)
      1. Women immigrants—Cross-cultural studies. 2. Women
refugees—Cross-cultural studies. 3. Gender identity—Cross-cultural
studies. I. Buijs, Gina. II. Series.
HQ1154.M473   1993
305.42—dc20   92–15999
                                                                    CIP

British Library Cataloguing-in-Publication Data
A CIP catalogue record for this book is available from the British Library

ISBN 0 85496 869 5

Printed in the United Kingdom by WBC Book Manufacturers, Bridgend,
Mid Glamorgan.

Contents

Acknowledgements   vii

1. Introduction
Gina Buijs   1

> Gender as a Dynamic Focus 1, The Experience of Exile 2,
> Space and Place 3, Gender Specificity: The Different
> Experiences of Female and Male Migrants 4, Violence
> Against Women 6, Changes in the Role and Status of
> Women as Mothers and Educators 8, Maintaining and
> Recreating Cultural Forms from the Home Society 10,
> Marriage in a New Setting 12, Women Migrating Without
> Men 13, Conclusion 18, References 19

2. The Gendered Dynamics of Quechua Colonisation: Relations of Centre and Periphery in Peru
Sarah Lund Skar   21

> Colonisation 21, Women and Mobility 25, Marriage and Kin
> Relationships 27, References 33

3. Reconstructing Life: Chilean Refugee Women and the Dilemmas of Exile
Marita Eastmond   35

> Chilean Political Exile 37, The Dilemmas of Exile:
> Liminality and Ambiguity 39, Exile and Identity 39,
> Preserving the Past, Creating a Heritage 40, Life and Death
> as Key Symbols 43, Life in the Barrio 45, Life an Work in
> Silicon Valley 46, The Changing Lives of Men and Women
> in Exile 48, 'Return to Life': The Dilemmas of Continuity
> and Change 50, References 52

4. Defining Gender in a Second Exile: Palestinian Women in West Berlin
Dima Abdulrahim   55

> Historical Background of the Palestinian Exiles 56, Political
> Asylum in West Berlin Until the Late 1980s 58, Economic
> Conditions of Asylum and the Definition of Gender
> Relations 63, Defining Gender in Exile 66, Women's Roles in
> Marriage and Divorce 72, Conclusion 76, References 81

5. **Patterns of Adaptation: Somali and Bangladeshi Women in Britain**
   Hazel Summerfield   83
   Similarities 83, Somali Immigration History 89, Work
   Patterns 91, Linguistic Skills 93, Economic Performance 94,
   Politicisation 94, Conclusion 98, References 98

6. **Identities Constructed and Reconstructed: Representations of Asian Women in Britain**
   Parminder Bhachu   99
   Introduction 99, Asian Women's Economic Activity: Past
   and Present 101, The Current Labour Market Profile 103,
   Commoditised Consumption and Cultural Patterns 105,
   Appropriation and Transformation of British Asian Identities
   and Cultures 108, Conclusion 112, References 113

7. **International and Internal Migration: The Changing Identity of Catholic and Hindu Women in Goa**
   Stella Mascarenhas-Keyes   119
   Introduction 119, Background 121, International
   Migration 124, Internal Migration 126, The Effect of
   Migration on Catholic and Hindu Women 127,
   Conclusion 141, References 141

8. **Vietnamese Refugees in Hong Kong: Behaviour and Control**
   Linda Hitchcox   145
   Introduction 145, Migration from Vietnam Since 1975 148,
   The Journey 151, The Detention Centres of Hong Kong 154,
   Insecurity and Protection in the Camps 154, Official
   Perceptions of Asylum Seekers and the Feminine Stereotype
   157, Conclusion 159, References 160

9. **Female Migration and Social Mobility: British Female Domestic Servants to South Africa – 1860–1914**
   Cecillie Swaisland   161
   References 177

10. **Women Alone: Migrants from Transkei Employed in Rural Natal**
   Gina Buijs   179
   Conclusion 192, References 194

Notes on Contributors   195

Index   197

Acknowledgements

Most of the chapters in this book had their origins in seminar papers delivered at the Oxford Womens Series seminars held in the Hilary Term of 1990 under the auspices of the Centre for Cross-Cultural Research on Women, at Queen Elizabeth House, Oxford, and organised by Helen Callaway. I should like to thank Shirley Ardener and Helen Callaway, General Editors of the series, for their initial suggestion of combining the papers into a book and for their help and encouragement thereafter. I have benefited from discussions with my colleagues in the Department of Anthropology at Rhodes University: Michael Whisson, Chris de Wet, Robin Palmer and Julia Segar, and also Donal Lowry. Most of all, I would like to thank the contributors for their patience and forebearance in coping with the demands of a long distance editor. Ann Hayward has been a very helpful word processing assistant.

Gina Buijs
Department of Anthropology
Rhodes University, Grahamstown

1

Introduction

Gina Buijs

Population movements on a grand scale have become a prominent feature of contemporary society, but there have been as yet relatively few attempts to look beneath the surface of the mass movements of people and to disentangle the specific experiences of women. Morokvasic (1983) and others note that until the mid-1970s women were invisible in studies of migrancy, and when they did emerge tended to do so within the category of dependants of men.

The contributors to this book are concerned with the dynamics of change in gender relations which have been brought about by migrancy, and several chapters have been written by women social scientists who are themselves migrants. The different chapters examine the varied and complex responses of women to migration; whether they were forced by political circumstances, as in the case of refugees, or driven by the need to escape poverty and destitution, as happened with most of the economic migrants. The boundaries of the title are at once geographic, moral and metaphysical. J.B. Jackson notes (1975: 20) that the original meaning of boundary is 'that which binds, which holds together', and that, traditionally, boundaries, whenever ritually established, had the power to regulate and consecrate relationships between people.

Gender as a Dynamic Focus

The Quechua women of Matapuquio, Peru, whom Skar discusses in her chapter, are an example of how gender serves as the dynamic focus in articulating relations between the highland centre and the lowland periphery in Peru. The women from the village of Matapuquio are oscillating migrants in the sense that their journeys with their husbands to the city or the jungle, the periphery of their world, always involve a return sooner or later to the village, the centre of life. Skar sees these women as dynamic agents, binding the dispersed male *mit-*

1

maqkuna or colonisers with the mother community in the highlands. Women in Peruvian Indian society have gender-specific rights and obligations which are part of the social code of morality. Control over land and its ownership in highland Peru is crucial since the Quechua are subsistence agriculturalists. The sending of agricultural produce by the women to their menfolk in the city and the jungle is a symbolic exchange which serves to bind the absent *mitmaqkuna* with their lands and family in the village. Skar notes that these women are 'the constant figures in an equation characterized by the movement of men and women out to the periphery and back.' Matapuquio men view their relations with village women with a respect which they do not feel towards city women.

The Experience of Exile

Many of the women whose experiences are discussed in this book were forcibly driven from their homes but hoped to retain, in their place of refuge, the essentials of the culture and lifestyles which were theirs at home, and they looked forward to their return to their countries of origin at some future date. However, the exigencies of being migrants, and sometimes refugees, forced them to examine their preconceptions and to adopt both social and economic roles, which would have been rejected at home. This remaking of self was often a traumatic experience that was exacerbated by the necessity of adjustment in their relationships with their husbands and other menfolk, sons, brothers and fathers. As Eastmond points out: 'The commonality of the refugee experience may be seen to lie in the forced uprooting from familiar patterns of everyday life, involving multiple loss and a struggle to recover continuity and control.'

For most of the women whose experiences are recalled in this book, the move to another country was not optional. Many were political refugees (Eastmond, Hitchcox, Abdulrahim) who had been victims of torture and repression in their native lands, or economic migrants whose position, whether as mothers, widows, wives or single women, had brought them to virtual destitution (Buijs, Swaisland). The apparent exceptions are the Asian migrants discussed by Bhachu and Mascarenhas-Keyes. However, even the East African Sikhs arrived in Britain originally as a result of growing hostility to their entrepreneurial activities on the part of governments and citizens throughout East Africa.

Space and Place

Among others, Anwar (1979) has written of the 'myth of return' existing among Pakistani migrants in the United Kingdom, and part of the process of crossing physical and metaphysical boundaries for migrants and refugees is an investment in an idealised perception of the society of origin or homeland. Thus Eastmond notes that, in exile in the United States, Chile and Chilean culture became a symbol of the losses suffered by the political refugees. Poetry and music and song contributed towards the construction of a collective identity.

Exile necessarily involved change, but for the Chileans change was a deep moral dilemma as integration into United States society was associated with betrayal of political commitment and of those left behind. In this way the dichotomy of time and space infuses the exile experience. Eastmond mentions that attempts to reconstruct what is familiar are a well-known psychological means of coping with the forced separation and loss experienced by refugees. Wollheim (1986: 62) notes that iconic mental states have an important part to play in the way we lead our lives.[1] They are crucial to the way in which the past exercises an influence over the present, and we draw upon them when, in the present, we try to predict or anticipate or control the future.

In the world of the female exile or migrant, as in the Proustian world, it will be not God, but simply the past which confers on the present its authentic existence. As Poulet notes: 'it is the already lived that saves the living. If familiar places are sometimes able to leave us, they are also able to come back to our notice, and, to our great comfort, to retake their original place. Thus one can see that places behave exactly like past moments, like memories. They go away, they return' [My translation]. (1983: 163).

Connerton (1989: 22) writes: 'our past history is an important source of our conception of ourselves; our self-knowledge, our conception of our own character and potentialities, is to a large extent determined by the way in which we view our own past actions.' What is important about the kinds of memories and recollections of the past and country left behind retained by migrants and refugees is that, as Connerton says, the kind of association that makes possible retention in the memory is not so much one of resemblance or contiguity as rather a com-

---

1. Iconic mental states are complex in character, incorporating different sense modalities: a certain kind of memory which is event memory, dreams and phantasy (Wollheim 1986: 63).

munity of interests and thoughts.' It is not because thoughts are similar that we can evoke them; it is rather because the same group is interested in those memories, and is able to evoke them, that they are assembled together in our minds' (1989: 37).

Gender Specificity: The Different Experiences of Female and Male Migrants

For Chilean refugees, exile emerged out of a political crisis which involved personal crises in the lives of individuals. Eastmond notes that socio-cultural change in conditions of forced migration is both more complex and more ambiguous than is assumed in linear models of 'refugee adaptation'. Although return and reintegration into the host society is part of the ideology of exile, it is far from assured. Exile is thus open-ended, generating increasing dilemmas and uncertainties as it is prolonged.

The role of Chilean women refugees in creating a sense of exile in the United States was essentially one of support to their menfolk. The Chilean refugees were mostly working class, used to a social life centred around the barrio or neighbourhood, but in the United States they settled in the heart of the electronics industry in California which forced restructuring of social relations.

Entering the job market in the United States meant acquiring new skills for Chilean women, not only in electronics but in their new language, in driving a car as well as earning an income. These skills increased the women's self confidence and domestic authority. Gender relations between men and women altered, as did role expectations; lives and identities became more individualised. After a decade or more of exile the possibility of return to Chile was, for these women, no longer the imperative it had been when they had first arrived in the 'belly of the beast' as they characterised the United States. In contrast, Chilean men had more difficulty adapting to the new setting; lacking trade unions and political activity, their lives had lost a vital dimension. In addition, the long-term psychological effects of torture often meant that the exiled men were unable to resolve the problems of the past in order to forge a new identity. Over the years the children of Chilean exiles became assimilated and many no longer wished to leave the United States. Their mothers were able to reconcile themselves to a continued stay if this meant being close to children and grandchildren.

Colson notes (1991: 9) that 'women refugees and other women migrants appear to show greater resilience and adaptability than do men', and it has been suggested that this is because they have the responsibility for maintaining household routines which provide them with occupation, and also that they are less conscious of status deprivation associated with the failure to find positions comparable to those they left.

Not all exiles, however, were as successful in their new lives as the Chilean women. Abdulrahim argues that for Palestinian women refugees in West Berlin social relationships were conditioned by overall historical circumstances of power, gender and class. Her analysis suggests that assumptions that change leads towards more egalitarian relationships as a result of Westernisation must be treated with caution.

The conditions under which refugees from Palestine were allowed to apply for asylum in Berlin effectively excluded them from the labour market while meeting their basic domestic needs through a system of cash and other benefits: conditions which resulted in the social and economic marginality of the Palestinian women being legally sanctioned. Phizacklea notes that migrant women in general in Europe are 'confined to certain sectors of the labour market because they are women, racial discrimination and/or legal controls intervene to ensure their subordination to men' (1983: 2). Male household heads lost their role of provider for the family and their continual presence in the home restricted the movement of unmarried girls, as well as the opportunity of wives to visit other women. The domestic arena became a means, in West Berlin if not in the camps in Lebanon, to increase control over women and to enhance the ideology of gender relations.

An important point, which Abdulrahim makes, is that norms which regulated the behaviour of women were turned into a mechanism to maintain group distinctiveness and separateness. The category 'woman' determined and defined exclusive boundaries. It was thus with the accommodation provided for the refugees in Berlin, which did not allow a rigid distinction between private and public domains (for instance, bathrooms had to be shared between families). Arabic-speaking households divided up the accommodation in space and time so that kitchens were defined as exclusively female domains and use of showers was separated into a time for women and a time for men. Courtyards were also deemed female-only areas at certain times of the day so that women could meet there.

The supposedly transient and temporary nature of the refugees' stay in West Berlin, where they were continually faced with possible imminent deportation, encouraged the community to distinguish and separate itself from the outside world. Even when, in 1989, Palestinians were granted residence permits in Berlin and were thus liable for compulsory education and eligible to seek employment, parental opposition to young women working outside the home continued. Since most Palestinian women, like the men, were unskilled, they could only occupy menial and badly-paid jobs which did not lead to an improvement in their domestic situations. Colson (1991:10) notes that men and women appear to find different kinds of situations particularly stressful and respond with different kinds of physical symptoms. Men appeared more vulnerable to economic stress and to the strain of trying to gain or hold social status when they lacked the required resources, while women were strongly affected by stress linked to family events which were associated with the burden they bore for managing family relationships and domestic affairs.

The constraints imposed by the host society may well be the major factor influencing the adaptation of migrant women to their new surroundings. Summerfield reveals that Somali migrant women in London were to a large extent able to become independent of their seamen husbands as they found employment as hospital cleaners and factory workers, occupations which gave them immediate contact with the white community. These women were able to rely on each other for friendship and companionship and to set up systems of initiation and introduction for newcomer Somali women which later formed the basis for formal women's groups.

By contrast the near neighbours of the Somali women, Bangladeshi immigrants to Tower Hamlets, were circumscribed by their lack of formal education and their inability to speak English. These factors meant that Bangladeshi women spent their lives within the confines of their homes where, if they did have work, it was piecework, machining garments. Even simple chores such as household shopping were often carried out by menfolk. For Bangladeshi women, unlike Somalis, divorce or separation were rarely realistic alternatives to unhappy marriages, as a divorced or separated wife would be ostracised by her community and culturally unable to ensure her economic survival.

Violence Against Women

Women's vulnerability and ways of protecting themselves in their new environment differ from men's experience of and reaction to violence. While men may be subject to racist attacks, they are rarely subject to assaults by women.

Abdulrahim concludes that there existed no real alternative to the family and community for Palestinian women in West Berlin – only isolation and marginalisation. A few Palestinian girls rebelled against the strict moral code imposed on them by their parents and indulged in an illicit social life with school friends. Although these social activities did not involve sexual relationships, the girls felt guilty and occasionally tension escalated into violent family confrontations. In a few cases the girls left home and took refuge in women's centres, although most soon returned to their families.

Summerfield draws attention to the fact that while both sets of migrants came from the middle income brackets of their home communities, the Bangladeshis were mainly small landholders while the Somalis were nomads. The first Somali migrant women to arrive in the United Kingdom had often had jobs in Aden or considerable domestic responsibility in Somalia. The conditions prevailing in the host countries did not always circumscribe the lives of migrant or refugee women as much as did their relationships with their male kin. Both the Somali and the Bangladeshi women living in Tower Hamlets were Muslim, but the circumstances of their lives in the London borough were quite different.

Both Bangladeshi and Somali women were subject to domestic violence. Somali women undergo circumcision and are ritually beaten by their husbands on their wedding night. Although the Bangladeshi marriage contract sometimes includes a promise by the husband not to 'torture' his wife, this refers only to a very severe beating. While Somali women in Tower Hamlets are able to leave a violent husband and to receive support from their own kin, such an option is not available to Bangladeshi women. Summerfield suggests that the positive adaptability of Somali women and their better mental health *vis-à-vis* their Bangladeshi counterparts springs from their relative independence.

Henrietta Moore has noted in her study *Anthropology and Feminism* that 'gender relations and in particular conflict between men and women are central to any understanding...of how and why women experience changing social and economic pressures differently from men'(1988: 95). Hitchcox shows that for Vietnamese women in detention centres in Hong Kong a feminine stereotype of helplessness and dependency, while according with administrative objectives, was likely to encourage male residents to take advantage of their physical weakness and vulnerability.

The circumstances prevailing in the detention centres encouraged from the women these stereotypical feminine responses which incorporated idealised virtues of Vietnamese females. Hitchcox reminds us that in Vietnam, however, this idealised model co-exists with other histories which show women as war leaders, critics, poets and satirists. While early Vietnamese history records women in positions of political and military authority, from the fifteenth century onwards their overall subordination to men was conspicuous, both in terms of lineage and authority. On the other hand, there were fewer restrictions on women in Vietnam than in China; Vietnamese women were legally equal to men in property inheritance and, under the French, education was open to them. Continuing warfare over a long period has meant that women have frequently been left in charge of economic matters and the home.

Like Vietnamese men, female Vietnamese refugees suffered severe hardships through prolonged imprisonment and persecution in their native country. They risked their lives to escape, as did men, by undertaking long journeys in often unseaworthy craft across the South China Sea to Hong Kong. (It is such journeys that have given the name of 'boat people' to these refugees.) Once they arrived in the camps in Hong Kong the women found themselves subject to an authoritarian regime which looked favourably on passivity and compliance as female attributes. Conversely, the want of work for Vietnamese men in the camps and their inability to be responsible for their families led to an increase in violence directed against women, arising from the men's sense of powerlessness and lack of what they assumed to be their male roles. Hitchcox notes that Vietnamese society is by custom patriarchal, deeply influenced by Confucian principles which make women subject to the authority of their husbands, fathers, sons.

One of the few ways in which men could gain power in the camps was to join criminal gangs, whose members were often prison inmates in Vietnam. Gang members threatened women and one of the ways in which a single woman could guard herself was to acquire the protection of a male resident. In circumstances of extreme poverty and overcrowding, prostitution or theft might become the only way a woman could make a little money.

Changes in the Role and Status of Women as Mothers and Educators

A growing literature refers to the question of whether migration leads to a loss or gain in the status of women as a result of changes in the distribution of power within the family, and the answers vary according to the immigrant context and cultural background. In some situations new economic and social responsibilities have been the basis for a woman's increasing importance within the family. In others, her role in the family has been undermined, especially for non-working women, isolated from an extended family network, who find themselves dependent on their children. This is particularly so if, like Palestinian women in Berlin and Bangladeshi wives in London, they themselves do not know the language of the host country.

Abdulrahim notes that Palestinian girls in West Berlin sometimes turned to schoolwork to compensate for a lack of the social activities which were permitted to their brothers. Although Palestinian fathers might say that daughters did not need an education since they would marry, she observed that a number of teenage girls were used as interpreters and intermediaries with the host society. Generational conflict between Palestinian parents and children in West Berlin was also gender-determined conflict. Palestinian youths were not subject to the same control as their sisters and did not have to conform to the image of an 'ideal' Arab as girls did. The category 'woman' determined and defined exclusive boundaries.

However, for East African Sikh women in London an improved education has, as Bhachu shows, enhanced their ability to find well-paid jobs and, similarly, educated husbands. Good salaries are spent building up dowries, over the contents of which they assume greater control than in the past. This is associated with a shift from extended family households to nuclear family households and an emphasis on the married couple, rather than the kin group. Successful migration has meant, in some instances, a striving by husbands and wives to improve the status of their children through improvement in educational qualifications.

Mascarenhas-Keyes analyses migration patterns both within and outside Goa in terms of changes in the identity of Catholic and Hindu women, especially married women. The Portuguese rule of Goa for several centuries until 1961 resulted in both economic and socio-cultural changes in the direction of Westernisation. These changes affected Catholic more than Hindu women and among the Catholics led to an emphasis on bourgeois values and especially on education. Increasing job opportunities for those Goans with some education, both in India and overseas, led to substantial migration, most spectacularly to the Gulf states and elsewhere in the Middle East where large sums of money could be earned and remitted. In the case of Catholic Goans it has been largely men who have migrated, with wives joining husbands for short periods or holidays.

The level of associational migration (wives accompanying their husbands) has been low in the case of Goan Catholic women because of the tremendous focus both husband and wife place on the education of their children. Mascarenhas-Keyes has dubbed this focus the concept of 'progressive motherhood'. Catholic Goan women see themselves as having not only reproductive and nurturing functions but also responsibility for the education of children; this includes skills and attributes such as familiarity with English, the ability to deal with teachers, supervise homework and to make effective use of psychological techniques to sustain their children's interest and diligence in school work. Good school performance reinforces the mother's concept of herself as 'progressive' and husbands, teachers and peers evaluate her performance critically. Hindu women are less likely to have international migrant husbands or to be able to support their children educationally.

Maintaining and Recreating Cultural Forms from the Home Society

Recent writers on migrant women insist that careful attention must be paid to the cultures of the societies of origin and to the way in which the status and roles of women are defined in them (Simon and Brettell 1986; Phizacklea 1983; Morokvasic 1983). It is important to distinguish between status and roles at the level of ideology and status and roles in practice as the two do not always coincide, for change in the context of the roles of women may also mean improved status. Bhachu shows the way in which East African Sikhs in London have altered the content of the marriage dowry bestowed on their daughters without altering its overall structure. The dowry here consists of clothes, china and high status consumer items such as a food processor, meant for the sole use of the bride and not cash or items for the use of the couple. As the young women themselves are now using their own earnings to build up their dowries they assume greater control over the contents than in the past, meaning that they can choose items and add to basic ones. However, change for immigrant women is neither simple nor unidirectional. Bhachu makes the point that certain cultural forms which Westerners might suppose to be oppressive, such as the dowry system and even arranged marriages can be 'liberating' for the women involved. She argues that women can be empowered through their experiences within their communities and with 'ethnic' cultural forms, even though these are presented by outside agencies as pathological and oppressive. She refers to the *transformative* powers of Asian women in generating and manufacturing their cultural systems (1985).

East African Sikh women move freely around London and are not subject to the same restrictions as most Muslim women. Many spend considerable time in religious activities in the company of other women. Bhachu notes that this ability to move around freely is a consequence of the expansion of their contacts as a result of employment. Independence and earning power make these women central figures in the gift exchanges which are associated with weddings, especially earning brides who contribute to their own dowries.

The earning capacity of East African Asian women is one of the most important factors influencing the escalation of the dowry system in Britain. Dowries provided exclusively from the parents' incomes to non-earning brides contain only the basic twenty-one items and none of the highly esteemed luxury goods. While the components of the dowry into which working brides inject their capital have not changed, they have been able to improve both the quality and quantity. Wealth has thus been translated in a classical manner and not, for instance, into cash for a deposit on a home. The East African Sikh women's acquisition of economic power and wealth has been channelled into areas over which they have the greatest control and from which they enjoy the greatest benefit. They can do this because before marriage few demands are made on their earning capacity.

Bhachu concludes that independent wage labour has a strong impact on both the negotiation of power within the domestic sphere and on traditional patterns. Asian women in Britain have acquired greater control over cash than they ever had in the past, whether in India or East Africa. She feels that the double or triple subordination model of analysis often used in the study of black and Asian women implies that the cultural values of these women are themselves oppressive to those who hold them. Triple oppression is understood here as the status of one subordinated by class, gender and, as a migrant, minority group member. She therefore suggests that there is a lack of understanding of the cultural construct from the perspective of the Asian or black woman herself because the debate has been focused too much on what seem, from an ethnocentric perspective, to be static and unchanging traditions. What is overlooked, Bhachu says, is that Asian women may actually choose to accept the traditional forms of the societies to which they belong.

By looking at the migrant women's status from their vantage point we come to understand that conditions an outside observer might classify as oppressive, do not always appear that way to the women themselves, (Simon and Brettell 1986). Rather than dismiss these attitudes as 'false consciousness' we should try to uncover the complex and subtle shades of meaning and perceptions with which migrant women view the world.

Some, but not all the links with the society of origin may be viewed in a positive light by women migrants. Palestinian women in West Berlin, in an effort to create boundaries with the surrounding German society, made and baked their own bread, for which traditional ingredients were hard to come by and which took up considerable time. They did so to avoid having to eat German bread, which they considered inferior.

Dress may also denote separateness from the host society. Asian women in Britain typically wear clothing representative of the areas their families originally came from in the subcontinent. Such clothing makes a statement of identity which is gender-specific, similar clothing is rarely worn by men (with the exception of the Sikh turban). The numerous ceremonies and rituals which East African Sikh women attend in London also reinforce gender difference as well as ethnic identity.

Marriage in a New Setting

Marriage for migrant women and men may involve issues which did not arise at home. For instance, the mothers of Bangladeshi men in Tower Hamlets often put pressure on their sons to marry girls from Bangladesh, rather than Bangladeshi girls brought up in London. This has been so because the women feared that the latter would be insufficiently socialised into the duties expected of the Bangladeshi bride, chief among which was taking over household tasks from her mother-in-law. Palestinian men in Berlin attempted to demonstrate their independence of the norms of their old society by marrying later and having both sexual and non-sexual relationships with German women. While Palestinian girls still submitted to arranged marriages, albeit with the possibility of rejecting a disliked suitor, Palestinian men were able to have a type of polygamous marriage. Such marriages occurred when the Palestinian or other Arab wife was legally divorced in the courts and her husband married a German wife. The divorce was not recognised in the Palestinian community and the husband effectively circulated between two households. Such marriages were approved as the man acquired residence and work permits through his German wife and social benefits accrued to the divorced woman's household. Bhachu relates that East African Sikh brides in Britain were content with arranged marriages and saw advantages in them which Western 'love matches' did not have, provided that there was a possibility of veto if the woman found the suitor unacceptable.

Buijs relates how in South Africa attitudes to marriage were influenced by poverty and virtual destitution which forced some women to migrate alone. Transkei women who migrated to work as agricultural labourers in Natal were often either widows or deserted wives. Their view of marriage was of an institution which had provided them with little comfort and less security and few wanted to remarry, preferring casual liaisons which did not affect their ability to move to areas outside Transkei in search of work.

Women Migrating Without Men

Late nineteenth-century English society was marked by a progressive isolation of the sexes and of different classes from each other. The economic and social upheaval of the times was controlled by erecting clear boundaries and the influence of women was largely based upon preconceived ideas of female characteristics. A woman could have power as a wife and mother, but only within a carefully delimited sphere. An ideal of domesticity masked the exclusion of women from political, economic and social power (Vicinus 1985).

Swaisland shows how, in the case of British women between 1860 and 1914, emigration was often undertaken in order to cross class boundaries and/or to achieve the goal of marriage which had proved elusive in England.[2] Few of the women whom she mentions would have deliberately chosen South Africa as a haven: the United States, Canada or Australia were preferred, but those who did manage to leave England could consider themselves fortunate, for not all who wanted to go were able to do so.

Middle-class commentators such as W. R. Greg considered the plight of the single woman to be symbolic of the larger social disorder brought about by industrialisation and urbanisation, and considered that emigration offered better marriage prospects for some women. Judging by correspondence to and from South Africa, many female emigrants thought so, too.[3] Lucie Duff-Gordon, writing from the Cape, noted that marriage claimed many immigrants soon after arrival.

The inevitable decline in social class suffered by women who were forced to work was thought by female emigrants to the Cape to be capable of remedy or even improvement. Many domestics, as Swaisland

2. Ethel Colqhoun (1913: 315) stated that the actual disproportion between the sexes in Britain in 1913 was 1,027,00 more women, but of them many were widows.

3. See also Van–Helten and Williams 1983.

notes, found it possible to renege on their contracts on arrival and sell their services to the highest bidder and 'most importantly, the new-comers quickly realised the value of their white skins. For the first time in their lives they encountered a class of people who ranked low-er than themselves and they were not slow to take advantage of it'. White servants 'gave themselves airs', and refused to undertake tasks which they had previously taken for granted, resulting in Lady Hely-Hutchinson describing the immigrant servant as 'flighty, self-assert-ing, ignorant, lazy and inefficient'.

Middle-class women who emigrated often fared little better in the end. The attraction of emigration for the desperate was that, in a country where they were unknown and far from the criticism of family or friends, they could do work which would have appeared unseemly or beneath them in England. Such women often occupied the category of 'lady-help'; a kind of superior domestic servant, who shared the family accom-modation. While some 'lady-helps' were a success, others were not.

The South African Colonisation Society said of many of the women who emigrated as lady-helps that they were 'unemployed because un-employable, decayed gentlewomen...who have gone out to South Africa with the idea that the inefficient will prosper better there than here'. The real problem was that the middle-class woman who fell on hard times often had little education and few skills, and unless she was prepared to work hard in South Africa was unlikely to find placement.

Both the middle- and working-class women who emigrated to South Africa were attempting to escape the rigid boundaries of their class and social position in England, which often meant virtual destitution if a male breadwinner died or was unable to support his female dependants. However, very few of these women were successful in throwing off the shackles of the past and assuming new identities in a far-away place. Emigration societies received frequent complaints of unsuitable women, unsuitable either because they were found to have a 'past' (generally meaning to have borne an illegitimate child) or to be unwill-ing to do heavy domestic work. These women were trying, by crossing the physical boundaries of nation and ocean, to place themselves within the invisible but all too real boundaries of middle-class respectability.

Cherryl Walker comments that it is a rhetorical commonplace that black women in South Africa suffer a triple oppression of gender, race and class. Although white women are discriminated against as women, 'their membership of a privileged racial group softens the impact of gender discrimination and works against their identification with black women as women, with shared problems (1990: 11). Certainly,

Swaisland notes the alacrity with which white domestic servants who emigrated to South Africa from Britain used their white skins both to distinguish themselves from black fellow servants and to align themselves as far as possible with their white mistresses.

While the emigration societies and concerned upper-class women like Lucy Duff-Gordon and Lady Hely-Hutchinson have left documentary evidence of the impact of white domestic emigrant women on South African settler society, the absence from the historical record of black women's voices is pronounced (Walker: 1990). Indeed, mission records or organisations of literate or middle-class women are often the only means of hearing black women's voices. Shirley Ardener has expanded on the theme of 'mutedness' and 'muted groups' first proposed by Edwin Ardener in 1978. This theory suggests that there are dominant modes of expression in any society which have been generated by the dominant structures within it: 'In any situation, only the dominant mode of the relevant groups will be "heard", the "muted groups" if they wish to communicate must express themselves in terms of this mode, rather than in ones which they might otherwise have generated independently' (S. Ardener 1978: 20).

Ardener's observation illuminates the position of women from Britain emigrating to South Africa in the nineteenth century, the situation they were leaving in Victorian England was one that had created a symbolic triad, binding a woman to extremes: she was either the ideal mother/wife, or a celibate spinster or promiscuous prostitute' (Vicinus 1985: 5), but the black South African women about whom Buijs writes may also be considered a 'muted group'. Moore suggests (1988: 9) that while women in a variety of societies share similar experiences and problems, these similarities have to be set against the widely differing experiences of women worldwide, especially with regard to race, colonialism and the rise of industrial capitalism.

Although these black women shared with the domestic servants whom Swaisland discusses the imperative of economic migrancy, that is, they were forced to leave their homes in search of work in order to survive – they were in other respects differentiated. Apartheid legislation prevented black women from taking better paid, albeit unskilled, jobs in factories or shops in urban South Africa and condemned them to manual labour in the agricultural plantation sector. Like the earlier Victorian ideology, the patriarchal order of traditional Nguni society proclaimed that the only suitable life style for a young woman was an early marriage combined with the domestic and field duties of her in-laws' homestead.

The women who made their way illegally to do casual work on the sugar estates were casualties of drought, desertion and death. While many middle-aged women had been married, their husbands had either died, deserted them, or, in a few cases, married a second wife who was preferred. Younger women often had one or more illegitimate children whom they could not support without migrating. In all cases the household unit could not survive in Transkei without the mother emigrating to seek work elsewhere. Guy comments that while work in pre-capitalist African society was heavy for women, 'it took place within a community which provided substantial security...Oppression in these pre-capitalist societies was certainly very different from the isolation and alienation which forms of exploitation through the wage create and which provide the impressions we have today of the concept of oppression'(1990: 46).

Women exercised control over the agricultural process in pre-capitalist times, and by virtue of the central importance of their fertility to society, enjoyed considerable status and a degree of autonomy not appreciated, or replicated, within colonial society (Walker 1990: 8). Once wages or cash income earned in external markets became more important, then the pre-capitalist era could be said to have passed and with it the structural centrality of gender in the organisation of society. While the old patriarchal authority was undermined, the price women had to pay for their new independence was a devastating increase in economic and emotional insecurity.

The effects of rural decline could be seen in the growing number of African women who moved out of rural areas of South Africa from the late nineteenth century, in defiance of both law and custom. Bonner, in his discussion of the movement of Basotho women to the Rand, brings out the economic forces at work, linking the high level of female migration from Basutoland to the relatively advanced degree of rural pauperisation and social breakdown in Basotho society. Thus, while rural African women were able, as a result of labour migration, to assert themselves as *de facto* heads of households, they were also forced to assume more and more of the burden of an increasingly attenuated household production (1990: 234). African marriage became less stable as an institution, with women gaining personal independence at the expense of the economic and emotional security within the precolonial family network.

An important point that Walker makes is that African women did not have the same interest in rural society as men, even while the burden of rural production came to rest more heavily on them. The lack of an independent interest in rural society explains what Bryceson (1980) has termed the 'voluntarism' that has characterised the movement of women off the land throughout the subcontinent. For female migrants, therefore, migration was more likely to represent a means of escape than either a means to reinvest in the rural economy or a process of dispossession, and Walker insists on the theme of women 'running away from their allotted place' and uses the term 'escape' to characterise a major component of female migration from the start of the twentieth century.

The women most likely to 'escape' in this way were those least adequately accommodated by the rural society and the women most disadvantaged socially. Thus the categories of female migrants described by Bonner were women who were experiencing difficulties in their marital situation and were particularly vulnerable to the forces of landlessness, impoverishment and marginalisation within rural society. These were women in unhappy marriages, widows and women whose husbands had deserted them. In the first half of the twentieth century these women fled from areas like Basotholand and Bechuanaland which were among the first to feel the hardships caused by labour migration. Later, areas like Pondoland, where the rural economy was initially stronger (Beinart 1982), succumbed as well.

Anthropological studies of southern African societes reveal that by the early decades of this century the African rural family was clearly in a state of crisis, showing unmistakeable signs of instability and a weakened ability to order relationships between the sexes and generations. Schapera (1947) documented the evidence of stress in the African patriarchal family and the emergence of new patternings of relationships within the household. His work highlighted the destabilising effects of migrant labour in the form of marital breakdown, rising illegitimacy rates and the loss of respect for elders among the young. Abandoned women were an increasingly common outcome of elopement. Without transferring a large proportion of the bridewealth payment, which had become so heavy that most men could not afford it, men enjoyed only limited rights over their children and a much weaker bond was sustained between husband and wife. The migrant women from Transkei discussed by Buijs are one part of the mosaic which is the story of the disastrous effects of enforced migrant labour throughout southern Africa.

Conclusion

Whether they were refugees or economic migrants, most of the women whose lives are examined in this book were forced to leave their original homes by circumstances beyond their control. The concept of 'home' became for many a reference point or lodestone to be remembered or summoned up as occasion demanded. Along with memories of the homeland left behind was often rekindled a desire to remake the abandoned way of life, whether by demarcating space in hostels in West Berlin or organising festivals in Californian suburbs.

This remaking or refashioning did not, and could not hope to replicate the past, but was an attempt to construct a meaningful identity in the context of life in alien and often, but not always, oppressive circumstances. The enforced humility and passivity of the Vietnamese women in the detention centres in Hong Kong is echoed by the restrictions which were placed on young Palestinian women in Berlin by their menfolk. In both cases women were forced to comply with male definitions and stereotypes of correct or appropriate female behaviour which were at odds with their previous lifestyles.

The boundaries which were crossed by the women in this book were not always traversed unwillingly. The wives of international migrants from Goa and enterprising East African Sikh brides in London eagerly seized the opportunities offered by education and paid work to improve both their own circumstances and, most particularly in the case of the Goan wives, those of their children.

Thus, the conditions available to refugees and migrants in the host countries shaped and mediated adaptation and facilitated in some cases the ability of women to take control over their own lives, as demonstrated by the Somali wives and Chilean refugees. Restrictions on movement in the host country and lack of access to even elementary adult education appear to be the most inhibiting, even paralysing, factors which resulted in women being bullied into conforming to imagined and unrealistic criteria of what constituted 'ideal' feminine virtues. None the less, for those strong enough to resist such imposed identities and who managed in the face of considerable odds to accommodate new life styles, the boundaries which they crossed provided hope and inspiration for the future.

References

Anwar, M., 1979 *The Myth of Return,* London: Heinemann

Ardener, S., 1978 'Introduction: The Nature of Women in Society in Ardener, S. (ed), *Defining Females: The Nature of Women in Society,* London: Croom Helm. Revised edition Berg: Oxford, 1993

Beinart, W., 1982 *The Political Economy of Pondoland: 1860 to 1930*, Cambridge: Cambridge University Press

Bhachu, P., 1985 Twice Migrants: East African Sikh Settlers in Britain, London: Tavistock

Bonner, P., 1990 'Desirable or Undesirable Basotho Women? Liquor, Prostitution and the Migration of Basotho Women to the Rand, 1920–1945', in C.Walker (ed.), *Women and Gender in Southern Africa to 1945,* London: James Currey

Bryceson, D., 1980 'The Proletarianization of Women in Tanzania' *Review of African Political Economy*, Vol. 7

Colquhoun, E., 1913 *The Vocation of Women,* London: Heinemann

Colson, E., 1991 'Involuntary Migration and Resettlement in Africa 1991', Carter Lectures on Africa University of Florida at Gainesville March

Connerton, P., 1989 *How Societies Remember,* Cambridge: Cambridge University Press

Guy, J., 1990 'Gender Oppression in Southern Africa's Precapitalist Societies, in C.Walker, (ed.),*Women and Gender in Southern Africa to 1945,* London: James Currey

Jackson, J., 1975 'The Meanings of Landscape', unpublished manuscript

Harrell-Bond, B., 1986 *Imposing Aid: Emergency Assistance to Refugees,* Oxford: Oxford University Press

Leeds, A., 'Women in the Migratory Process: A Reductionist Outlook' *Anthropological Quarterly,* vol.49, pp. 69–76

Moore, H., 1988 *Anthropology and Feminism,* Cambridge: Polity Press

Morokvasic, M., 1983 'Women in Migration: Beyond the Reductionist Outlook' in A. Phizacklea (ed.), *One Way Ticket: Migration and Female Labour,* London: Routledge & Kegan Paul

Phizacklea, A.(ed.), 1983 *One Way Ticket: Migration and Female Labour,* London: Routledge & Kegan Paul

Poulet, G., 1983 *L'Espace Proustien,* Paris: Gallimard

Schapera, I., 1947 *Migrant Labour and Tribal Life: A Study of Conditions,* London: Oxford University Press

Simon,R.J and C.B. Brettell (eds), 1986 *International Migration: The Female Experience,* Towtowa, New Jersey: Rowman & Allenheid

Van-Helten, J.J. and K. Williams, 1983 'The Crying Need of South Africa: The Emigration of Single British Women to the Transvaal, 1901–10', *Journal of Southern African Studies,* vol. 10, no.1, October

Vicinus, M., 1985 *Independent Women: Work and Community for Single Women 1850–1920,* London: Virago

Walker, C., 1990 'Women and Gender in Southern Africa to 1945: An Overview' in C. Walker (ed.), *Women and Gender in Southern Africa to 1945,* London: James Currey

Wollheim, R., 1986 *The Thread of Life,* Cambridge: Cambridge University Press

2

The Gendered Dynamics of Quechua Colonisation: Relations of Centre and Periphery in Peru

Sarah Lund Skar

Colonisation

By calling this chapter 'The Gendered Dynamics of Quechua Colonisation', I am at the outset attempting to focus our attention on a specific way of looking at mobility from a Quechua cultural vantage point. As a means of clarifying this culturally specific way of looking at resettlement I am also restricting that viewpoint to certain areas in which gender relations come most to the fore. It would seem that the word 'colonisation' may pose problems in communicating some of the interpretation which is to follow. The overriding negative overtones this concept has for most Africanists has been brought to my attention in discussion as evoking that sense of colonialism in which a foreign (European) power imposes control over an area by subjugating the local populations and bringing them under its jurisdiction. From this perspective, colonisation emphasises the assymetrical relationships between two groups of people; the colonisers and the colonised.

Also, in the history and ethnography of South America, colonisation carries a connotation of subjugation. As with Africa there is a colonial experience in which the Spanish and Portuguese subjugated the vast indigenous populations of the continent. In addition there is considerable documentation about pre-hispanic colonisation practices used by the expanding Incan Empire both as a technique of subjugating their enemies and a method of insuring an even distribution of agricultural produce over a vast area (Murra 1972; Espinoza Soriano 1973; Pease 1982). To this day, colonisation is seen as a legitimate means of settling the vast jungle areas east of the Andes, a region perceived by national governments to be largely uninhabited (see Shoemaker 1981).

21

All of the Andean republics have looked to their jungle lowlands in the east as the source of undiscovered wealth offering limitless development potential for the nation. The rubber boom of the last century, the discovery of oil reserves in the 1970s, and the extraction of precious metals and exotic wood during most of this century, have all served to maintain the image of a regional El Dorado in the attitudes of these countries. They have all, because of this, looked east for a solution to many of their economic and demographic crises.

In Peru, particularly under the populist president Belaunde, vast colonisation programs were part of official policy. The overcrowded capital city of Lima became an especially important recruiting ground for colonisers willing to be resettled in the jungle areas east of the Andes. It is a case of internal colonisation in a multi-cultural context. The settlers are called *colonos* (colonisers), and on the basis of over-riding national interests can be given legal title to their homesteads regardless of the extent to which these might have encroached upon traditional land claims in the area. For the purported good of the nation, indigenous minority rights in an area are overlooked for the sake of development. Thus, examples of colonisation with the connotation of subjugation can certainly be found within the context of the nation in a post-colonial period.

However, aside from this view of colonisation so strongly associated with the historical process of colonialism, there is another, more neutral meaning to the word. Colonisation in its original sense, untainted by the many negative political overtones, means the settling of unoccupied areas by a mother community. From this internal perspective, colonisation becomes a process by which a centre of perceived power and authority holds, or at least struggles to hold, dominion over produce and personnel at its periphery. This is an internal view of colonisation, a perspective which can be well suited to a kind of inside view of spatial mobility and resettlement. As I shall attempt to justify in this chapter this kind of perspective is of particular relevance in characterising Quechua settlements.

Over the course of a decade, I have carried out fieldwork with villagers from Matapuquio in the southern highland department of Apurimac.[1] In later years this work has focused on resettled groups

1. My fieldwork has been funded by various institutions. The original fieldwork in Matapuquio in 1976-7 was funded by the Norwegian Council for Research in the Social Sciences and Humanities. Later fieldtrips in 1984 and 1986 were made possible by a generous grant from the Swedish Research Council for the Social Sciences. I gratefully acknowledge the support.

living in Peru's eastern jungle, or *montaña* as it is called, and with villagers in the coastal capital of Lima. In interpreting the material my task has been to try and understand the kinds of cultural transformations taking place in the two displaced communities of Matapuqeños. Though initially I approached the material by using migration as an important analytical perspective, after a time I felt compelled to abandon this approach altogether. In fact, for my purposes at least, I found the use of the word 'migration' to pose more questions than it answered.

Originally, my interest in colonisation as an analytical tool derived from John Murra's (1972) vertical archipelago model; an ethno-historically derived explanation of Incaic resource production and redistribution in the extremely contrasting ecological situation of Peru's Andean highlands, the coastal desert and the dense jungle of the eastern Andean slopes. Murra has shown how under the Incas, and probably before, altitude-specific products such as fish and cotton from the coast, potatoes (in dehydrated form) from the highlands and coca from the jungle were circulated throughout the kingdom by means of a centralised system he has termed 'archipelago'. With the power always retained by the highlands, segments of Andean village populations were resettled both to the west of the highlands on the coast and to the eastern jungle. These resettled people were called *mitmaqkuna*, a term also applied to loyal Incan subjects resettled in newly conquered enemy territory to consolidate control and discourage uprisings. Particularly rebellious groups would also be forcefully moved into peaceful areas to subdue them. The populace of all these resettlements were called *mitmaqkuna* a term that is found repeatedly in the colonial records glossed with the Spanish *colonos*.

To ethno-historians it has come as a surprise to learn that the word *mitmaqkuna* is currently used in Matapuquio to designate that part of the village population which is outside the village in Lima or in the montaña area of Chanchamayo. Despite the impact John Murra's work has had on anthropologists working in the region, to my knowledge migrants have never been referred to as *mitmaqkuna* in the literature on contemporary Andean migration. Thus, up to the present, I have no comparative ethnographic illustrations of how this concept is used today in other locations or contexts. For example, my Quechua teacher from Ayacucho did not know the term except for its historical meaning of resettled peoples during the reign of the Inca.

I first became aware of the contemporary relevance of the term in a completely different context. A discussion of *mitmaq* came about spontaneously during a conversation about another basic principle of

Quechua social organisation, that of *ayllu,* roughly glossed as family or community. The work of Harald Skar (1982) focused on this many-faceted principle of recruitment and applied its explanatory power in elucidating the upheavals brought about by expropriation and co-operativisation of the Pincos *hacienda,* Matapuquio's all-encompassing neighbour.

Beyond the context of close kin in a bilateral kinship system, *ayllu* is a flexible concept used to describe the group which joins with you in moments of conflict or crisis. In this way, it can designate the entire village (as it did when the land reform villagers joined forces to fight for control over the *hacienda).* Some relationships based upon *ayllu* are institutionalised as in the case of the village moieties of *hanay* (upper) and *uray* (lower), which together fashion much of the interdynamics of village political life. Essential to the principle of *ayllu* is the idea of the nestedness of groups, of varying degrees of inclusiveness which in an instance of lineages would be probably termed segmental. Finally there is an emotive sense of *ayllu* as place of origin in a community such as Matapuquio in which territory and kinship are inextricably bound.

Many of the questions about the nature of the *ayllu* arose again when we first revisited Matapuquio in December 1980. One evening we were discussing what *ayllu* meant in different situations, almost all of which had to do with intra-village relationships. Something made me break out of the discussion and begin to talk about my own feelings about Matapuquio during my absence. I even related some of the frequent dreams I had had about the village while away. Then I questioned the appropriateness of having such strong feelings when I was not really part of any *ayllu,* that is I had no kin-based connection.

This digression brought quite a response from our hosts, a family with whom we have had long and intimate contact but, at that point, no ritual kinship ties. Everyone assured us that we belonged to the *ayllu* even while we were in Norway. The fact of our return made this evident. My host, Julian, dipped his spoon into the soup cooking on the fire and threw out a bit on the packed dirt floor. He pointed to the concentrated drop of soup first and called it *ayllu.* Then he indicated all the many droplets spread around about the larger drop and called them *mitma.* All *ayllus* have many parts spread out in both space and time. To be a *mitma* in relation to an *ayllu* is to be a part of a larger whole. 'I am your *mitma,* I am a part of you *(yo soy su mitma, yo soy su parte)'*, Julian explained. In referring to the droplets someone then said: 'everything is *ayllu,* everything is *mitma (Todo es ayllu. Todo es mit-*

ma)'. In other words, everything is a part of something else. What is *ayllu* at one level is *mitma* at another.

Drops of soup on a dirt floor become a metaphor for highly complex ideas about the nature of parts and the whole, and about the significance of boundaries between centre and periphery. The 'map' poses many issues, among which the most fascinating for me in the present context is that of being of the same essence (the soup) but separate. The nature of separateness is a central question in the relationship between an individual and larger social groupings, between a mother community and her colonies.

Julian's map is about colonisation. It demonstrates a particularly Quechua view about resettlement. The *ayllu* is always the encompassing whole to the *mitma*/colonisers. In practical terms this is most clearly played out on two levels. In both, *ayllu* is clearly anchored in the highlands, *mitma* dispersed to the periphery. In one instance, *ayllu* is the community of Matapuquio, the *mitmaqkuna* the cluster of settlers that have together formed a social group in a subservient relation to the village in the highlands. At a more individualised level, the *ayllu/mitmaqkuna* relations are played out in the context of an elaborate set of rights and obligations within the extended family. For the remainder of this chapter, I shall concentrate on this latter instance because it is the best example of how gender serves as the dynamic focus in articulating the relation of centre and periphery.

Women and Mobility

Elsewhere I have discussed the breakdown of marriage relations among Matapuqeños in Chanchamayo (S.Skar 1993). In that discussion the point was made that village women are held to be the guardians of culture in Quechua society (cf. Allen 1988). While free and forceful agents within the context of their own village, Matapuquio women who have moved away from the valley especially into areas of mestizo cultural dominance,[2] are held to be lacking in morality and are suspect.[3] In general they are seen to lack the attribute of humility deemed desirable in a marriage partner, whether man or woman, and it is frequently assumed that they are prostitutes.

2.The term *mestizo* is used here in the cultural sense to indicate hispanicised people of the towns who are integrated into Peruvian culture but have some affinities with the Quechua culture of the countryside.

3.This moral boundary is easily transgressed. Women who had resettled in the nearby hacienda in the valley were ascribed the same stigma that characterised those who had moved further afield (e.g. Skar, S. 1980)

The many women who are colonisers moving with their families to Lima or Chanchamayo are placed in a compromising light which causes conflicts and often places them in a no-win position. Others are left in Matapuquio as a form of safe keeping or even brought back to the village when their husbands find their situation in the colonies too objectionable. Still others find it impossible to make the adjustment to life in such different environments as coastal desert or jungle-clad foothills. They are sent home again for their health's sake, for homesickness is considered a serious physical illness which could easily threaten their lives.

Thus there is a lot of shifting back and forth and much of this movement involves women. I propose to look first at the women in Matapuquio who have, in one form or another, close family members residing out in the jungle or in the city. I do not want to look at their situation from a perspective of household survival strategies or development cycle considerations but, rather, I want to address the question of how these women serve as a kind of dynamic agent in binding the dispersed *mitmaqkuna* or colonisers with the mother community. In order to be able to view these inter-relationships in terms of an integrated whole, we must gain an appreciation of the kinds of gender-specific rights and obligations that are part of the social code of morality in Matapuquio. This touches on wider issues of Quechua society.

Not surprisingly, a crucial factor in the matter is land. The Quechua are agriculturalists whose subsistence economy is based largely on the cultivation of maize and numerous tubers and for whom animal husbandry plays a secondary role in household economy. In Matapuquio, land is inherited by both sons and daughters, an inheritance which should be received at marriage. Agricultural produce is not marketed, the idiom of village interdependence being largely expressed through the sharing and in some cases bartering, of agricultural foodstuffs within categories of socially defined kin. Beyond the boundaries of the village such produce is sent to colonisers as a kind of symbolic exchange which is seen to physically bind the absent *mitmaqkuna* with their lands and family in the village. I shall return to this exchange in greater detail.

In animal husbandry, village women have a dominant role. They care for the animals, have a deciding voice in herd management, and gain access to their own money through the buying and selling of animals and animal products. Milking is explicitly restricted to women, one of a few such rigid distinctions made in a system of otherwise largely interchangeable division of labour. As they range far and wide on the mountain slopes in search of sufficient pasturage village women are moving about in their own space, highly visible and in no way hampered in their relations with other villagers, men or women. Sexual relations before marriage are common and are associated with this life away from the village proper where youths and young girls can meet in privacy.

Marriage and Kin Relationships

Marriage, on the other hand, is another matter, because it involves the necessary strategy of combining the land resources of two families. Marriage in the village is about 97 per cent endogamous, and young people who defy their families to marry outside the village for 'love' are completely ostracised. One marries the land in Matapuquio and considerable effort is made to reunite bordering fields into new units. As described elsewhere (S. Skar 1993), marriage is a family matter in which two bilateral groups become ritual kin with the many obligations this implies. Individual men and women, husbands and wives, are overshadowed by wider group considerations.

Rights and obligations in Quechua society are loosely differentiated in terms of the degree of closeness or distance of *kin/affinal ties*, of age and gender and of the degree of closeness or distance of *ayllu* relations. Different forms of work exchange are highly institutionalised, so that in most agricultural endeavours, people outside the immediate family are recruited to help out. These exchanges have a largely social and political role in building up clusters of interdependent families in a community where formal political leadership is muted. In cases in which married men are absent, their wives are responsible for keeping both their own fields and those of their husbands under cultivation.[4] Frequently this is made possible only with the help of the wider *ayllu* group. In the absence of a half-grown son who can participate in work exchanges, the woman will have to rely on drawing extra help from her ayllu by holding a *minka* in which she provides bountiful food and drink, coca and cigarettes in exchange for labour. To acquire sufficient labour at critical times, she will have to pay some workers day wages

4. The constant pressure for land means that single women unable to keep their fields under cultivation are vulnerable to having their fields encroached on by their husband's and occasionally their own siblings. I have known several dispossessed women who have not been able to retain control over their own lands; rights in land are thus not through private ownership but though use, and so it is absolutely crucial to keep the fields under cultivation.

as well. In addition, when the village holds its frequent work parties for community projects, she will either have to pay a fine or find a brother, brother-in-law or son who will work in place of her husband. In this way she will be covering her husband's responsibilities towards the village as well as towards his family.

For his part, the absent husband supports his wife by sending a commission through other travellers, which can consist of money or, more commonly, purchased items unavailable in Matapuquio, things which are valued for their novelty more than their utility. The husband in Lima sends clothing, the most important responsibility of a man in the family being to clothe his wife and daughters. He may send foodstuffs as well, such as noodles and rice, which are seldom eaten in Matapuquio. If he trusts the person who is taking his commission, he may also send money, but the truly symbolic content of the message is held in the items that are felt to be an indication of the man's ongoing commitment to his responsibilities in the village. The men say that they are sending the commissions in order to keep their women content.

In turn, the women reciprocate by sending off bundles of agricultural produce to the jungle and city when the opportunity arises. One such commission which I saw was made up of seventy smoked cheeses, twenty guinea pigs, *qora*, (the specially prepared corn for making beer), roasted corn, corn for cooking and wheat. All of this food is treated with an attitude I would have to describe as reverential when it is handed over in Lima and Chanchamayo. There is an obvious statement in the exchange implying that the woman continues to uphold her marriage obligations by covering the man's responsibilities in the village. More importantly, however, the food is the physical manifestation of the land that, through eating its produce, all Matapuqeños view as intrinsically part of their own person.[5] In Matapuquio you not only marry the land, you also eat it.

In a situation much like that Murra described as archipelago, agricultural produce from the highlands is sent down to the coast and jungle while, in turn, products typical of those regions are sent with villagers travelling back to the highlands. In both cases money, which is seen as being a part of life on the periphery, can also be included. In Matapuquio money still has a relatively marginal role, so that, in fact

5. Within the context of Quechua ideas about contiguity, which stress the identity of substance between parts of a larger whole, food conveys an essence bound up with the land which produced it. Through eating the food produced in the village, resettled villagers renew their bond with their land. On sharing food from the same fields, separated families become substantially bound in essence.

receiving money from *mitmaqkuna* outside is not necessary to maintain the family. What is needed are workers, and when the access to labour becomes precarious women call the men back. If the message gets through, it usually holds quite some authority as it is usually brought by other family members who bring considerable pressure to bear on the man to return home.

Messages, like the circulating food, clothing and money, are sent with travellers leaving the village. The post has for the most part no access for most resettled Matapuqeños and there is no postal service in the village either. In fact, for Matapuqeños letter writing is a disturbing form of communication: it both gives authority to the message but requires a medium, someone who can put the words down on paper in a foreign language, Spanish, and in a proper form (S. Skar, forthcoming).

On numerous occasions I have served as courier and have an appreciation of how the demands are placed. The women must find someone who is literate, pay a small fee for the service and provide the writing materials. Usually the sensitive contents of a letter are camouflaged behind stylised Spanish, formal in tone, which always begins by inquiring after the health of the addressees and other family before passing directly on to the real matters in hand. The pleas that are made are often concluded by some kind of implicit threat to the effect that if the message goes unregarded the marriage relationship will be considered broken. In the many cases of the mother writing and begging her son to return, this threat is replaced by an appeal to a sense of guilt, as children are responsible for maintaining their parents. Mothers promise to find unmarried men good wives and provide everything they will need to establish a new household if they will only come home. In such situations, the son has as often as not left over the issue of marriage, his parents having refused to let him marry because they wanted to delay the division of their fields.

Many men have only chosen to leave because they wanted to learn about the ways of the wider world. When they are needed they often return gladly, loaded down with such status items as radios, wristwatches, hopelessly inadequate clothing and the occasional lantern. With the return, foreign ways are gradually put away so that over the course of a few months the returnees are rendered virtually unrecognisable, at least to this anthropologist.

A father and son had been working together in Lima for some years on construction sites. It was considered an important part of the boy's education, carefully supervised as it was by his father. The son went to evening school and through his work managed to put some money by for his return to Matapuquio to marry. The wife/mother remained in Matapuquio with the younger children and kept the farm going largely through the combined efforts of her brothers-in-law, both her husband's brother and her sister's husband. When she found the appropriate wife for her son, again with help in the negotiations from her relatives, she recalled both husband and son from Lima.

They arrived in fine state wearing shoes and bringing with them festive clothing for the wedding celebrations. The father also had enough money to buy and have transported in sufficient dry goods to set up a rudimentary store in his house. At the time of their return these men were highly visible, dynamic personalities. On meeting them again after a prolonged absence, I truly did not recognise them. Their dress and ways had entirely reverted to those of the village. while the little shop in the corner of their house was reduced to a few dusty cans of tuna fish. When I exclaimed over the change they shrugged it off: 'It's impossible to change things here', Honoroto Altimirano said, 'trade is impossible. No one wants to pay you and everyone insists on having favours [i.e. getting credit].' On being asked if they regretted the return, however, they had no hesitation in replying that no, they could not possibly think of living outside Matapuquio. Money was easy to get in the outside world, but everyone went along eating it up as they went anyway *'en Lima la gente van comiendo su plata'*, I was told. The newly-wed son also explained that 'the women here in Matapuquio seem so precious and sweet *(preciosa/miski)*. When I'm away, I think differently of women ...without respect. It's a bad way to be.'

For another newly-wed couple, the conflicting attitudes had created problems of another kind. Andreas had been working in Lima. He returned to Matapuquio to marry Felisitas and together they went back to Lima. What had been a very good relationship at the beginning went from bad to worse. The husband could not come to terms with the changes in Felisitas on bringing her out of Matapuquio. She began to wear slacks and learned to speak Spanish. When they discovered that Felisitas was pregnant, Andreas insisted on her return to Matapuquio. There she lived with his mother. When I knew Felicitas, she no longer wore slacks, though she admitted to having several pairs amongst her things packed away at the house. 'It's the women', she told me, 'they talk and criticise you for wearing slacks. It's impossible to stand up against them.' Felisitas asked me about the adult literacy classes that were being held at the school during that time. She really wanted to go to them but her husband, who was still in Lima working, had absolutely forbidden it.

Women as Anchors

Obviously within a traditional framework that values complementarity between men and women, there is little flexibility on issues arising from outside that value system. The relatively equal status of men and women in Matapuquio seems compromised when women take on outside attributes deemed inappropriate. It is, however, viewed as appropriate for there to be motion in the men's lives. Articulating different cultural modes is an accepted aspect of their movement. The anchored place given women in this value system restricts them to one cultural mode only. In socialisation, the women are to pass on to their children the Quechua ways, just as the men must prepare youths in the ways of working both inside and outside the village.

As ideally stationary figures in a situation defined by movement, women in Matapuquio are 'holders' of property as well as guardians of Quechua culture. This 'holding' arrangement is an elaborate ritualised agreement, with certain aspects of a credit institution, usually made between women who leave with their husbands, and the other women who remain in the village. Though, in a similar way, both men and women can dispose of their fields, the women's arrangements for the care of their animals are by far the more frequent kind of agreement, making criss-crossing networks of co-operating kinswomen and merging herds.

As we have seen, animal husbandry is that part of the economic domain associated with women. Far more than money, animals are valued as accumulated wealth. The proliferation of the herds is both an indication of personal skills as well as the favour of the mountain gods. Animals are rarely sold off when someone leaves the village. They are 'deposited' in another woman's care and she in turn gives money (not equivalent to a sale price) as security for the animal. Food and drink are also given to the departing pastoralist who must eat and drink this ritualised form of offering denoting honour and respect.

To reclaim the animal at a later date, the returning woman must return the money given as security for her cow. Witnesses to the agreement and sufficient kin to back up the demands are crucial in reclaiming animals boarded out during one's absence. No particular compensation is made for the work of caring for these animals except for the potential of their offspring. Of course, there is the chance that the owner will never reclaim the property and they then become incorporated into the other woman's herds. Obviously there is much to-ing and fro-ing between highlands and colonies concerning the shifting of these animals. The real locus of wealth in Quechua terms is always retained in the highlands. Money as wealth resides on the periphery in the realms of that other way of life where human relationships are so suspect.

Matapuquio husbands leave their lands in the care of their wives while departing women leave their animals in the care of other village women. Like the cattle they guard, these village women are themselves held as precious. For men relations with village women are infused with respect. Women are the constant figures in an equation characterised by the movement of men and women out to the periphery and back. In order to bring family back to the central life in the village, it is the women who frequently place the demands while their male kin travel out in search of the villagers needed at home.

I have attempted to give some indication as to how, in the process of colonisation, men and women of Matapuquio seem to have certain gender specific parts to play in the relations between mother community and colony. Men, who are the main actors in the movement outwards, are largely responsible in taking young boys of the village to introduce them to the ways of the wider world and to teach them to work and acquire skills outside agriculture as well as to become farmers. Women, who are ideally the stationary figures in this drift to the periphery, are often drawn out to the coast or jungle to help other families in difficulty or to accompany husbands and establish their own homes. Very frequently, however, village women are returned to Matapuquio to avoid the implicit dilemmas inherent for them in a bicultural situation. After a sojourn out, many men and women return to Matapuquio complaining of not being able to tolerate the climate or the food and simply of being so homesick that their health was threatened. Wives who cannot adjust to living away from home but whose husbands want to continue living on the outside, can return to their families with their marriage dissolved.

The women left behind are trustees of a way of life as well as guardians over what are the most esteemed forms of wealth from a Quechua perspective: animals and the inherited lands linking the present generations with the ancestors. However, far from being a kind of *clenodia* (trinket) safely tucked away on some *bric-à-brac* shelf, these women are crucial elements in the retaining of the pre-eminence of the centre over its colonies.

In addressing the problem of Quechua movement and resettlement out of the highlands in terms of colonisation, one of the central questions must remain 'how does the centre situated in the highlands retain its ascendancy over its settlements on the periphery?' It seems evident to me that as long as village women are held to be the bearers of the kind of Quechua identity least perverted by outside influences and that a preponderance of these women while remaining in the village constantly reaffirming their ties with the kin on the periphery, Matapuquio will retain a kind of pondus in this centre/periphery equation.

Of course, movement is crucial to this dynamic. Personnel must be constantly shifting in and out to uphold the highlands as the ground spring of group identity. Whether in terms of personal relationship or property, people on the periphery must retain a sufficiently meaningful stake in the centre for them not to drift outside the scope of rights and obligations bound up in these interacting spheres. Stepping outside the context of one's social responsibilities effectively means a kind of social death; no longer a part *(mitmaq)* of a greater whole *(ayllu)*, one must put aside the traditionally Quechua view of the world as an integrated spatial and temporal experience where the past and the future merge and the centre and the periphery are but different aspects of an ultimate totality.

References

Allen, C. 1988 *The Hold Life Has: Coca and Cultural Identity in an Andean Community,* Washington, DC: Smithsonian Institution Press

Collier, G., Rosaldo, R. and Wirth, J. (eds), 1982 *The Inca and Aztec States 1400–1800,* London: Academic Press

Espinoza Soriano, W. 1973 'Colonias de Mitmas Multiples en Abancay: Siglos XV y XVI',*Revista del Museo Nacional* (Lima), vol. 39, pp. 225–299

Murra, J. 1972 'El Control Vertical de un Maximo de Pisos Ecologicos', in *Visita de la Provincia de Leon de Huanuco en 1562* by I. Ortiz de Zuniga, Huanuco: Universidad Nacional Hermilio Valdizan

Pease, F. 1982 'The Formation of Tawantinsuyu: Mechanisms of Colonization and Relationship with Ethnic Groups' in G. Collier, R. Rosaldo and J. Wirth (eds), *The Inca and Aztec States 1400–1800,* London: Academic Press, pp. 173–98

Shoemaker, R. 1981 *The Peasants of El Dorado; Conflict and Contradiction in a Peruvian Frontier Settlement,* Ithaca, New York: Cornell University Press

Skar, H., 1982 *The Warm Valley People; Duality and Land Reform among the Quechua Indians of Highland Peru,* Oslo: Universitetsforlaget

Skar, S., 1980 'Quechua Women and the Agrarian Reform in the Pincos Valley; a Case from the Southern Highlands of Peru', unpublished Mag. Art thesis, Institute of Social Anthropology, University of Oslo

—1993 'Marry the Land, Divorce the Man; Quechua Marriage and the Problem of Individual Autonomy' in V. Broch-Due, I. Rudie and T. Bleie (eds.), *Gender: Symbols and Social Practices,* Oxford: Berg

—Forthcoming 'On the Margin: Letter Exchange among Andean Non-Literates' in E. Archetti (ed.) *The Multiplicity of Writing. The Meaning of Marginal Texts in Anthropological Analysis.* Oslo: University of Oslo Press

3

Reconstructing Life: Chilean Refugee Women and the Dilemmas of Exile

Marita Eastmond

This chapter addresses the dilemmas of exile as experienced by Chilean refugees in the United States, and the ways in which men and women reconstruct their lives and identities in exile. The study is based on fieldwork carried out in 1985 in northern California in a community of Chileans expelled by the Chilean regime ten years earlier. It is particularly concerned with the experience of women, how forced migration affects their lives and perceptions of themselves. It is often assumed that refugee women, as women, are more vulnerable than men.[1] My study suggests that this is not invariably the case, and that we need to clarify the contexts and forces which shape different experiences. In so doing, we also need to take account of how refugees themselves define their experience and how such definitions may be transformed in the course of exile. These processes will be examined below in the context of collective ideology and discourse that give exile structure and meaning in the community. In particular, I will explore their struggle for cultural continuity as Chileans and supporters of a political movement, and the different roles and perceptions of men and women in this process.

Refugee situations, their causes and consequences, are complex and varied. The impact on lives and identities occurs in the interplay between historical, political and sociocultural background factors and the settlement context of each refugee population. Similarly, the refugee experience may be a different one for different kinds of social actors in that population, as each bring specific perspectives and expectations into a new situation, as, for instance, do men and women or members of different social classes. Nevertheless, the commonality of the

---

1. For example, the World Council of Churches defines refugee women as the most vulnerable group.

refugee experience, may be seen to lie in the forced uprooting from familiar patterns of everyday life, often involving multiple loss, and a struggle to recover continuity and control. The chances of restoring a sense of continuity may vary greatly between different refugee situations and between different social actors.

For instance, when Moçambicans or Angolans, fleeing the guerilla attacks of Renamo and Unita, cross the border to Zambia and settle with kinsmen in villages on the Zambian side, there is a long history of voluntary movement for marriage and other forms of exchange between members of their ethnic group residing on different sides of the national boundary. Although the guerilla incursions on their villages, families and fields have destroyed or disrupted their bases of livelihood and local community, they are no strangers in the Zambian villages and can settle with relatives and people who share their culture and language (Spring 1982).[2] For many other refugees, crossing a border often means that lives must be reconstructed in circumstances and cultures alien to their own. For the Chilean refugees, the United States as host country was not only alien, offering only minimal support on arrival, but was also perceived by them as the historical political enemy, which inevitably had implications for their adjustment. However, in both cases, women have generally fared better than men in the host community. The African women through marriage to Zambian kinsmen, are able more quickly to recover an economic base and become socially integrated. The villages are used to brides coming in to settle, to be welcomed and outfitted and given access to land. The refugee men, in contrast, landless and penniless on arrival, have few chances of coming up with a brideprice or the other necessities for marrying. With these constraints to rebuilding an economic base, the men tend to remain poor wage workers in the low-paid sector for many years (ibid.).

The lives of the Chilean women refugees are transformed as drastically as those of the men in exile, but in ways in which new roles and identities are more easily reconciled with their past. Continuity, then, does not mean absence of change, but to be able to integrate change in culturally meaningful ways. To understand the different implications of social and cultural change in the new country for Chilean men and women we must look more closely at their social worlds and bases of identity in Chile. The process of change must also be examined within the broader context of the exile community and what may be called the 'social con-

2. The situation changed with the new refugee policy in Zambia which restricts Moçambicans from settling spontaneously in villages and, instead, transfers them to government settlements.

struction of exile' – that is, the negotiations in which the social meaning of exile is defined and a collective exile identity is formulated. This social construction must, in turn, be related to the nature of political exile and the particular conflict it generates between continuity and change.

Chilean Political Exile

The military coup in 1973 and its repressive aftermath, the political events which forced the Chilean Left to leave the country, structured much of life in exile. The history of the popular movement's involvement in the political struggle also provided its social meaning for its supporters. The military coup had been a deep tragedy for this movement which had brought the Popular Unity (a coalition of left-wing and centrist parties) to power in 1970 under its socialist president, Salvador Allende. The Popular Unity had generated enormous hopes for a better and more just society with its 'Chilean Road to Socialism', an unprecedented attempt at a peaceful transformation to a socialist society. It was the first time a marxist president had been elected into office; but the Popular Unity entered its hazardous road to democratic socialism with only a slim victory at the polls. Set on reversing this transformation of Chilean society, the military repression and violence that followed the coup was massive, involving thousands of deaths and large numbers of opponents forced into exile.[3]

The one-hundred families that made up the community of my study were rank and file militants and supporters of the Left. In the intensive years of Popular Unity, women and men had, in different ways, been part of its project of 'constructing socialism' in Chile. The men, as skilled or semi-skilled industrial workers, had also been active in trade union politics in Chile. Many workers saw their parties and trade union organisations grow and become more militant in the years of Popular Unity, pressing for change. Industrial workers were given a key role in the mobilisation of the masses and in social transformation. The women, as with most working-class women in Chile, were housewives for whom their families and households were their main responsibility. Few of them had been directly involved in trade union or party politics, but many had participated in the government's popular mobilisation projects such as housing or family health in their *barrio,* or local neighbourhood.

3. As many as 30,000 are estimated to have been killed in the military takeover, and about 80,000 were taken political prisoner in the first six months (Angell and Carstairs 1987).

In the months preceding the coup in September 1973, the political unrest and increasing tension were forebodings of the defeat of their project. However, few were prepared for the massive brutality with which it was to be carried out. When they arrived in the United States in 1975, both men and women were marked by the traumatic experiences they had suffered. The men had almost all been imprisoned and exposed to torture and other forms of violence. The women, on the outside, had had to fend for themselves and their families, assuming economic and other responsibilities, under extremely difficult conditions. Many of them had suffered long periods of uncertainty about the fate of their husbands or sons, and had been forced to confront the authorities in their search.

The refugees had been released under the so called *extrañamiento* programme: two years after the coup, in response to mounting international pressure, the Chilean regime issued a decree which permitted some political prisoners to commute their sentences to exile. Most of the refugees in this study had applied for asylum to countries other than the United States, but the urgency of their need to get out of prison and be reunited with families and the painful slowness involved in processing applications, put pressure on them to accept the first country offered. Moreover, going abroad was seen as taking only temporary refuge during what was anticipated to be a short-lived military rule in Chile. Admission as refugees to the country seen as responsible for their plight held its own particular paradox for the supporters of the Chilean revolution. A central symbol in their political struggle, the United States was the imperialist giant, and the refugees referred to their new position with the words of the Cuban poet Jose Martí as being 'in the belly of the Beast'. Their position was marked by a great deal of uncertainty. The admission of Chilean leftists was surrounded by much political controversy and caution at the highest levels of the United States Administration, and they were given only a temporary status as 'parolees'. There were also restrictions on their political activity and financial support, and the Chileans had to rely on a local Catholic church and on their own self-help activities for settlement in the new country. For their part, the refugees welcomed a minimum of intervention by North American authorities, fearing that any contact would facilitate surveillance by the Chilean intelligence. Their shared experience as survivors of an ordeal, as refugees in the United States who yet had a strong commitment to return, formed the basis of a close-knit and cohesive community, which drew a strict boundary between itself and the host society.

The Dilemmas of Exile: Liminality and Ambiguity

Exile, as problematic reality, was intensely discussed and defined by
the members in the community, especially in the first years. Norms
and values concerning how to live in exile were formulated in an
emerging discourse on exile and related to the struggle to maintain
their identity in exile.

For the Chilean refugees, exile was a highly temporary state, a life
in waiting for return and a resumption of normal life when conditions
back home allowed. The concepts of *destierro* and *destiempo,* being
out of normal place and time, in the Chilean exile discourse (Riquelme
1987) illustrate this conception of exile as suspended existence well.
The condition is similar to that of liminality, a term coined by van
Gennep (1908) in analysing rites of passage from one social state or
identity to another, and later elaborated by Turner (1967; 1969).
Liminality refers to the phase between separation and reincorporation.
The liminal state is replete with ambiguity, marked by the undefined
identity of those in transition, existing and yet not existing as social
persons in society. The Chileans perceived themselves to be, and in a
real sense were 'betwixt and between' social realities. Their undefined
social position, divested of their rights as Chilean citizens with only
conditional status in the United States, was a precarious reality.

Exile and Identity

In particular, the essential ambiguity of the liminal state as described
by Turner is useful for understanding the dilemmas of exile. However,
in contrast to the predictable outcome of a ritual order, in which separation is always followed by reincorporation, exile is open–ended. As
a response to the disruption of the social order itself, it is unplanned
and involuntary, and there is no guaranteed return. This open-ended
quality compounded the ambiguity of Chilean lives and identities over
time, as a growing conflict between their Chilean past and the North-
American present. Exile necessarily involved change, sometimes profound transformations of individuals' lives and identities. But change
was a deep moral dilemma, though, as integration into the United
States' society was associated with the betrayal of political commitment and of those left behind. Individuals' survival guilt, the psychological result of leaving others behind while they themselves were escaping, was closely intertwined with political commitments in which
'the dead acted as fiscal prosecutors guarding against integration'
(ALAM n.d.).

For refugees, forcibly removed, and with a moral commitment to return, life is put on hold in exile. Looking forward is always looking back. This dichotomy of time and place infuses the exile experience. Like the guards of Dante's inferno, whose heads and bodies were facing different ways, their tears running down their backs, the exile exists in two societies, yet not fully in either. Over time, life threatens to become permanently provisional, leaving the refugee in limbo if he is 'unable and unwilling to become fully part of his life in exile for fear that in doing so he will forfeit his life in his "native place"' (Abu-Lughod 1988: 62).

Preserving the Past, Creating a Heritage

Continuity was thus a strong concern of the Chileans in exile, reflected in the intense activity with which they rebuilt the bases of their social and cultural life. To reconstruct the familiar is a well known psychological means by which refugees cope with forced separation and loss. For a community of uprooted people, organisation and collective symbolic expressions can also be a means of resistance; for the Chileans they were not only an important dimension of the struggle for democracy in Chile, but also in resisting absorption in North American society. In this process, culture takes on a special significance: it forms a lifeline to the home country, a basis for group identity in the diaspora and for political claims to their homeland. As Worsley and others have shown, culture can become an effective political weapon for 'movements of the disinherited' (Worsley 1968, cf. Kapferer 1988).

In exile, Chile and Chilean culture became the paramount symbol of all that had been lost and must be regained. Mementos of Chile decorated the walls of Chilean homes and the verses of the poet Pablo Neruda, the 'patron' of the cultural movement in Chile and one closely associated with the Popular Unity, were widely read and cited in the community. In his vibrant and powerful homages to his country, often personified as a body, Chile attained an almost physical presence in the distance. Other aspects of life, such as language, forms of address, food and dress, which at home had been rather unreflected aspects of everyday life, now became conscious values as symbols and markers of Chileanness. The way of life and thought to be preserved by Chileans in exile was debated and defined at numerous meetings in the community, in particular in the first few years. The collective identity was essentially fashioned out of the values of the popular movement and Marxist political ideology. The values of solidarity, collectivity, a simple life as workers rejecting the consumerist lifestyle of United States' society, were vital components in the ideal of *no absorbarse,* not being absorbed by 'the beast' and becoming part of its system. Transmitting these values to the children was seen as a crucial task. As in Chilean exile communities elsewhere, a Saturday school was started for children, to teach them Chilean political history and maintain the Spanish language. A dance group was also formed which taught the children Chilean folklore.

The formulation of their cultural heritage necessarily involved a selection of elements from tradition and history. As such it was a creative act, a collective reconstruction of the past in new contexts, which involved a rearrangement of traditional symbols for new functions. The primary function was that of political opposition to the Chilean regime, to preserve the identity of the popular movement. But in exile, these symbols also formed the basis for community, and acted as boundary marker to other groups in the host society. For instance, the politicised dimension of their collective identity as refugees was often articulated to mark their difference from the low-status Mexican labour immigrants in the area.

Defining a collective identity and a heritage as part of a political process to legitimate claims, often involves revitalising or 'inventing' traditions (Hobsbawm 1983). The first years saw an intense and vibrant activity in the community, with a variety of cultural expressions. Traditional music and dances were performed in numerous internal and public events in support of the struggle in Chile. These expressions drew almost exclusively on the traditions of the cultural movement which had emerged in Chile and other parts of Latin America in the 1960s. Emerging in support of political revolutionary change on the Latin American continent, and inspired by the Cuban revolution, this movement identified its heritage in a pre-Hispanic history, postulating a state of Andean harmony and unity before Spanish conquest and imperialism. One of its most well known expressions is the music of *la nueva canción* (the new song). It adapted indigenous musical forms and instruments, revitalising them and giving them new meanings in the new contexts of contemporary Chilean society and politics (e.g. Fairley 1984; Eastmond 1989). Such rediscovered indigenous traditions, real or imagined, lent legitimacy to the ideological vision of the Left in search of political liberation, unity and an authentic national identity. This 'root identity' was then reflected and recreated in a variety of forms in music, art, handicrafts, in the names of song groups (such as the internationally known *Inti Illimani*) and even in the naming of children among the supporters of the Left. For political opposition at home and abroad, these traditions were further elaborated to lend legitimacy to their claims to power and the right to live in their own country. Groups in exile also reflected local traditions: *Kamanchaka,* the musical group which emerged in the community in this study, subsequently incorporated local musical traditions of the politicised Chicano culture and began articulating a wider Latin American identity.

In this concern to preserve traditions of the political movement in exile, there was a tendency to draw on idealised patterns of past political practice, that is, to postulate traditions which had been more in the way of ideological goals than actual political practice at home. The ideals of family and collectivity (at times backed by quotations from Lenin on the nature of the universal worker family), were emphasised with an ideological puritanism that did not correspond to patterns of social relations in everyday life at home. Kay (1987) noted a similar process in her study of Chilean refugees in Scotland. Family matters, such as the socialisation of children or domestic violence, were to be debated and resolved collectively by the community members. That way, what had been more private and personal in Chile became highly politicised and public in exile, facilitated by the transparency of lives in a small and socially isolated community. Similarly, *compañero* ('companion') or *compañera* as a form of address had become common during the revolutionary years of Popular Unity, to foster solidarity and equality in the movement (Kay 1987). Now it took on a new significance and intensified use as a symbol of revolutionary heritage and egalitarian relations between the exiles.

However, with its focus on the political history and ideological content, the heritage thus recreated was defined most actively by men, as the more articulate and politicised social actors. In particular, old or aspiring new political leadership actively shaped the public discourse that developed in the community (although not without considerable competition and conflict among them). In this sense, men and not women defined and represented official 'tradition' in exile, even if women participated in its various expressions. While the political drama of Chile had certainly also shaped the fates of women refugees, they identified less as political actors, and their part in the struggle was seen rather as complementary.

Women's role in upholding Chilean traditions was a less public one, located as it was in the more private domain of domestic life. Here, their role as mothers was crucial, even if the father's role as guardian of the political heritage and the one responsible for transmitting to his children a 'political consciousness' took on greater weight in the new context of North American society. Women were also more active in maintaining ties to family and kin at home, while communications with political networks were almost exclusively handled by the men. A few young and single women who had some experience of politics in Chile and were growing disenchanted with the male aggrandisement of exile politics tried to start a women's political group but were effectively marginalised from the community. Most other women saw their political contribution as a more supportive one. Maria, a woman with a family of politically active men, reflected the view of those women when she referred to the meaning of exile as 'the sacrifice I had to make in order to save the lives of my husband and two sons. I had to leave my country, in order that they may live in safety'. This conception of women's role in politics, in particular the theme of sacrifice, is also represented in the symbolic discourse that emerged in the political opposition after the military takeover.[4]

Life and Death as Key Symbols

In this discourse, power relations and existence were central and closely intertwined themes, expressed in the key metaphors of Life and Death. The military regime was associated with death, a violation of democracy and of life itself. The message, presented in different kinds of collective manifestations, was that life is to death as democracy is to dictatorship. In the exile community, this theme was articulated most clearly in the annual commemoration of the victims of the military coup, in the form of a mass, which has remained the most important event to affirm a common fate and identity as exiles.

In the symbolism of the performance of the mass, which has been analysed in greater detail elsewhere (Eastmond 1989), life and death are key symbols which conflate different domains of meaning (political and religious) and, with their strong moral focus, integrate different groups within a broad opposition, from the Catholic Church establishment to the revolutionary Left. As they are overtly neutral and ambiguous they are difficult to attack, which has allowed a repressed opposition to express in an emotionally powerful way through them the political conflict between the two political systems. In this mass the

4. In the apocalyptic discourse of Chilean politics in the 1970s and 1980s, the increasingly polarised political struggle has been depicted as a battle between forces of life and death. The discourse has been analysed in greater detail in Eastmond (1989).

religious and the political, the eucharist celebration of resurrection and the eschatology of Marxist revolution, reinforce one another in a celebration of how death/dictatorship will be conquered, the victory of life and democracy over death. In this political discourse, the symbolism of life and death also alludes to the notion of women as lifegivers. In Chile, the group known is *La Agrupacion de Familiares de Detenidos Desaparecidos* (the group of relatives of the detained and disappeared), composed and organised mainly by women, articulates this theme most clearly. In their public manifestations against the military regime, the demand for social justice and democracy was legitimated by referring to their moral force as wives and mothers. Their slogan *dar la vida por la vida* (to give life for life) refers to their potential sacrifice, risking their lives in a confrontation with the regime, in order to reclaim the lives of their loved ones. At the same time, they make a public political statement (Vidál 1982). This challenge to the military authorities was a familiar one to many of the refugee women, from the time when they had been trying to locate their husbands detained after the coup. Like the acts of the *Agrupacion,* it meant assuming a new role, making a new experience. With their husbands in prison, women had learnt to make the important domestic decisions and take public action, and later, in exile, they were unwilling to revert to a more dependent female role. However, the family ideal promoted by the political groups implied a return to the traditional division of gender roles. To many women's dismay, the men seemed to devote their time to political activity, in endless debates and meetings, while expecting their wives to resume the traditional responsibility for the household and children. But now, without their social support network at home, women wanted men to take greater responsibility for the adjustment of the family to the new situation. Thus, women did contest and challenge male constructions of exile reality, in areas of particular relevance to them, but they usually did so less publicly: at home, or by seeking support from other women. Such different expectations, in the context of turbulent change, placed a heavy strain on many marriages in the beginning, resulting in domestic quarrels, even violence and divorce in some cases. Subsequently, however, readjustments in gender relations in support of women's perspectives were brought about by the demands of life and work in the United States. In order to understand the different impact on men and women of the encounter with the new society, a brief and somewhat simplified outline of their different social position in Chile is necessary.[5]

5. For a fuller account, see, for example, Kay (1987) or Eastmond (1989).

Life in the Barrio

In Chile, the social milieu of working-class families was mostly that of the *barrio*, the local neighbourhood, which formed a closely interconnected social network consisting of neighbours, kin, workmates and political associates. The women, as housewives, were oriented mainly to running the family and the household, but had close interaction with the other women, as relatives, neighbours and friends in the local neighbourhood. Men's roles as principal breadwinners and workers took them beyond the *barrio*, into the world of production and party politics.

The Torres family lived in such a typical working class *barrio* in the capital, Santiago. It carried the name of the nearby industry which employed Eduardo Torres and many of the other men who lived in it. His wife, Maria, was a housewife who also occasionally contributed to the household economy by taking in laundry or sewing. Like most of the other women in the neighbourhood, Maria was not an organised militant of any political party but supported the political work of her husband and the new policies of the Popular Unity government. From her perspective its significance for the local barrio was this:

> We were like one big family, in our *barrio,* we always helped each other out. We managed, but there was much poverty around us, people struggling to make ends meet. Under Allende I saw many of them coming out of their misery, getting jobs and higher wages. Children were given free milk every day now and had proper health care ... Everybody was involved, participating with the government, even the children at school. People belonged to different political parties but most of us supported Popular Unity. We organised a neighbourhood council to improve housing conditions, and there were local health and educational programmes. The men spent a lot of time at the factory, in meetings and committees with new responsibilities. Everybody seemed to be talking politics, we learnt that the people had rights. All these things made us believe in Allende. We had great confidence in him.

The coup brutally crushed these hopes. One night, shortly after it, the *carabineros* (military police) came to the Torres' house and picked up the husband and the eldest son. Maria spent three weeks searching for them. As with many others detained in this period, there was no information available on their whereabouts.

> Twenty-four hours a day I was enquiring about them – at police headquarters, at the military regiments, the Red Cross, the Ministry of the Interior, hospitals and mortuaries. I walked through all the streets where corpses

had been thrown out and searched for them. Those were twenty days of an-
guish. I finally found them, in a concentration camp, in a terrible condition.
Both had been beaten and tortured badly.

The persecution and flight following the coup shattered the worlds
of both men and women. 'We arrived *desnudos*', meaning dispossessed of everything, expressed the sense of vast loss many refugees
suffered on being forced to leave relatives and friends, their country
and familiar culture for an uncertain existence elsewhere. Almost
every family had lost a close relative or friend in the massive killings
of the opposition. Having nothing and being nobody in the new country, they entered the United States with a strong apprehension about
life in 'the belly of the Beast'. But the sense of loss and concern for
the future had a somewhat different focus for men and women. The
men tended to centre on the political defeat and the ordeal they had
suffered in prison. After the coup men were displaced from their roles
as political actors and as breadwinners, both important bases for male
identity and self-esteem. The women, on the other hand, grieved the
loss of their social world, the network that made up their daily life in
the *barrio*. Concerned about her children, Patricia reflected the mood
of many women in the beginning: 'The first year was terrible and full
of grief. I missed so much my *barrio* and my country. I was afraid my
children would take a bad road in the US. In Chile we have this idea of
this country as being the centre of drugs and perversion'.

Life and Work in Silicon Valley

The prolonged exile required some accommodation, however reluc-
tantly, with the new society. The tentative quality and intensely political focus of the first years was gradually challenged by the construction of another compelling reality, that of everyday life. In this
process, some contexts of new experience had more impact than others. Work and economy in northern California's electronics industry
centre (known by its nickname 'Silicon Valley') was the principal
point of interface with the host society, which in decisive ways re-
structured social relations in the community.

There was initially a strong resistance to entering the United States'
labour market. Apart from the ideological implications of economic
integration they also felt a sense of vulnerability as newcomers not
speaking the language and having to start in the low-status occupations. However, the strong demand for labour in the electronics indus-

try and the availability of job training persuaded a majority to accept training and employment as assemblers and technicians in electronics companies in the area. Two incomes were necessary to survive in the high-cost area of the Valley and after some time women too entered the labour market, at first doing unskilled manual work in the local canneries. Employment was new to them, as few women had worked outside of the home in Chile. Later, many of them entered and completed training courses in electronics assembly, and a small number subsequently moved on for more qualified training as technicians. Employment also required learning other skills such as a new language, driving a car and mastering the culture and technology of modern bureaucracy and high-tech enterprise. For the women, earning their own living and acquiring new skills was an important part of gaining more confidence as well as greater domestic authority.

New work patterns affected gender relations and role expectations in the household. Men's and women's work roles, which had been relatively complementary in Chile, became more similar and exchangeable, blurring the traditionally stricter division between male and female domains. As women went out to work along with their men, a new division of labour became necessary at home: men were forced to enter the domestic domain of childcare and housework, as their wives were on alternative work shifts, or refused to shoulder the double work load. The surrounding society provided alternative models of gender relations and women began to question traditional male privileges. The differences in social position between men and women, so taken for granted at home, became more visible in the new context. Men's resistance to such change now exposed more acutely the uncomfortable gap between the political rhetoric of gender equality and the actual, traditional practice. Nevertheless, women continued to hold a greater responsibility for the household. In the absence of the support network at home, their overall workload did increase.

Relations between families in the exile community also changed as a result. In contrast to the social organisation of the *barrio,* where households were integrated by patterns of mutual support and daily interaction, each household was transformed into a more self-sufficient economic and social unit. In this process, husband and wife became more dependent on each other for emotional support and companionship, and the demands of busy working lives provided less opportunities for external relationships. The exile community, initially a close-knit support network, increasingly took on the function of an interactional social network, with families socialising on weekends for leisure or special celebrations. Such occasions were often different kinds of solidarity events for Chile. As exile politics was successively reduced to a solidarity function, and as active party politics declined, such events opened up a space for women to assume new and active organisational roles. The contribution to the struggle in Chile was modest but increasingly recognised as concrete and broad-based in contrast to the more rhetorical and partisan politics of the men. Such activity was facilitated by the fact that it could be combined with family responsibilities and interaction with friends. For instance, a women's group formed and worked successfully to support the women of the *Agrupacion* in Chile, organising benefit events and their handicrafts which they imported from Chile.

For all, however, lives and identities became more individualised. This represented a significant change from the close-knit networks of working-class life in Chile. The change also conflicted with the ideological norms of collective concerns and community in exile. However, the authority of political parties and other leadership was successively eroded by a complex of problems relating to exile politics (Eastmond, 1989), as well as by the increasingly self-sufficient households.

The Changing Lives of Men and Women in Exile

Compared to their positions as working-class wives in Chile, women's social world expanded in the new society, as they gained a broader repertoire of roles, including a greater participation in economic and other public spheres. Employment brought not only their own income and a necessary contribution to the family economy, but also an occupational identity, together with greater self-reliance and confidence. Although new working lives away from the social network of kin at home meant greater loneliness and less emotional support, at least initially, many women welcomed the absence of social control exercised by such networks. Most importantly, in their new position, women were largely able to reconcile their new roles with the traditional expectations and concerns held of them and by them as mothers. Contrary to their initial misgivings about raising their children in the United States, their children were doing much better than expected and benefitted from the educational advantages available to them compared to their peers in Chile. Thus, the sacrifice that Maria and other women claimed they made for their families when they chose to go into exile had not been in vain. Now, through their own incomes they could contribute even more actively to their children's education and future wellbeing.

In contrast, men's worlds contracted in comparison to their situation in Chile. Their lives became more private, and disconnected from the public sphere as they knew it at home. Although content to be able to provide a good life and education for their family, men felt that a deeper meaning of work was lost in the way of life they had come to. For these workers and active trade unionists, politics and work used to be closely connected in Chile, where there was a strong solidarity between workmates. In the United States' companies, which had neither trade unions nor a tradition of collectivity, this vital dimension was lost. For Ramon, a miner, and others, life was now a secure but tedious existence that lacked the urgency of political struggle that had pervaded his life and work at home. Eduardo complained that he felt he was 'merely existing, not living ...if there is nothing to die for, there is nothing to live for, either'. Political struggle had made work roles meaningful and dignified in Chile, and had provided a source of status and identity. Exile politics increasingly marginalised them from the national arena as political actors and party activity dwindled.

The discrepancy between their past and present roles and identities was more problematic for the men. Their inability to resolve the conflict must also be understood in the context of their history as victims of torture and organised violence and its problematic relation to political commitment as a basis for identity. To question convictions for which they had suffered and many comrades had died was unsettling and painful. This past was not easily relinquished, in particular not for what appeared to be a comfortable, middle-class life in the United States. Renouncing their role in the struggle would also be a victory for the regime, and their personal sacrifices would have come to nothing. Furthermore, torture is a profound and lasting assault on a person and those who survive are inevitably changed (see, for example, Turner 1989), the experience may remain as a troubled inner reality along with outwardly well-adjusted lives. Many exiled men were caught in a paradox which can be expressed as the torment of remembering and the fear of forgetting. While their convictions helped to make suffering more meaningful, sustained through the revolutionary heroism of their political discourse, holding on to this past also tended to inhibit its resolution. For the men, more than the women, exile appeared to harbour an irreconcilable duality, in which the preserving and the relinquishing of one's political past was equally problematic.

'Return to Life': The Dilemmas of Continuity and Change

After a decade in exile, the lives of refugee men and women had been irretrievably changed. For the large majority, the transformation was taking its toll. Adaptation to life in the United States remained a moral and ideological conflict with respect to Chile and commitments made to those who remained at home. Ageing parents, unemployed relatives and the growing poverty of the Chilean working-class under the Pinochet regime constituted an inescapable reality in stark contrast to their own secure and comfortable life styles in California. The ambiguity of their existence persisted as exile remained open ended. The dilemmas were brought to the fore acutely when political changes in Chile began opening the doors for exiles to return. This seemed the moment of truth, but choices were no longer so clear-cut: Chilean society had been transformed during their exile and returnees were likely to find themselves economically and socially marginalised. They, too, had changed in their absence from home. For those who eventually returned, reintegration would mean another battle and their state of exile may well continue at home, yet would those who chose to remain still be exiles? The ambiguity of definitions and the struggle over time with identities, compounding legal, ideological and existential dimensions, reflect the essence of the exile condition. Whereas the legal and political status may change, the condition for the individual may, in existential terms, last a lifetime (Tabori 1972).

The commemoration mass held every year in the community represented an attempt to resolve, symbolically at least, these contradictions of exile, postulating the necessity of return. In this mass, life and death as political metaphors were elaborated with special reference to the exile condition: the symbolic conversion in which life conquered death through resurrection represented the reconquest of a democratic social order, but also referred to the return home of the exile. While exile was depicted as non-life, as merely 'existing, not living' and in its extension holding the threat of social death, return home held the promise of reconquering a 'full life' *(una vida plena)*. Or, as the old Argentinian exile in Solana's film 'El exilio de Gardél' put it, 'Exile is absence. Extended absence is death.... *hay que volver o morir!* [you have to return or you die!]'. This annual event was an institutionalised attempt to reaffirm unity and continuity, to reiterate collective obligations, to hold firm processes of disintegration and change in the community. However, as official ideology, the discourse no longer unambiguously reflected Chileans' personal experience of exile. The very basis for collectively defining reality was eroding, and ideological schemes and concerns no longer adequately explained or resolved the struggles of personal life. In attempts to renegotiate the meaning of exile in the community, it was agreed that return, once a key element in this official ideology, was to be 'a personal decision', no longer open to moral judgement by other members of the community. Nevertheless, this was a process loaded with discomfort and tension between collective interest, official ideology and individual experience (cf. Jacobson-Widding 1989).

The ultimate dilemma of exile may be the emerging doubts about one's own cultural constructions of reality. It was, for the Chileans, not only a crisis of social meaning but also, for the individual, a crisis of identity, of coming to terms with Chile and the past. The theme of social death and estrangement, of forgetting and being forgotten, was a recurring one in many exiles' dreams, often represented by images of death. Julio, for instance, often dreamt that he returned to his hometown, full of joy to see the familiar streets and the faces of his loved ones but, rushing to greet them, he found that nobody recognised him or knew his name. The dream left him with a feeling of never having existed. Having severed close social bonds in Chile without creating new ones in the host society, his fear was that of being doubly marginalised, of having forfeited a full life in both worlds. Laura, who although like Maria was fairly reconciled with staying in the United States if it meant being close to her children and grandchildren, still reflects the sense of loss associated with defining new roles and identities in the present. In an unsettling recurring dream she observed, from a distance, her own deathbed. All her family and kin at home were gathered around her, they were all crying. She was dying, without any physical pain, but with 'an unbearable sadness'.

The diminished authority of the official ideology of male politics made more salient women's experiences and perspectives. The women seemed less attracted by the idea of return than their husbands, even if ambivalence afflicted them all. Many women feared losing the gains they had made in terms of a more independent social and economic position, one that would be difficult to maintain back home. Moreover, the option of return presented a new dilemma, one which threatened to nullify the sacrifice many women felt they had made, successfully, to keep the family together throughout years of turbulent change. Many children felt more at home in the new country, some had started families of their own and did not share their parents' dream of returning to Chile. Insofar as children also represented continuity and life for

women, seen as 'life-givers', the affirmation of life would be to remain where their children and grandchildren chose to be.

Thus for the Chilean refugees in California, 'return to a full life' no
longer necessarily means a return to Chile. It may be a question of creating new meanings and identities out of the contradictions between
past and present. While these contradictions seem to be an inevitable
mark of the exile experience, this study demonstrates a case in which
refugee women have been relatively successful in integrating their past
into a meaningful present. In so doing, they have been able to reconcile traditional role expectations with the demands of the new society,
and collective concerns with personal experience and aspirations.

References

Abu-Lughod, J., 1988 'Palestinians: Exiles at Home and Abroad', *Current Sociology*,
   vol.36, no.2 pp.61–9
ALAM Ediciones (n.d.), *Situación de los Exiliados Latinoamericanos en Venezuela*,
   Stockholm
Angell, A. and Carstairs, S., 1987 'The Exile Question in Chilean Politics', *Third World
   Quarterly*, vol.9, no.1 pp.148ff.
Eastmond, M., 1988 'The Politics of Death: Rituals of Protest in a Chilean Exile
   Community', in S. Cederroth, C. Corlin and J. Lindstrom, *On the Meaning of Death.
   Essays on Mortuary Rituals and Eschatological Beliefs*, Uppsala Studies in Cultural
   Anthropology no. 8, pp. 77–94
—1989 'The Dilemmas of Exile. Chilean Refugees in the USA', unpublished PhD the-
   sis, Department of Social Anthropology, Gothenburg University
Fairley, J., 1984 '*La Nueva Canción Latinoamericana*', *Bulletin of Latin American
   Research*, vol.3, no.2, pp.107–15
Hobsbawm, E., 1983 'Inventing Traditions', in E. Hobsbawm and T. Ranger (eds), *The
   Invention of Tradition*, Cambridge: Cambridge University Press
Jacobson-Widding, A., 1989 'Personal Experience and Official Ideology. The Illness of
   the Double Bind', in A. Jacobson-Widding and D. Westerlund (eds), *Culture,
   Experience, and Pluralism. Essays on African Ideas of Illness and Healing*, Uppsala
   Studies in Cultural Anthropology no. 13
Kapferer, B., 1988 *Legends of People, Myths of State*, in W.I. Merrill and I. Karp (eds),
   Smithsonian Series in Ethnographic Enquiry, Washington DC and London:
   Smithsonian Institution Press
Kay, D., 1987 *Chileans in Exile. Private Struggles, Public Lives*, Edinburgh Studies in
   Sociology, Houndmills and London: Macmillan
Riquelme, H., 1987 'Latinoamerianos en Europa. Experiencia de desarraigo y proceso
   de identidad psicocultural', *Acta psiquiát. psicol. Amér. lat.* , vol.33, pp.281–95
Spring, A., 1982 'Women and Men as Refugees: Differential Assimilation of Angolan
   refugees in Zambia', in A. Hansen and A. Oliver-Smith (eds), *Involuntary Migration
   and Resettlement*, Boulder, Colorado:Westview Press, pp.37–47
Tabori, P., 1972 *The Anatomy of Exile*. London: Harrap
Turner, S., 1989 'Working with Survivors', *Psychiatric Bulletin*, vol. 13, pp. 173–6
Turner, V.W., 1967 *The Forest of Symbols. Aspects of Ndembu Ritual*, Ithaca, New
   York: Cornell University Press
— 1969 *The Ritual Process: Structure and Anti-Structure*, Chicago: Aldine
van Gennep, A., 1908 *Rites of Passage*, London: Routledge and Kegan Paul, 1960 ed.

Vidál, H., 1982 *Dar La Vida por la Vida: La Agrupación Chilena de Familiares Detenidos Desaparecidos*, Minneapolis, Minn.: Institute for the Study of Ideologies and Literature
Worsley, P., 1968 *The Trumpet Shall Sound*, London: McGibbon Kee

4

Defining Gender in a Second Exile: Palestinian Women in West Berlin

Dima Abdulrahim

Palestinians arrived in West Berlin from refugee camps in Lebanon. When they went to this European city it was not their first move. Since 1948 they have been subject to a long term process of forced displacement and transformed from a predominantly peasant population into landless refugees. Palestinians in exile have also undergone a process of social and economic transformation and reconstruction defined by the extent of their control over their own affairs.

My aim in this chapter is to look at some aspects of this process. In particular I will examine the definition and transformation of gender relations among Palestinians in West Berlin, by arguing that gender and social relations are historically specific. They are determined by social, economic, class, political, legal and ideological factors, as well as cultural and religious ones. I will argue, as does Messick, that subordinate discourses are historically specific. They exist in the context of particular power configurations of gender and class, and change as part of a more general process of historical transformation (Messick 1987: 216).

The historical analysis of gender relations among Palestinians in more than forty years of exile has shown that gender differentiation and subordination have been constant factors. Palestinians do not differ from other cultures and societies. However, though there may always have been inequality of the sexes, the position of women, their status and activities has not been the same at all times, but has been subject to transformation. In this chapter I thus aim to look at the conditions that maintained and reinforced subordination at certain times; or, on the contrary made the introduction of more egalitarian definitions possible and legitimate at others.

The analysis of Palestinian women in West Berlin has raised general questions relating to the effect of migration to the West on gender relations. Similar exercises have been undertaken cross culturally and many conclusions have been reached. The interpretation of changes towards more egalitarian relationships as a result of Westernisation, identified by the Tradition-Modernity approach has been criticised since the 1970s. More recent evidence has shown that supposed move towards achieving equality among migrant communities were not always what they purported to be. It is now assumed that both gains and losses took place (see, for example, the special edition on women of the International Migration Review 1984). Research has also shown that the effects of minority status and racism are lived differently by the various sectors of 'migrant' communities. It has identified class and regional location as some of the important factors that determined differences (see, for example, Afshar 1989: 211–23).

Analysis of the definition of gender relations among Palestinians in West Berlin has shown that they have undoubtedly been redefined, but not at all towards greater equality. On the contrary, migration has given rise to a more differentiated definition of gender relations and a traditional understanding of concepts of community and continuance. This traditional model, I argue, was formulated and sustained by the migration to a Western sexually-integrated society and by the marginality of Palestinians to the German state, society and economy.

Historical Background of the Palestinian Exiles

In 1948, the peasants and urban poor of Palestine were turned overnight into completely destitute refugees and were placed in hurriedly prepared refugee camps. In Lebanon, the status of refugee which they acquired marginalised them from the socio-economic structure of the Lebanese state and society. Refugees differed from foreigners in as much as they could not be deported, but were treated as foreigners in all other matters: they had no voting rights, required the same work permit as foreigners and employment was on a 'first-preference-to-citizen' basis. Palestinians had no right to receive social benefits or to join trade unions. The family has been analysed as a comprehensive social, psychological and economic system that helped Palestinians survive more than United Nations agencies did.

Between 1969 and 1982 Palestinians in Lebanon developed a higher degree of autonomous control over their own affairs than they had in the preceding centuries under Ottoman and British hegemony. Through the Palestine Liberation Organisation (PLO) Palestinians achieved representation on national and international levels, and developed an independent socio-economic and political structure orientated to their needs. The PLO provided both a welfare system and employment in productive and non-productive institutions.

The development of PLO institutions by refugee communities was accompanied by a process of social engineering. It did not unfold in an atmosphere of confrontation, alienation, or coercion but within the context of national and cultural reconstruction. The national movement initiated new ideologies of the social order and concepts of justice, and enjoyed a substantial measure of popular support. The national and patriotic context in which this process of reconstruction unfolded lent it an aura of legitimacy and made possible the introduction of new forms of social relations (Peteet 1987: 30–2).

A new definition of women's role in society emerged. Women were recruited in the agencies of the PLO and the idea of a new Palestinian woman was formulated. Their participation in the national struggle became legitimate and essential, for the struggle was based on the integration of all sectors of the society. A socialisation process worked through education and political education to allow for their participation in formal economy and polity. It was enhanced by the establishment of services such as day care centres and nurseries. Problems of women's economic participation in their society were addressed by the provision of employment and by the promotion of literacy, skills and technical training. On a local camp level, family opposition to the political participation of women generally met with the intervention of political cadres. Cadres often intervened in cases of domestic violence, the marriage of women against their will, matters of divorce and other crises.

The participation of women in their nation's struggle gave them legitimate public activity outside the household and often involved sexually unsegregated activities. An arena of social and political activity existed outside the family. The politicisation of poor refugee women implied their presence and participation in areas that had been defined as male domains. It implied legitimate contact between the sexes outside the context and the control of the family.

Although the position of women in society had been subject to transformation, the changes were by no means radical. The involvement and active participation of women in the struggle continued to be determined by traditional forms of patriarchal control and domination. The Palestinian political organisations placed considerable emphasis on the importance of the woman's and the family's reproductive functions, and gave these a patriotic meaning. No radical transformation of the division of labour took place, and thus no eradication of the asymmetrical nature of gender relations: a woman's involvement in the struggle was legitimate, but overshadowed her struggle for equality. Her stance was one of support and was dictated by her social position (although well known exceptions existed and were accepted). Nationalism, in other words, came at the expense of feminism (see, for example; Sayigh 1987, and 1989; Kazi 1987).

It was argued by S. Joseph in her analysis of a Peteet study, that the absence of a Palestinian state inhibited the liberation of women (Joseph 1986: 5). Between the late 1960s and 1982, however, the position of Palestinian women in the camps was not static; even if no radical change took place, the Palestinian woman in 1982 was very different from her counterpart of the late 1960s. Palestinian society saw itself as part of a general process of transformation. New models of community and continuance were developed, and, within them, social and gender relations were not defined by traditionalism, but by an attempt to create a new and progressive society.

Political Asylum in West Berlin Until the Late 1980s

Palestinian families started to arrive in West Berlin in the mid-1970s, as a direct result of the war in Lebanon. 'Migration' generally followed political tension, military attacks or massacres. After the Israeli invasion of Lebanon in 1982, Palestinians were joined by other groups from Lebanon, namely Kurds, Shi'ite and Sunni Muslim Lebanese. Around 15,000 asylum seekers from Lebanon were estimated to be living in the city in the mid-1980s (*Evangelischer Pressedienst* 1985: 100). With the exception of a very small number of middle class students and professionals, Palestinians in West Berlin were poor refugees. In the majority of cases, they were semi-skilled or unskilled workers with little or no formal education. Illiteracy or semi-literacy was high, especially among older women.

Like many foreigners from the Third World, migrants from Lebanon were, until recently, asylum seekers. As the Federal Republic as it existed before German reunification did not recognise the division of the city, of which the then extant Berlin Wall was the physical emblem, entry to the Western sector of the city through the Eastern one was possible without valid entry visas or travel documents. There, like many others from the Third World, they applied for political asylum. The effects of the cataclysm that has taken place in Germany will be discussed in the conclusion.

Until the late 1980s, the vast majority of Palestinians in West Berlin were asylum seekers. Only a very small minority had acquired regular residence permits through marriage to German women or by arriving in the Federal Republic in the 1960s. These people were not subject to the procedures of asylum but had rights denied to asylum seekers. A few accumulated a small amount of capital and acquired businesses such as grocery shops, sandwich bars, cafes and restaurants. With family elders and political cadres, they formed the informal leadership of the Palestinian community.

'Measures of deterrence', in Federal asylum policies, were aimed both at making asylum seekers want to leave voluntarily and deterring potential new arrivals. The fact that asylum seekers from the so-called Third World had little if any chance of being recognised as persecuted political refugees, and also the development by the German Federal government of difficult living conditions. (For more on political asylum in the FRG see, for example, Goodwin 1983: 177–180; Marx 1983, 1984.)

Political asylum applications were the responsibility of the Federal Office for the Recognition of Foreign Refugees. Decisions to recognise an asylum seeker as a persecuted political refugee could be challenged by both the asylum seeker and the state in a process that could take up to four or five years. There was little or no chance for Palestinians to be recognised as persecuted political refugees. The conditions of the Lebanese war, however, meant that the deportation of Lebanese, Kurds and Palestinians to Lebanon was not always possible. The expulsion of rejected asylum seekers was often temporarily halted in which case they were then issued with Tolerance Permits, which did not confer a right of residence, but were temporary residence permits pending deportation.

The shadow of deportation formulated many of the considerations and calculations of asylum seekers from Lebanon. One young man summed up this feeling by stating that 'people felt that they were neither here nor there'. There was little relation between immediate action and long term consequence: long-term investment in Germany did not have a practical meaning. The shadow of deportation determined to a great extent the relationship of Palestinians with the German host society.

The procedures of asylum circumscribed the boundaries of social and economic action. They attempted to segregate asylum seekers from the majority German society by restricting rights to work, to freedom of movement and study. Basic contacts and communication were difficult for instance adults were not eligible to free education, not even German language classes.

The procedures of asylum determined many other aspects of the lives of asylum seekers. They had a crucial role in the definition of gender relations and the position and role of Palestinian women in society. On an official level, legal procedures contravened the international definition of the 'family unit' concept as unequal status was given to different family members (International Convention on Civil and Political Rights of 1966, article 23). In other words, husband and wife were defined as individual asylum seekers and not as a legal/bureaucratic unit. They had to present different proofs of persecution, had separate applications for asylum and could be deported separately.

Since 1978, upon arrival in West Berlin asylum seekers have been distributed among the various *Länder* (states) of the Federal Republic. Movement out of the allocated area without prior authorisation was illegal. The reallocation of asylum seekers among the various areas often took them by surprise as many assumed they would be able to live in the same city as their kin. What was most feared was being allocated to small villages in remote rural areas, where Palestinians and foreigners were rare.

The random allocation of individuals, in particular, women, to various areas of the Republic often caused problems. Those who suffered most were, of course, the most vulnerable. Unmarried women were in some cases allocated to remote rural villages in West Germany, although their parents or relatives lived in West Berlin. As social norms made it impossible for them to live on their own, they often lived illegally in the divided city. (The implications of their illegal stay will be clarified in the following pages.) The restriction of asylum seekers to allocated areas also had an effect on of a woman's ability to leave her conjugal household and to seek divorce, as will be discussed later.

From 16 January 1982, newly arriving asylum seekers were restricted to accommodation centres or homes *(Heim)* established in former military barracks, disused hospitals and schools, hotels and other such collective premises. These centres were designed to provide for the basic needs of the individual. The premises were divided between those in which cooked food was distributed in collective areas at particular times of the day, and those in which asylum seekers cooked their own food rations in communal kitchens.

Until the mid-1980s, living conditions in these collective premises were the subject of strong national and international criticism. Best known is the 1983 United Nations High Commission for Refugees

(UNHCR) internal report that was leaked to the press. It mentioned difficult living conditions and the restriction of inmates to very small spaces, often not exceeding four or five square meters per adult. It also mentioned the unhygienic sanitary conditions and psychological climate (UNHCR 1983). Over the years, living conditions and hygiene standards in these centres were improved. In the second half of the 1980s, a three phase system was introduced allowing asylum seekers to look for privately rented apartments after a period of five years.

Collective premises were also divided between those designed for single men or women and those for families. Families were given a number of rooms, depending on their size. *Heim* residents shared bathrooms, toilets and kitchens. In other words, private activities, such as bathing, had to be undertaken in collective areas. In a society which sanctions the contact between unrelated members of the two sexes, questions are raised about the effect of the housing on social relations inside the collective premises.

People who did not know each other had to share living space. A rigid distinction between private/domestic and public domains was impossible. Physical space was thus redefined. In one of the collective premises visited, Arabic speaking households divided the Heim in space and time. Kitchens were, predictably, defined as exclusively women's domains, and the use of showers was divided by the asylum seekers themselves between a time for women and for men. This practice was common to most collective premises. Sources of tension were foreseeable: conflict often centred around the use of public spaces and facilities, and concerned the level of noise made by children and the cleanliness of the kitchens and bathrooms.

Living conditions meant that real segregation of the sexes was not possible. To be able to conform to gender relation norms and to accommodate the new living conditions, social relations between households also had to be redefined. A new relationship was established between the residents in this *Heim* turning strangers into neighbours *(Jiran)*. This relationship could be interpreted as honorary kinship. It allowed for a fluid interpretation of socio-physical boundaries between households and maximised the domestic and private space.

In one of the collective premises four households lived in the eastern wing of the second floor of some converted offices. As each of these households was allocated a certain number of rooms, movement from one room to the other had to be done through the collective corridor. To make movement possible, the corridor between the various rooms was defined as part of the domestic space of all households. Within it, informal movement and domestic activity was legitimate. It was, in other words, possible for adults and adolescents to be seen in their night clothes on the condition that they were modest. In summer, the doors of the various rooms were often left open. Domestic and other activities were conducted in the collective space.

This shared domestic space was well defined. It covered the eastern wing of the floor and was separated from the western wing by the staircase. The stairs separating two floors, or the gangway separating two sections of a building defined the strict boundaries of social activity. Movement in the shared domestic area of a different floor was more formal and subject to different social rules. In other words, although households shared these collective areas, they were part of the domestic domain of those who were situated there only. A number of collective areas were defined as neutral areas, that is they were not part of the domestic arena of any household. These were turned into areas for exclusive female use on a temporary basis. In the afternoon, the women of the *Heim* sat together in large hall-ways, for instance.

By 1987, the great majority of asylum seekers did not live in collective premises. They lived in privately rented apartments, the rent for which was paid by the asylum authorities. Palestinians and other asylum seekers lived, predictably, in the poor working class areas inhabited by other foreigners. These offered social and psychological advantages such as the possibility of movement with less racial harassment, protection of other foreigners and access to familiar foods, mosques and community centres. They also offered collective control of the group over the behaviour of individuals, especially women.

Arabic speaking women, who generally lived near other households from Lebanon, established between each other the privileged relationship of neighbourhood. As the street was a public area it was also the scene of intense social interaction and became a basis for intimacy. Women's networks were one of the main determinants of the street or area. They had a large local importance, extended throughout the neighbourhood, and incorporated Lebanese, Palestinian, Kurdish and other Arabic speaking women.

Women offered each other help and services. Newcomers were taught how to use the public transport system and how to use shops. Many activities, such as visiting shopping areas, were often done collectively with other women. They thus not only offered each other company but also social control, protection and chaperonage. Networks established rules that newcomers had to adopt, and they organised, through gossip and exchange of information, controlled domains. Women knew through these networks of the whereabouts of their husbands; whether they frequented bars or saw other women. Arabic-speaking women also informed each other about the movement of their daughters and so had greater control over them.

Women's networks were potentially wide reaching and extended beyond the kinship group and neighbourhood. In this way they thus maximised access to services. Women's networks also forged the means for establishing contact between men and so households. By defining controlled domains and providing services, a certain degree of control over men was enabled by these networks.

In the various residential quarters women defined exclusive collective public domains in which they could meet. In a small number of buildings inhabited only by Arabic speakers, women met daily in summer in the internal courtyard of the building. The courtyard was considered by them, and the men, to be an exclusive female area in the afternoon. Corners of parks and squares in the immediate vicinity of the houses also often took on the same role.

Economic Conditions of Asylum and the Definition of Gender Relations

On 18 July 1980, asylum seekers lost the right to work for the first two years of asylum; this period was extended to five years in 1986. An asylum seeker had the right to take paid employment after this period, but only after a job had been advertised for three months and had not been taken by a German citizen or the holder of a regular work permit. Palestinians were effectively excluded from the regular labour market. They depended on a type of social aid or 'Help for Survival' introduced in January 1981. Its value in West Berlin was around 20 per cent less than that given to non-asylum seekers, although this discrimination was declared illegal in March 1985 by the Federal authorities.

In collective premises, benefits were given, as far as possible, in the form of cooked food, food rations, clothing and vouchers to be exchanged for clothes. Individuals were also given a small amount of cash, amounting in 1987 to DM 70 per head of household. Asylum seekers in private apartments received their monthly allocations in the form of cash or vouchers. Monthly benefits in 1987 were DM 405–410 per adult head of household and less for other adults and children. The dependence of Palestinians on asylum benefits and their exclusion from the regular labour market had a number of implications. Laws relating to asylum seekers did mean that their basic needs were met: they were fed, clothed and housed. Their social and economic marginality was, however, legally sanctioned. The dependence on social benefits, had a number of other implications and affected intra- and inter-household relations.

The absence of employment meant that the male head of household lost his role as provider. Benefits meant that other members of his household – especially women – were economically independent of him. This does not mean that the lack of economic activity and the equality of benefits seriously affected gender relations (in reality it meant a further marginalisation of women as will be discussed below), but whether the social order was affected or not, the men's perception of their loss of authority was significant. It was often accompanied by a loss of self-esteem which they saw as resulting from their economic inactivity and dependence on benefits. One father of adolescents asked: 'How can my children respect me when I do not respect myself? How can I respect myself when I do not work but sit and do nothing the whole day?'

The presence of the unemployed father in the household restricted the movement of girls and young unmarried women and limited their freedom of movement. Mothers were generally more lenient and allowed them to go out more easily; they reprimanded their daughters for staying out later than allowed, but often tolerated it and did not punish the adolescents. As solidarity existed between mothers and their daughters, absent fathers would not be informed. The presence of the father in the home meant a different set of rules. As one seventeen year old girl said: 'When my father is at home, I cannot do anything'.

The communal living of the older women, characteristic of life in the camps they had left in Lebanon, was transformed. The economic inactivity of men also affected their movements in West Berlin and made contact between them more difficult. The presence of the man in the household made it more difficult for his wife to visit other women or be visited by them. Visiting did, however, take place, but women avoided doing so at times when the husbands were at home. Some categories, however, were regulated by different social relationships. The relationship between a woman and the husbands of her close neighbours and friends was redefined; it was transformed into a tie of honorary kinship and made informal contact legitimate.

The weather in West Berlin also contributed to the isolation of women and increased the difficulty they faced in sustaining network relations. In the long months of winter, it was too cold to meet in the open air courtyards, squares and parks. To a large extent, women lost their control over the street, the area they dominated in the camps in Lebanon and which was defined – socially and physically – as part of the domain of women. In the camps, women lived to a large extent collectively and not in privatised units. In West Berlin the Arabic video films came to occupy a large part of the spare time of women.

Women's domestic activity was also subject to transformation. First and foremost, they lost much of the help they had from other women – especially kin – in domestic work and child rearing. A state in which there was much less co-operation came to exist and fewer possibilities for carrying out domestic chores with other women. The arrival of Palestinian women in a Western city did not make their domestic activities any easier; some chores, on the contrary, were added to their burden. For instance, women spent many hours baking bread, one of the main staple foods, as they could not afford to buy the necessary quantities nor did they see the bread sold in the market as an alternative to their own. Despite men's economic inactivity, their unemployment did not result in any important contribution to domestic work.

Daughters, especially the eldest, were expected to do a large part of the housework and to care for younger children. Mothers depended very heavily on their help. In addition to household work, the eldest daughter was expected to play the role of translator and bridge between her parents and officials, doctors and German society in general. She was especially necessary for a mother who often spoke no German at all and who was, in many cases, illiterate or semi-literate even in Arabic. This role did not empower daughters, instead it effectively reduced the role of their mothers in the household.

It is interesting to note that it was women who undertook much of the regular contact with West Berlin officials and employees of the various legal aid and welfare organisations for refugees. U. Haupt, who was director in 1987 of one of these organisations, said that men often initially reconnoitred the offices to assess whether the environment suited the presence of women, from which time on, if the decision was positive, it was their wives who came. Women were thus given the responsibility of dealing with many legal matters and seeking advice on a number of issues. It was women generally who collected social benefits from the relevant offices.

Although legitimate economic activity was circumscribed by asylum procedures, an alternative economy was developed by asylum seekers. Social benefits were, therefore, not the only source of income, as illegal work was a common way of increasing cash flow. Employment was generally occasional, and was found in the services sector, restaurants and bars for example, often involving cleaning work or work in the kitchen. Cash supplemented social benefits and made the acquisition of consumer items possible, but it did not effectively change living conditions.

For a number of reasons the employment of women in West Berlin was less frequent than it had been in the camps in Lebanon. The work of the married women in West Berlin was, more than previously, seen to be incompatible with domestic activity and most particularly with child rearing. It is also important to remember that women were not allowed to work in factories, spoke little German and had few marketable skills.

While the employment of an unmarried woman was tolerated and often necessary in the refugee camp, social benefits distributed in West Berlin meant her basic costs were covered and that her employment was not vital to the livelihood of the family. The nature of the illegal employment available also excluded her participation. Work was mainly available in bars, cafes, restaurants and other areas where alcohol was served. Often, it meant working evening shifts. While work in fast food chains was tolerated in some cases and employment was also found in the cleaning sector, it was characterised by arduous conditions, bad pay and low status. Analysis of the employment patterns of both the married and unmarried women also raises issues of gender and class.

The analysis of Palestinian women and income generation in West Berlin confirms many of the conclusions reached by other researchers in different groups in the Federal Republic of Germany and elsewhere. As with the case of Turkish women, the study of Palestinian women cannot ignore the relationship between gender and the insecurity of residence and work, including the non-availability of work permits (see Munscher 1984: 1230–46). It cannot automatically assign to women the role of dependent and analyse this dependency as also applying to the country of origin (Morokvasic 1984: 888–93). As the Arabic-speaking community defined women as having only a domestic identity, a public identity was not made possible through employment or education in West Berlin. Women were restricted to the domestic arena and this became the norm.

Defining Gender in Exile

Asylum seekers denied an integrated public identity found collective identity in the private and domestic sphere. The domestic arena was not integrated with the public and the political as had been the case in Lebanon. On the contrary, it was lived in West Berlin as the means to protect women, and, by extension the community. Migration to Berlin thus led to a domesticisation of kinship and of the household in as much as kinship and other communal relations had an almost exclusive role in regulating social and gender relations, especially for women. They regulated the position of women by insulating them from the public world of the majority German society.

As Palestinian women assumed a new domestic role and identity, they were turned by the community into a means of defining collective identity. Norms that regulated the behaviour of women were turned into a mechanism to maintain group distinctiveness and separateness. Women determined and defined inclusive boundaries and conducted their lives in such a way as to secure the legitimate reproduction of these boundaries. The moral value attributed to the sexual behaviour of women was a measure by which the community reaffirmed its self worth and value. The redefined sexual culture was perceived as the universal one and other cultures as deviant. Through it, the community measured its superiority over the dominant Western culture and reaffirmed to itself its self worth in the face of economic, social, political and legal subordination.

The movement of the community to a Western society redefined the ideal woman as well as concepts such as 'shame' and 'honour'. The ideal Arab woman was partially constructed on the community's conception of the German woman. The former, in other words, was everything which the latter was not: the one was modest, the other promiscuous. Society was not perceived as based on the integration of males and females in a joint struggle, as it had been in the camps in Lebanon. The integration of the sexes was, on the contrary, seen as a threat to women's honour. To this was added a new perception of the sexuality of the Palestinian woman in West Berlin as an aggressive element that would threaten the equilibrium of society if not controlled. The contact of Arab women with men was identified as assimilation to the majority community, the loss of Islamic and national identity which would ultimately lead to the destruction of the community.

The interaction of women with men, especially non-kinsmen, was subject to very strict control. No legitimate and neutral areas existed, such as had been provided by the Palestinian organisations in the camps. No legitimate, that is non-sexual, reason for contact existed, and any contact was viewed with suspicion. This control over the movement and action of women started the moment she was perceived as a young adult *(Sabbiyeh)* and vulnerable.

School posed a particular problem, as it exposed adolescent women to subjects such as sex education and physical education. It placed them in the presence of young men without providing adequate control. The school of a bright female student was often chosen by parents on the basis of its proximity to their house and not on the standard of education it offered, a possibility institutionalised by the German system.

It has been very noticeable that girls and adolescent women generally performed better in school that their male counterparts, despite the pressure exerted on them to participate in domestic work. Time spent on studies was often considered as wasted time and was sometimes actively discouraged. 'A woman', said a father, 'does not need degrees to work in the kitchen and raise children.' Samiha, his fifteen year old daughter, explained her interest in education as a chance for acquiring knowledge, and the fact that 'I am not allowed to go out very much and have nothing else to do. My brother goes wherever he wants. He considers studying a waste of time.' Girls also perceived education and knowledge to be a way to improve their situation.

Not all parents viewed the education of girls and young women in this way. As with other manifestations of gender relations, analysis should not fall into faulty over-generalisations but has to emphasise the differences which existed between families and which defined structures as much as the patterns and trends did. One couple, Abu Lu'ay and his wife, placed much emphasis on the education of their daughters, three of whom were top students. In other cases, too, a positive attitude to female education could be analysed in terms of the age of the parents, their political/ideological orientation and socio-economic status in both Germany and before migration.

More than anything else, schooling exposed the young women to German culture and society. Conflict between the schoolgirl and her family was often the result of a difference in interpreting norms and differences in understanding the nature of gender relations. Adolescent women regularly complained of being unjustly reprimanded for talking to their male peers. What the parents considered to be an infringement of moral codes was seen by the young women as normal. Young women said that they related to most male classmates as friends, free from any sexual connotation, while the older generation considered all relationships across the gender divide to have sexual aspects.

Observation showed that some young women have used the misunderstanding of the parents as an excuse to violate norms. One sixteen year old girl said:

I was punished by my father when I was seen by a neighbour walking down the road from school with a number of classmates, including boys. I had done nothing wrong; they saw me and came to talk to me. I could not ask them to go. Then I decided, that if I was going to be punished, it might as well be for a real reason.

This adolescent woman, despite family and community norms, developed an illicit social life with her classmates. Her social life included activities with male peers in forbidden areas. As with a small number of other adolescent women, she resolved her inability to participate in social life outside the domestic arena by circumventing the truth and lying about her movements. Activities outside the norms involved social activities with a group of young people but generally did not involve sexual relationships. This young woman visited German classmates and went with them to the cinema and parties. Although she justified her violation of the norms as being ultimately innocent (not involving sexual activities), yet she also saw them as a crime. She said she was often terrified of being seen and felt guilty.

The tension caused by this behaviour was observed in a discussion with a group of adolescent women between the ages of twelve and seventeen. The girls condemned their own behaviour in an indirect way. As they did not want to admit either to me or to each other that they did violate their community's norms, they used the example of Turkish girls – subject to a very similar code of behaviour – to talk about themselves. Turkish girls, they said, often 'committed immoral acts' while pretending to follow the moral code. Girls from fundamentalist Muslim families, they said, often removed their head scarves and pulled their skirts up to shorten them when outside family control. They also had illicit relations with boys.

The young women said in the same discussion that German women were 'honourable', more so than their Turkish counterparts. German girls they knew from school did not lie, and generally treated male classmates as brothers. By means of their discussion of German and Muslim adolescent women, the young Palestinians showed their perception of two different sexual cultures and two definitions of gender relations. What they regarded as primarily 'dishonourable' was not the German sexual culture but the violation of their own.

The violation by girls and women of their normative and sexual codes, and the subsequent escalation of violent conflict with the family, has, in a small number of cases, led to the desertion by the young woman of the family household. Instead of the traditional method of taking refuge with relatives or neighbours, young women had the opportunity of turning to German women's centres. Women, in the majority of cases, returned to the family household, but a small and increasing number of exceptions is significant. Taking refuge outside the community, even if temporarily, indicates that an alternative to family organisation now exists for women. By using it as a threat, young women have increased their power in a conflict situation.

The return of women to the family, however, shows that this alternative was not viable in a majority of cases. The threat of deportation was, for many years, one of the first restrictions on alternatives. Refuge centres for the young and women provided them with immediate protection from family violence, but women were aware that the consequences of their act was deportation to Lebanon. Other reasons also prevailed. The total desertion by a young woman of her parents' household not only implied the loss of contact with her parents, but also her ostracisation from the community as a whole. Although German society offered an alternative to the family, there was no alternative for the family in the community.

The relatively recent creation of a Palestinian-run organisation to deal with the problems of young run-away women could allow them to make a move without burning their bridges with their families. Although important help has been extended over the years to distressed young women by German individuals or organisations, much of it has not taken into account the relationship of these young women with their own communities.

Boundary maintenance between German and Arab societies was often perpetuated through (German) social workers, youth and community workers, feminists and other well-meaning persons. As was observed in Britain, these people often immediately assumed the family and culture to be mainly repressive. Like Sikh youth in Britain, Palestinian youth often easily found support with German friends, teachers or doctors and were often encouraged to move away from home altogether, abandoning their family and culture. Yet the idea of becoming German, in a cultural sense, was almost universally rejected by Palestinians and other young people from Lebanon (see R. and C. Ballard 1977: 45–6).

Much of the problem cannot be isolated from an undifferentiated German perception of an Oriental/Arabic/Muslim society put forward by Western popular media. This perceived culture disregarded historical, socio-economic, political, legal, national, ethnic and cultural variations, and did not allow for differentiation. Muslim women have been much used by the host society as a means to attack minority cultures;

this was very much in the vein of 'integrate or go home'. On a more general level in the popular debate, the emancipation of the Muslim woman and the revision of Muslim moral values has been identified as a necessary condition for integration (Wilpert 1983). The role of the socio-economic conditions in Berlin which also defined her position, have too often been completely ignored or conveniently forgotten.

This does not mean that cultural and religious factors should be ignored in any analysis. On the contrary, Islam undoubtedly also defined models of the community and of domestic and collective identity. Palestinian women shared with Turkish and other Muslim women the Koran and their minority status. In a Western society that separates church from state, and in what is also a predominantly Christian society, Islam was pushed into the realm of the domestic. Its marginalisation gave it a new importance and turned women into measures of adherence to the *Shari'a* or Islamic law. An analysis of gender relations also has to look at the contemporary and local meaning of Islam. Head scarves will be used here as a light example to illustrate a discussion of more serious issues. The resurgence of Islam as a political force in the early 1980s gave rise to a new Islamic political identity both in the East and among Muslim minorities in the West. The head scarves fashionable today, like the ones made famous (or infamous) by the British and French schools controversies, are modern *Shari'a;* scarves were not the traditional head dress. They represented a modern politicisation of Islam. Understanding the use or lack of use of these scarves sheds light on issues of identity and identity construction.

Generally, older Palestinian women in Berlin covered their heads outside the house or in the presence of strange men, but used the traditional scarf to do so. Although a number of young Palestinian women covered their heads, most did not. Several reasons explain this discrepancy. Islam as a political identity was not adopted by the majority of Palestinians in Berlin, even if it partially defined personal, household and communal identity.

In the camps in Lebanon, from which the Palestinians in Berlin had come, it was observed that Palestinian ethnicity had little religious content (Rubenberg 1989: 107). Moreover, in Berlin, although the nature and form of political participation had changed from from what it had been in Lebanon and had greatly decreased, political identity continued to be based on allegiance to the political organisations of the PLO. These organisations, while not defined by their secular nature, did not have any religious identity. Political identity was defined by national identity, by ideology and by the individual's relationship to the PLO. Taking an Islamic identity in Berlin would have been perceived as assuming an alternative identity as well as rejecting the national struggle led by the PLO, and was thus unacceptable.

Moving away from an Islamic political identity in Berlin was accentuated in the mid-1980s by the relationship of Palestinians to the Sh'ia Lebanese. The conflict which took place in Lebanon between Palestinians and Lebanese Shi'ites, the 'War of the Camps', was transported to inter-Arab relations in Germany. Lebanese Shi'ite families were in most cases sympathetic to political organisations which defined themselves – to varying degrees – as Islamic. Islam was the political identity of the household as much as religion and domestic identity.

Whereas Shi'ite Lebanese women often tended to cover their heads, the fact that Palestinian women did not was a means of affirming the difference between the two groups and placing visible boundaries. This process is probably not dissimilar to the one observed by Ruth Mandel in her comparison of Sunni and Alawite Turkish groups in West Berlin (1989: 66–8).

The relatively limited role of Islam in the definition of public and political identity among Palestinians in Berlin should also be seen in relation to other factors. Palestinians lived in West Berlin with the awareness of their possible deportation; their stay was considered temporary. They did not need to claim and and reaffirm a distinct religious and cultural identity. They were not interested in the long term struggle for recognition as a religious minority which could empower a Muslim community to negotiate for itself with the authorities and take over in a unified fashion the education of children, rites and ritual. Although Palestinians supported these demands, they were mainly the demands of Turks and other established minorities. The Palestinian knowledge of their temporary position in Berlin did not turn Islam into a symbol of ethnic salience as observed among other groups in the Federal Republic and elsewhere. Future research should look at changes in the role of Islam in the definition of identity, especially as the Palestinians have recently been granted a more permanent status in the city (see conclusion).

Women's Roles in Marriage and Divorce

Observation of the Palestinians in Berlin has shown that Islam on its own cannot explain the position of women at marriage. What was the role of migration? The presence of the community in Berlin did not lead to a liberalisation of the laws of marriage, but on the contrary, seemed to have reduced the possibility for a woman to choose her own husband. As cultural and religious factors cannot on their own explain the early age of marriage for women, the impossibility of employment and further education cannot be ignored. The analysis of working class and poor communities elsewhere similarly shows high instances of the early marriage of adolescent women (see, for example, Rapp 1982: 173).

The presence of the community in a Western context did not increase the average age of marriage of women, but encouraged even earlier ones. There has been, however, an increasing trend towards the late marriage of men. More men are expressing their wish to 'live freely' before being tied down by marriage and marry in their late twenties or early thirties. The attitude of young men to marriage has been described by a number of older people as becoming like that of Germans. As they were not tied down by the same sexual norms as women, men were able to participate in activities open to German youth and to have non-marital sexual and non-sexual relationships with women.

Contrasting with the situation Palestinians had left in the camps in Lebanon, where it had been possible for women to meet men legitimately through the political organisation, the two sexes had little opportunity for legitimate interaction in Berlin. Marriage was turned into a measure to prevent the corruption of women and was arranged by the two families. Women often found difficulties in rejecting a suitor, especially on more than one occasion: this raised the suspicion of their having an illicit relationship or of hiding the loss of virginity.

Despite the difficulties, it was still possible for young women to reject a particular suitor. Rejections took both direct and indirect forms. A few women insisted on a very large *Maher* (dower) to deter potential husbands. Others threatened to desert the family household or made alliances within the family, especially with brothers and other kin. The marriage of a woman against her will was often prevented by persons outside the kinship group, where she found support and intervention. Help was sought with friends and their families, neighbouring women or influential and liberal persons in the community.

In the majority of cases, however, young women saw advantages in marriage. Marriage provided one of the only means to change their status and to increase their power, authority and movement. Once married, the rule of the woman inside the household was, to a great extent, undisputed. Married women acquired progressively more freedom of interaction with men and movement. With age they lost their sexual vulnerability and older women were perceived as asexual. Mothers kept a strong influence over male children when they grew up and, in fights between wives and mothers-in-laws, husbands generally sided with their mothers.

Only a few polygamous marriages existed in the Palestinian refugee camps in Lebanon. They were too expensive and generally seen as 'backward' and 'reactionary'. It was thus ironic that the presence of the community in the West lead to a increase in polygamy. Analysis of polygamy in West Berlin has to go beyond a strict interpretation of the concept and, despite their increase, such marriages remain rare. Polygamous marriages, as such, were not conducted in West Berlin, but existed, and were sustained, by the dual interpretation of both Federal and Islamic law. Palestinian and other Arab women were judicially divorced in the German courts from their husbands, who, in turn married German women. The German divorce was not recognised inside the community, and relations, including sexual relations, with the Arab woman continued to be regulated by the rules of the Islamic marriage.

Polygamous marriages of this type were tolerated, as the man acquired a residence and work permits through his German spouse. They did not constitute an economic 'burden' on the man, as social benefits covered the basic expenses of the divorced Arab woman's household. They were tolerated as they allowed for the continuation of the relationship between the man and the household, and solved problems of care, custody and education. Moreover, despite the cultural importance of mothers, it was fathers who were seen as being able to exert any real control over adolescents, and young women in particular.

The households of a polygamous man often had specialised functions. Community activities were conducted in the Arab woman's home, while activities associated with the German culture, such as drinking parties, were conducted in that of the German woman. The men saw their role and position as husbands, differently in each household. They helped the German wives in domestic work and conducted social and public activities with them. They did not, however, share the chores of the Arab women who spent much of their spare time with other Arabic speaking women. Polygamous men applied two sets of standards. Their relationship with each of the women was determined by their perception of her culture. It was this contrast in treatment that was often the cause of criticism, and sometimes described as contrary to Islamic law, especially by other women.

Divorce continued to be relatively rare in West Berlin and the ability of women to instigate it, was limited. The ability of a woman to seek refuge with kin or friends outside the conjugal home at the time of conflict with her husband was, however, neither uncommon or new. A process of mediation between the spouses and of pressure generally returned the woman to her conjugal household. Her return was, however, often preceded by a detailed agreement between the spouses on duties and rights towards each other. Stipulations against domestic violence were often enclosed. Conditions were wide ranging. One woman demanded that her husband should spend the evenings with her and not his friends, and that he should take her out on Sunday afternoons.

The preventative nature of the early marriages of women in Berlin ironically led to a small rise in the number of divorces instigated by young women, who had often been married off as soon as possible. Parents frequently found that taking time to find a suitable husband for their daughters was a risk. Less importance was placed on the opinion of the woman, or her perceived compatibility with the man. The young women, however, partially socialised in German schools and within the German culture, viewed marriage as romantic; their ideal man was often very different from the one chosen by the family.

A divorced woman was often looked upon as a social disgrace, and was the target of gossip and suspicion. Tremendous pressure was generally exerted by the family of a young woman who deserted the conjugal household to return to her husband. In later years, however, a number refused to do so despite pressure and mediation. One young divorced woman talked of having resisted return although she was aware of the implications of her future status as a divorced women. She stated:

> I am an old woman now, my life is over. I cannot marry again, but I will kill myself if my father forces me to return to my husband. I know that after my divorce I will not be able to work outside the house, will be forced to do all the household chores and become a servant of my brothers.

A divorced woman – that is young and non-virgin – in a 'corruptive' Western society was seen as being in an extremely vulnerable, and easily exploited position. Her violation of the norms was perceived as a very real threat. A young divorced woman was placed under stricter control than her unmarried sisters and was often excluded from attending weddings and other social and public functions.

The ability of a young woman to divorce ultimately depended on the approval of her parents, and was not determined by her. As it was socially impossible for her to live outside a kin or conjugal household, her divorce was a collective decision, and most particularly a decision taken by her father and other close relatives. Without their agreement, a woman faced the choice of deserting both her conjugal and natal households and thus being ostracised from the family and community as a whole. A woman was able, however, to exert some pressure over her parents' decision by asking for the intervention of mediators on her behalf. Her ability to seek refuge outside the family and household was, as for the unmarried women discussed above, very limited despite access to Federal laws and institutions (such as refuge centres for women). Married women who had arrived in West Berlin as adults or adolescents faced additional problems as many were not very fluent in German, not familiar with the culture and had little possibility or wish to integrate with the majority society.

In addition to these problems, the possibility of finding temporary security in women's refuges was foreclosed by the fear of deportation. After taking refuge in one of them, a woman who returned to her conjugal home said: 'even if I can survive here on my own, he [her husband] will find me in Lebanon. God knows what he will do there, he might kill me'. Furthermore, the allocation of asylum seekers to the various *Länder* often caused problems to women who wanted to divorce. A young woman from Berlin was married to a kinsman in another part of Germany. After negotiations with the relevant authorities, her police papers were transferred to the new *Länder*. When her marriage broke up, she managed to arrive at her family home in West Berlin, only to be told by the police to return to West Germany. Her inability to leave the *Länder* to which her husband was allocated came to reinforce the position of her parents, who did not allow her divorce.

Not all divorces instigated by women were, however, conducted in this manner. Women subject to physical abuse or wives of addicts and alcoholics, for example, often had the support of their families even though they were aware of the social implications of divorce. A small number of conflicts resulting from divorce were well known in the community. Conflict between spouses escalated to conflict between families or, as observation has also shown, within the same kinship group.

Conclusion

In the late 1980s Palestinians and other asylum seekers faced new conditions. In October 1987 and again in June 1989, asylum seekers from Lebanon were subjected to a change of status. Beneficiaries of this change were given a right of residence, for many this came after they had been living in the city for fifteen years. As for the very small number of asylum seekers who had benefited from a similar change in 1986, they were taken outside the procedure of asylum. The change in status meant that they were not to be deported, yet did not imply that they were recognised as political refugees. Thus, the changes did not set a legal precedent for potential new arrivals. As asylum seekers moved out of the procedures of asylum, however, they acquired rights previously denied, such as the right to movement, easier employment conditions, the right to study and to equality of social benefits.

With the directives of 1987 and 1989, Palestinians became the holders of residence permits given to foreigners. This very important change will undoubtedly have immediate and long term effects. These rights have freed Palestinians from the fear of deportation to Lebanon. For the first time in many years, they know that they have the possibility of remaining in the country. A new relationship has developed between immediate action and long term consequence.

The immediate and long term transformations in the attitude to education will be interesting to observe. As discussed earlier, Palestinian children have not been subject to compulsory education. Neither Palestinian children nor adolescents have previously had much incentive to work hard in schools. New conditions came with the new residence permit. Education gave the theoretical possibility of socio-economic mobility and the improvement of living conditions. As mentioned earlier, it has been noticeable that girls and adolescent women showed more interest in education and performed better in schools than boys. Education gave women a relatively legitimate reason to justify their presence in unsegregated German public areas: technical colleges and universities, and established an alternative to early marriages. The newly found possibility of further education posed a potential source of conflict within the household between young women and their parents. A small number of young women enrolled in technical colleges and universities; for them, education will also have personal and social importance. Very few though they are, they will make a social precedent.

The novel discovery of access for young women to technical training and education continued to be restricted by the household, family and community. Women, it was often said, had to be prepared for being housewives and mothers. Girls continued to have heavy chores and were discouraged from spending time doing homework. The household and family, however, did not have a monopoly over the definition of female education. The education of Palestinians, and other ethnic minorities in West Berlin, was regulated by other factors. From the first day at school, the migrant child was disadvantaged in basic skills and often fell into the vicious circle of bad school performance, lack of training and skills, unemployment or low pay (Hoft: 1983). Although a small number of Palestinian women will undoubtedly achieve mobility through education, comparison with other ethnic minority women makes one predict that education will not radically change the overall position of women.

Another important change brought about recently was the access of Palestinians to the labour market. Although the advantages of this change are far reaching and obvious, this new found possibility has not changed employment patterns. As employment was sought, and found in the majority of cases, little difference existed between the nature of the previous illegal work and that of the new legal one. Palestinian youth and adults, who until recently were denied the right to technical training, had few or no skills and continued to be employed in the services sector, generally in unskilled, badly paid work.

As the economic conditions of Palestinians in West Berlin have been subject to change in the late 1980s and early 1990s, a number of questions are posed. How will the right of employment affect women and their position inside and outside the household? How significant will changes be? Within a household headed by an employed male, it can be argued that women have lost the economic independence previously determined by the distribution of social benefits for asylum seekers as they do not depend on social benefits any more, but on the employed male. Employed men have found, once again, their role as economic providers and have regained the economic basis of power over other members of the household.

The legal possibility of employment does not necessarily imply that radical changes in the employment patterns of women will take place in the forseeable future. A number of fathers who had relatively well paid jobs have been reported to have refused permission for their daughters to take paid employment on the grounds that it was less necessary than ever. Parental opposition to the employment of young women has been reinforced by the nature of work available to them. When they were given the right to work, the majority of women – like men – were unskilled or had few transferable skills. Generally speaking, their employment has continued to be found in badly paid jobs, often in difficult conditions in low status sectors: in fast food restaurants, in cleaning services and other similar activities, for example. Such employment has not encouraged women's work outside the household, and has not encouraged them to stand up to family opposition.

The few young women who were employed greatly valued their ability to generate some income, and working outside the domestic arena. The nature of employment, however, did not lead to any empowerment inside or outside the household. Similarly, no real alternative to the family and community existed for women, only isolation and marginalisation.

Although the change in status has meant that Palestinians are now less marginal to the socio-economic structures of the majority German society, this relationship has continued to be characterised by institutional discrimination, by education policies and employment which disfavoured foreigners and by individual racist behaviour. Thus, however important the changes in the legal position of asylum seekers, Palestinians continued to be defined by their position as a 'visible' non-European socio-economic and ethnic minority.

If the community encouraged the segregation of the sexes and the isolation of women from public activities, the West Berlin socio-economic and political structure did not allow their integration. Moreover, the oppression of women in Berlin as asylum seekers/foreigners/minority group was more sharply felt than sexual discrimination inside the household and community. Changes in the position of the woman and her social empowerment within the household and family cannot be dissociated from her lack of empowerment in German society at large.

The changes that have taken place in Eastern Europe will undoubtedly have direct and indirect effects on the Palestinian community in Berlin. The catalytic changes that have shaken up societies in the second half of 1989, and most particularly that of the former German Democratic Republic, cannot be ignored. The changes have lead to the influx of a large number of its citizens to the actual territory of the Federal Republic including West Berlin, as well as the political reunification. The presence of non-European ethnic minorities is resented by the German community more than ever before. Their cheap labour is no longer needed for menial jobs as they compete with the large pool of skilled migrants from the East. The position of Palestinians and other minorities will also be dependent on the policy towards foreigners in post-1992 Europe.

Analysis cannot forget the political developments that have taken place on the Palestinian level in the second half of the 1980s either. In the last years, images on German television of the Palestinian *Intifada* (uprising) in the occupied West Bank and Gaza strip have revived in West Berliners' minds the perception of the position of women that Palestinians asylum seekers had developed a number of years before in Lebanon. Images of Palestinian community on the television screens have emphasised the active integration of the Palestinian woman in the national struggle and public society. These images have challenged those developed by the Palestinian community in West Berlin heretofore. Palestinian women of the *Intifada* were not defined by their need for protection and *Sutra,* but by their participation in the national struggle and their presence in an integrated society. Where the segregation of the sexes in West Berlin was perceived as a means of adhering to the *Shari'a* and was thus transformed into a symbol of identity, an opposing and equal symbol of identity was found in images of the Palestinian uprising in the media portraying, once again, the integration of the sexes within the PLO. In the 1990s, the Palestinian community in Berlin entered a new phase of development. Legal changes in the status of asylum seekers in Berlin combined with the Palestinian Uprising in the West Bank and Gaza Strip have placed new elements in the definition of the position of women in Berlin. The Berlin state has given them the limited possibility of integrating themselves with the socio-economic structures of the majority German society. Through the *Intifada,* the PLO gave their participation in the social, political and economic world a degree of legitimacy. What will be the effect of these factors on the role, position and status of the Palestinian woman of the 1990s in Berlin is a question that can only be answered by future research.

Observation of the historical transformation over the last forty years has, however, shown that the eradication of gender differentiation cannot be found in the PLO or the German state alone. On the contrary, the role of the state in maintaining gender differentiation has been revealed in both cases. To conclude on a personal, political note it must be stated that the thesis of this chapter was based on the assumption that a woman's problem exists outside a national, class and minority/majority problem. Questions basic to the understanding of gender relations must address the relationship between the two.

References

Afshar, H., 1989 'Gender Roles and the "Moral Economy of Kin" among Pakistani Women in West Yorkshire', *New Community* Vol. 15, no. 2, January 1989, pp. 211-25

Ballard, R. and C., 1977 'The Sikhs: the Development of South Asian Settlement in Britain', in J. Watson (ed.), *Between Two Cultures: Migrants and Minorities in Britain*, Oxford: Basil Blackwell

Davis, J., 1979 *Understanding Minority-Dominant Relations*, Sociological Contributions, Illinois: AHM Publishing Corporation

Evangelischer Pressedienst, 1985 *Flüchtlinge aus dem Libanon*. Zentralredaktion Frankfurt am Main: Haus der Evangelisches Publizistik

Goodwin, G., 1982 The *Refugee in International Law*, Oxford: Clarendon Press

Haddad, Y., 1980 'Palestinian Women: Patterns of Legitimation and Domination' in K. Nakhleh and E. Zuriek (eds), *The Sociology of the Palestinians*, London: Croom Helm

Hoft, D., 1983 'The Children of Aliens in West German Schools: Situation and Problems', in C. Fried (ed.), *Minorities: Community and Identity*, Dahlem Konferenzen, Berlin: Springer-Verlag, and New York: Hiedelber

Joseph, S., 1986 'Women and Politics in the Middle East', Merip Middle East Report, no. 138 January–February, Washington DC

Kayser, C., 1984 'Le Sort precaire des refugies du tiers-monde', *Le Monde Diplomatique*, August

Kazi, H. 1987 'Palestinian Women and the National Liberation Movement: A Social Perspective', *Khamsin* special edition on women *Women in the Middle East*, London: Zed Press

Mandel, R., 1989 'Ethnicity and Identity Among Migrant Guestworkers in West Berlin', in N. Gonzales and C. McCommon (eds), *Conflict Migration and the Expression of Ethnicity*, Boulder, Colorado: Westview Press

Marx, R., 1983 'The Political, Social and Legal Status of Aliens and Refugees in the Federal Republic of Germany', in C. Fried (ed.), *Minorities: Community and Identity*, Berlin: Springer-Verlag

—1984 *Asylrecht*, Band 1, Rechtsprechundessammlung mit Erlauterung, Aufflage, Baden Baden

Messick, B., 1987 'Subordinate Discourse: Women, Weaving and Gender Relations in North Africa', *American Ethnologist*, vol. 18, no. 2 May

Morokvasic, M., 'Birds of Passage are also Women' in *International Migration Review* vol. 18 no. 4, Winter

Munscher, A., 1984 'The Workday Routines of Turkish Women in the FRG: Results of a Pilot Study' *International Migration Review*, vol. 18, no. 4, Winter

Peteet, J., 1986 'No Going Back: Women and the Palestinian Movement', *Merip Middle East Report*, vol. 16, no. 138 note 1, pp.20–24, January-February, Washington DC

—1987 'Conflict Resolution in the Palestinian Camps in Lebanon', *Journal of Palestinian Studies*, vol. 16 no. 2, Winter, Beirut

—and R. Sayigh, 1986 'Between Two Fires: Palestinian Women in Lebanon', in R. Ridd (ed.), *Caught up in Conflict*, Basingstoke: Macmillan

Rapp, R., 1982 'Family and Class in Contemporary America: Notes Towards an Understanding of Ideology', in B. Thorne and M. Yalom (eds), *Rethinking the Family: Some Feminist Questions*, New York: Longman

Rubenberg, C., 1989 'Lebanon's Protracted Conflict: Causes and Consequences', in N. Gonzales and C. McCommon (eds), *Conflict, Migration and the Expression of Ethnicity*, Boulder, Colorado: Westview Press

Sayigh, R., 1987, 'Femmes Palestiniennes: Une Histoire en quete d'historiens', *Revue d'Etudes Palestinienne* no. 23, Spring

—1989 'Palestinian Women; Triple Burden, Single Struggle', *Khamsin* special edition

on women *Palestine: Profile of an Occupation*, London: Zed Press
United Nations Higher Commission for Refugees, 1983 'Mission
to the Federal Republic of Germany, 6/10 June', Bonn, July 1983, internal
report
Wilpert, C., 1983 'From Guestworkers to Immigrants: Migrant Workers and their
families in the F.R.G', in *New Community* 1 and 2, Autumn and Winter

5

Patterns of Adaptation: Somali and Bangladeshi Women in Britain

Hazel Summerfield

The origin of the paper on which this chapter is based was my observation that a major factor defining my female clients' mental health was their ability to divorce men with comparative impunity. My material was obtained over three years of working as an immigration and refugee advisor with immigrant communities in Tower Hamlets, East London. Tower Hamlets includes the old port of London dock area, where, traditionally, immigrants arriving by ship disembark and settle. For hundreds of years it has been the first point of settlement for immigrants in London. Immigrants who arrive by air gravitate towards existing communities of their own ethnicity, thus Tower Hamlets continues to receive the bulk of new immigrants from older immigrant communities. Tower Hamlets is one of the poorest and most socially deprived boroughs in London. The two main ethnic groups whom I serve are the Somali and the Bangladeshi communities. It was the difference in the behaviour patterns of the women from the two communities which led me to the above conclusions on divorce. Somali women appeared to have much lower depression rates and be more in control of their lives than men.[1]

Similarities

The two most immediate and striking differences between these two groups of Muslim women were, first, the ability of Somali women to divorce without incurring the disapproval of their community, and, secondly, the support the community gives to divorcees and their children. Thus my initial reaction was that a large component of the mental health of women depends on their ability to divorce with minimal

1. I am aware that I have not defined 'depression' or 'mental health' medically. I am using the terms as a lay person.

negative consequences either to their social status, economic well being and family structure. However, I think that there may possibly be other factors contributing to the apparent comparative well being of Somali women to Bangladeshi women and this chapter is an attempt to check my original reaction that women who can divorce easily tend to be 'healthier' and to look at other factors which may contribute to the different patterns of adaptation exhibited by women from the two ethnic groups.

First, let me deal with the background to these two groups of immigrant women, beginning with what they have in common: both groups are actively polygamous Muslims who have arrived in the United Kingdom over the last hundred years. Both waves of migration were started by seamen (recruited from empire and commonwealth countries to serve in the Royal Navy in wartime and the Merchant Navy in peacetime) who settled in the dock areas of London. Although the Somali community predates the Bangladeshi, in both cases female immigration began in the 1960s.

The first generation of immigrants of both groups never intended to settle permanently in the United Kingdom, but to make their fortunes and return to their country of origin. This dream, of becoming rich and of return, was to have profound effects on their pattern of adaptation and integration in the United Kingdom. I use the term 'integration' advisedly to mean non hostile interaction with other communities here in the United Kingdom and not to mean assimilation with the host community.

Both waves of immigration began, as has been said, with men coming over and leaving their womenfolk behind. Initially, and not infrequently, the men married into the white community. Bangladeshi men tended to be single when they arrived, though for tax reasons they informed the authorities they had families in Bangladesh. Somali men often already had one or two wives in Somalia. Somali men would normally send back the offspring of mixed marriages to be brought up in the Somali way in Somalia. For instance I have traced a family whose connection with England began around 1880 when the great-great-grandfather arrived as a British Merchant Navy seaman from what was then British Somaliland (now northern Somaliland),[2] and married a Welsh girl. The offspring of this union were, in childhood,

2. In 1991 the Somali National Movement drove government forces from the north of Somalia and declared the Independent State of Somaliland. There has been no diplomatic recognition of the secession of Somaliland but *de facto* Somalia no longer exists. The south is in a state of anarchy while the north has its own government and state structure formed by the SNM. The former Somalian embassies throughout thr world are closed or

returned to Somalia, but were brought over as adults to work in the United Kingdom. No further mixed marriages occurred in the family but the pattern of childhood in Somalia and working adulthood in the United Kingdom has continued. As the community in the United Kingdom expanded the practice of intermarriage became unusual and was disapproved of by both the Bangladeshi and to a lesser extent the Somali communities.

Both sets of migrants came from the middle-income bracket of their home communities and were by no means from the lowest status groups. The Bangladeshis were mainly small landholders from Sylhet (a wealthy but inherently politically unstable area of Bangladesh) (Carey and Shukor 1985: 1406) and the Somalis were Isaak nomads from what is now northern Somaliland. Nomadism is considered the ideal by Somalis (see Lewis 1981) and I will illustrate later that part of the difference in adaptation is the different cultural expectations of settled farmers to nomadic herdsmen.

Let me now turn to the differences between these two groups: first, the Bangladeshis tended to be cooks on the boats and the Somalis boilermen, (although I have been told that sometimes whole ships were crewed by Somalis except for the officers who would have been white and British). These different skills have contributed to a divergence of on shore employment. Approximately 90 per cent of 'Indian' restaurants in the United Kingdom are Bangladeshi owned and run. The catering industry is a very important source of wealth and employment for Bangladeshis, while Somali men have almost nothing to do with the catering trade.

Although Bangladeshi migration to United Kingdom was initiated by seamen, very few ever settled in the country and the Bangladeshis did not become a discernible group until the 1950s when they were actively recruited to fill gaps in the British labour market. The seamen's kinsmen were the first to come, and it is still true that the majority of immigrants are part of what I would call a transposed kinship group. By the mid-1960s most of the primary immigration was finished (by 'primary' I refer to the immigration of those arriving who had no previous close connection with the United Kingdom). The 1971 Immigration Act, which became law in 1973, effectively prevented any further primary immigration into the United Kingdom. Since 1973 only those with close relatives (elderly parents, spouses and children)

---

manned on a voluntary basis by former employees who choose their own allegiances. I do not believe that any embassies are open in the former capital, Mogadishu, which is situated in southern Somalia in the old Italian protectorate. Northern Somalia, now known as Somaliland, was formerly a British protectorate. Somalia existed from 1961 to 1991.

in the country here have been allowed to settle. The 1971 civil war which resulted in East Pakistan becoming Bangladesh marked the last major influx of primary immigrants from Bangladesh.[3]

As the situation in Bangladesh deteriorated economically and politically the men already settled in the United Kingdom began to give up their hopes of returning to their country of origin. This trend was exacerbated by the economic recession and rising unemployment in the United Kingdom. Bangladeshi men realised that they would never be able to accumulate sufficient wealth to 'retire' in luxury to Bangladesh. Thus, although they continued to remit money home, and to acquire land in Bangladesh, they began to try to bring over first their sons and then their daughters and wives. This trend occurred throughout the 1970s and 1980s. Estimates from the 1981 census suggest that there were then 26,000 Bangladeshi in Tower Hamlets and that the ratio of women to men was 1:1.9 compared to the overall figure in the population of 1: 0.98.

Immigration still continues in the 1990s, although the new Immigration Act of 1988 brought into force in July 1989, reduces the right to bring in close family members. However, many potential immigrants still qualify, either because their fathers became British citizens before their birth (so that they are British citizens by descent), or because they are still minors (under eighteen years) whose parents can maintain and accommodate them without recourse to public funds.[4]

Even when a man has decided to bring his wife and children over to the United Kingdom the 'myth of return' is still harboured. This is exhibited in three main ways, the first of which is observable in the course of my work during which I frequently have to establish the domicile of a man. This is a legal concept which is not, as many people imagine, synonymous with permanent residence, but looks at where a person ultimately associates most closely with, for instance where he would like to be buried.[5] For both Somalis and Bangladeshis the answer is normally their country of origin.

The second way Bangladeshis express their emotional allegiance to their country of origin is that though children are frequently brought to

3. Immigration Act 1971, Statement of Changes in the Immigration Rules 23 March 1990 HC 251 HMSO and Statement of Changes in Immigration Rules HC169 HMSO.

4. Please note that there are other criteria under which immigrants can enter the United Kingdom, in particular by marriage or under the 'other relatives' provisions of the im- migration rules.

5. To establish domicile as opposed to residence the Home Office send out a lengthy questionnaire and one of the questions on it is 'Where would you like to be buried?'

the United Kingdom to establish residents' rights they are immediately returned to be educated in Bangladesh. This is particularly true of girls, who are not expected to become economically independent of their families in this country, but will attract a greater range of marriage suitors if they have residence rights in the United Kingdom. Religiously minded fathers will send their sons to be educated in Bangladesh as it is felt that one cannot acquire a 'good' religious education in Britain. Wives are often only brought over in order to establish the residence rights of the children and then returned to Bangladesh. (These women are known as 'carrier' wives.)[6] I will return to the position of wives later in this chapter. The third main way in which the preference for Bangladesh over the United Kingdom is exhibited is that even when, for practical purposes, a man has given up hope of a permanent return for himself he will choose a spouse from Bangladesh for his children. Even when a male child has been born and bred in the United Kingdom, the preference is still for him to marry a spouse born and bred in Bangladesh. This is partly for kinship reasons, for instance to facilitate the immigration of a kinsman who would otherwise have no right to enter Britain. However, the Bangladeshi spouse is often not a relative and is chosen in preference to a suitable kinsman already established in Britain. The most frequently expressed reason for this choice is that children are brought up better in Bangladesh, and that one can only find a 'good' son or daughter-in-law in Bangladesh. This is especially considered to be the case where the potential mother-in-law is in Britain. Traditionally young girls live with their husbands in their in-laws' compound. The girl is expected to work for and take orders from her mother-in-law. There is a great fear that if a son marries a Bangladeshi girl reared in England that she will not be sufficiently servile to either mother-in-law or husband. Bangladeshi girls educated in the United Kingdom are considered to have over liberal views as to the extent to which they can talk to and question male household members. Many prefer to work outside the family and thus are not as readily available to work for and obey their mothers-in-law and husbands. Often the girl will want to set up her own household rather than following the Bangladeshi custom and living in her mother-in-law's compound.

From discussion with both first and second generation immigrant women I suspect that what is an 'acceptable' level of domestic vio-

6. This is the Home Office description of such wives. Should a woman be suspected of being a 'carrier' wife then she and her children will be refused entry clearance even if they might otherwise qualify.

lence in Bangladesh is unacceptable to women reared in Britain. A reason frequently given to me by wives wishing to leave their husbands is that both the husband and his family are maltreating her. This situation is often exacerbated as the bride does not have her own family in the United Kingdom who may otherwise have intervened on her behalf to protect her. Another cause of friction is that Bangladeshi girls reared in the United Kingdom, if they do work, expect to keep at least part of their wages. This causes a great deal of ill-feeling friction as Bangladeshi husbands reared in Bangladesh often expect all the wages to be given to them or their families.

The demands of a mother-in-law are so strong that I frequently hear of older Bangladeshi women demanding that their sons give up their higher education in order to work so as to be able to bring over a young 'wife'. This will effectively facilitate the mother-in-law's retirement. A daughter-in-law will take over, or assist with, most of her mother-in-law's domestic chores, in return for which she will receive assistance with child rearing. Under Muslim law contraception is forbidden and within the community is frowned upon, so a son rapidly becomes enmeshed in supporting a young family and this is one way in which the community keeps itself within the ghetto and perpetuates its relatively low status and earning power. Sons are expected to earn as soon as possible. Of course, there are many other factors, both internal and external which contribute to a ghetto life style, in particular housing policy and racism.

To a certain extent the belief that control of the second generation of immigrants is being lost is borne out. Politicisation has occurred among the youths and they have taken control of their communities' political and social interactions with the host community by setting up 'youth groups'. These groups were originally established in the 1970s to respond to racist attacks, and to counter institutionalised racism particularly among the police and in housing and education policies. This is a distinct change from the traditional pattern in which it would have been the elders in the community who would have been the ones to decide the community response to events. Both the elders and the youth group leaders have 'lost control' of an element within the community and there are particular Bangladeshi housing estates (in common with some white estates) that now sport their own gangs who fight each other, are truants or unemployed and hang around the predominantly Bangladeshi all-female secondary school in the borough, harassing the Bangladeshi girls and on occasion dragging them off into cars. Neither the community nor the parents of these individuals seem to be able to stop their activities, although they strongly disapprove of them. However, to put this breakdown of traditional norms in context, the majority of second generation youths remain within and help their family units.

Somali Immigration History

I now turn to the history of Somali immigration and will follow this by looking at the different patterns of family organisation and female behaviour in each community. By the turn of the century there was already a distinct male Somali community in Docklands, centred around Queen Victoria's Seamans' Rest. The seamen followed their traditional pattern of having a wife in each area in which they had an economic interest, thus it was not unusual for a seaman settled in the United Kingdom to have a white wife. In Somalia his Somali wife would be looking after his herds with his agnatic nomadic kinsmen and perhaps he would have a second wife in Somalia, living in her own household but in close contact with agnatic relatives, looking after his economic interests, in Burrao or Hargissa, the main towns of the north (Lewis 1960: 8-11).

This pattern already represents a divergence in custom from the Bangladeshis who would typically be single and would marry on a return trip to Bangladesh after having established themselves in the United Kingdom. A wife in such a marriage would be left in Bangladesh in the husband's compound in the charge of a male relative; although she might have some decision making role in the economy of the household, it was generally minimal. Thus, traditionally, Somali women control their own households, but Bangladeshi women do not.

The first Somali women began to arrive in Britain in the early 1960s, (Somalia became independent in 1960 and was created from a former Italian colony in the south and a British protectorate in the north. From 1988 until 1991 the north, led by the Somali National Movement, the SNM, fought a very bloody civil war which resulted in 1991 in the overthrow of President Siad Barre, the destabilisation of the south and the formation of a newly independent Somaliland on the territory of the old Northern British Protectorate.) Most of these early arrivals were, in fact, Somalis displaced by the growing unrest in Aden. In 1967 Aden achieved independence from British rule and the dominant Arabs threw the Somalis out. The post-1967 period represents the first major influx of Somali women, who, rather than return to Somalia where they may never have lived, came to join their husbands in Britain. Interestingly, nearly all these women had had jobs in Aden. One of my clients, who arrived in London in 1962 from Aden, told me that there were only two other Somali women in London when she arrived. She said that as a result she was extremely lonely until the late 1960s when other Somali women came to London. She spoke with bitterness of her rejection by her Bengali female neighbours. Perhaps stemming from this early experience, a pattern of introduction for Somali women became established. Whenever a Somali woman arrived, whether or not she had any kinship ties or was known to the women in London she would automatically go to the household of a resident Somali female. The resident woman took the responsibility of initiating the newcomer, showing her round and sharing family burdens. Many of these early arrivals have told me that unrelated seamen would visit them and their children just for the pleasure of being in a family atmosphere. This type of contact is apparently allowed by their husbands. Bangladesh husbands would almost certainly consider this type of behaviour adulterous. There is an extraordinary 'sisterhood' amongst Somali women (in common with other African women), which appears to be extended to any woman whether she is Somali or not. This pattern of getting to know each other and forming strong, mutually supportive friendships laid the basis for the formal women's groups which were to emerge in the 1980s and about which I will enlarge on later.

In contrast, although Bangladeshi men will form friendships outside the extended family, almost no first generation Bangladeshi women will: they will only mix with their own kinswomen. The Bangladeshi women largely remain in purdah, only occasionally visiting relatives' houses either on feast days or for family celebrations. Men do the shopping and conduct any interactions which need to occur with the host community. Thus, Bangladeshi women, in contrast to the Somalis, remain isolated from one another and from the host community.

Slightly predating the first influx of Somali women there was an influx of high status Somali students (I have not yet been able to ascertain if any were female). These students were from the elite of Somali society and were the first generation to finish school in Somalia and be sent to university in Britain. They formed the Somali National Movement which now dominates the new Somaliland as they returned to become national leaders and government ministers when British and Italian Somaliland became independent Somali.[7] The government was a coalition of tribes including Isaaks from northern Somalia, which is the tribe of most Merchant Navy Seamen. From what I can gather the

7. The concept of greater Somalia predates colonial division and includes Djbati and the Ogaden.

student group had minimal contact with the seamen and Somalis from Aden; their aspirations were directed on Somalia.

Throughout the 1970s most Somali women in the United Kingdom were from Aden and they shared with their menfolk the belief that they would return to Somalia some day. Money was remitted to Somalia to acquire property, keep wives and children and increase their herds. The seamen also prepared for their return home by building houses in northern Somalia (now Somaliland). They mainly stayed in seamen's hostels in Britain, visiting Somalia every two years. It is worth noting that they kept up their 'idealised' nomadic existence by remaining seamen even when their wives were in the United Kingdom. The women from the start were, therefore, largely independent of their men and reliant on each other for support and friendship. A husband could not be depended on to do the family shopping if he was only at home once in every six months.

Work Patterns

Perhaps half the women whom I have met from this generation also obtained employment in the United Kingdom, mainly as hospital cleaners and factory workers. This gave them immediate contact with the white community. The majority of Somali women I have met have divorced and remarried at least once. Thus the women's experience and contact with the host community differs markedly from their Bangladeshi first generation counterparts who, if they work at all, do piecework at home. This is normally machining garments on a sewing machine rented to them by a factory owner (often a relative), so that they do not have to leave their homes to work, nor do they form new social relationships through their work. Nor can Somali women's work patterns be seen as synonomous with those of Bangladeshi men. Most Bangladeshi men work within Bangladeshi run industries, in the catering and clothing trade or as retailers in shops specialised to the needs of the Asian community, for instance Halal butchers, Bengali grocery stores or sari shops. Only the wealthier 'factory owners' would have any significant contact with the white community.

Most Bangladeshi businesses are family run, and this again contrasts markedly with Somali patterns. I have only learnt of one Somali 'family' business: a Somali-run cafe, now closed, where the wife worked in the kitchens. Somalis themselves cite this arrangement as exceptional as, normally, husbands and wives will not work together. This economic separation of husband and wife (although not complete, often a wife with young children will not work), is an important factor in Somali women's independence and sense of control over their own lives, allowing divorce to be a realistic mode of dealing with a dysfunctional marriage. It is also important that Somali women tend not to have jobs which are controlled by their menfolk; they do not work in family businesses but in jobs run and created by the indigenous population. Paid work and work outside community domination gives Somali women an independence within the home which is not available to their Bangladeshi counterparts. Another major advantage of such work for the Somali woman is that it forces her to learn English.

I will deal with the effects of linguistic isolation shortly but first I will complete the history of Somali immigration. From the late 1970s and throughout the 1980s civil unrest culminating in civil war has resulted in a steady trickle of high status Somalis fleeing Somalia either as refugees or as students who have never gone home. At the beginning of 1987, the estimated London population of Somalis was around 5,000. The civil war has led to British visas being issued at an approximate rate of 500 per month in the 1990s, and, in addition, about 150 Somalis are being granted asylum each week at Heathrow airport.[8] Since 1991 when the north seceded from the south there has been a movement back to Somaliland, but until the infrastructure has been rebuilt most will remain in the United Kingdom where, because of the dislocation in the north, most still consider their families to be safer. The civil war, which officially began in 1988 but which had its immediate roots in the 1974 famine and the compulsory relocation of northerners in the south, followed by a defeated and disaffected army returning from the Ethiopian wars in 1978, has introduced a period of exponential growth for the Somali population in the United Kingdom, which is presenting its own problems for the community. The new arrivals are being dispersed throughout London, mainly in Council 'bed and breakfast' accommodation. Thus the 'traditional' welcome and initiation by resident Somalis is more difficult to achieve both because of the numbers involved and geographic dispersion.

For the first time Somali women are accompanying their men out of Somalia. Although in the early and mid-1980s these refugees tended to be from the wealthy elite, unlike their student predecessors they have not remained aloof from the seamen and Somalis from Aden; they mix freely in the same organisations, especially the women, as will become clear when I describe the politicisation of the Somali community.

8. Unofficial Home Office statistic.

Since 1988 when the Dresden-style bombing of the north of Somalia destroyed the towns and forced the population to flee to Ethiopia, the seamen have given up hope of return to Somalia and have seen all their investments there disappear. It is now their families that form the bulk of the refugees entering the United Kingdom.

Linguistic Skills

A major factor in Somali women's adaptation to their new lives is their proficiency in spoken English. Until the 1970s northern Somali education was conducted in English. The Somali language was first written in 1972 and Latin script became the official script. In 1974 a mass literacy campaign was launched. Thus, prior to the 1980s, all northern Somalis, male or female, who had any education would have a good working knowledge of English.

Although many seamen and their wives are semi-literate or illiterate and do not speak much English my belief is that there is far more English spoken and written in the Somali community than the Bangladeshi. I often meet an older long term resident Bangladeshi woman who cannot communicate at all in English and I frequently meet Bangladeshi men who have been in Britain for thirty or forty years who cannot speak English. I occasionally meet a Somali seaman who cannot communicate in English, but have never met a Somali woman who has been in this country for more than three years who does not have a working knowledge of the language.

Probably there are three main reasons for the enhanced communication skills of Somali women. Two of these reasons may diminish as the population grows. First, unlike the work environment of their husbands or the Bangladeshis, theirs is unlikely to be predominantly Somali. It will be interesting to see if the rapid increase in the Somali population will lead to 'ghettoisation' and attendant loss of linguistic ability. Secondly, even when Somali women do not work they still shop, and their shopping is done in English. This is in contrast to the Bangladeshi men who, if they choose the right shopkeeper, may not need English. Thirdly, as nomads with little plastic art, linguistic skill is enormously important to Somalis (Lewis 1981). To understand Somali and Somali poetry is to know the essentials of Somali culture. Language is considered so important by Somalis that I am told there is an ambivalence towards strangers learning Somali; on the one hand they are flattered, but on the other it is considered to be an invasion of privacy and a means of control.

Economic Performance

The economic performance of the Somali community is fascinating. From the 1950s to the 1970s the community perceived itself to be well off and fully employed. However, nearly all Somali male employment was based on the British Merchant Navy. Up until the mid-1970s there were a few Somali restaurants and night clubs in Tower Hamlets, but these businesses appear to have been reliant on the wages of seafaring kinsmen. Employment at sea declined drastically in the mid seventies. By 1978 there was no longer a single Somali restaurant or night club in London. In 1987 the Somali unemployment figure was estimated to be 75 per cent (however, I find this figure suspiciously high, as do Somalis I have asked about it and I do not think it reflects women's employment).[9]

For the 1980s wave of refugees, unemployment is probably highest amongst the men. Many of the men held relatively high status jobs in Somalia and were wealthy. They are not prepared to demean themselves by taking low status jobs. However, it is considered less demeaning for a woman to take a low status job. Thus the wives, if they do not divorce, are likely to work as well as rear children, keep house, cook and defer to men. Many Somali women complain of this and several leave their husbands. Being single may actually relieve a women of some of her burdens. The community of the 1990s is being further impoverished by the refugee situation. Once a Somali man or woman obtains a visa for their relatives they will sell whatever they have to pay for the airfares.[10] They will also expect a wide circle of kinsmen to contribute as an outright gift and friends will lend money without charging interest. This lack of usury is in direct contrast to the Bangladeshi population in which, although Islam forbids it, it is common.

Politicisation

The politicisation of the Somali community is also important. As I mentioned previously, amongst the Bangladeshis it is the youths, often second generation, who have founded the community groups and are the political voice of the community. They run both Sylheti expatriate

9. Second generation Somali men and women appear to move rapidly up the socio-eco- nomic scale, often pursuing further education in technical subjects such as engineering or computing.

10. The United Nations High Commission for Refugees (UNHCR) should pay air fares for refugees and their families but since the summer of 1989 has failed to fulfil this in- ternational obligation.

politics and are becoming active in English political structures, such as the local council. This contrasts with the situation in Bangladesh itself where the elder men retain political control. Until the late 1970s the Somalis were, in effect, apolitical; there were no formal Somali community organisations. I am told that this was because as the men did not have their women and children in Britain and were uninterested in their political position in the country they saw their stay as temporary. Any political interests they had were directed towards Somalia and not the United Kingdom.

I believe that the first formal Somali association in London was founded in the late 1970s: the Somali Community and Cultural Association. This association was founded by two women, both Somalis from Aden. Initially the association was founded to bring women together whilst their husbands were away. This organisation is still the main Somali organisation in the borough of Tower Hamlets, but a number of other organisations are off-shoots, including the two other major Somali organisations in the United Kingdom, SOMREC, set up to provide relief to refugees in Somalia and the Somali Education Project. These organisations were also set up by the women who arrived in the 1970s. These women were later assisted by the elite women who arrived a decade later. Today all these organisations have been taken over by men.

The first Somali male organisation (other than the Somali National Movement, which is the political party that fought the north-south civil war, and which, though set up by disaffected students in London, has aims directed only at Somalia), was formed by the take-over of a Somali women's organisation, such as the Somali Community and Cultural Association. In the 1980s the women vacated the premises they had acquired for themselves as their menfolk had nowhere to meet and, although this association has now formed a subsidiary women's group, the pattern is one that has been repeated many times. The Somali Education Project was taken over by men when it received funding. Indeed, until recently it only employed men and the female founder, who desperately needed employment, remains as a volunteer. Thus, Somali women have initiated community organisations, but as soon as their efforts have gained a formal status they have 'allowed' the men to take over. However, as the Somali refugee crisis in the borough deepened all organisations became more effective and now include competent members of both sexes.

The organisations, which are effective in female hands, are often nearly emasculated by the internecine quarrels of men. This happened to SOMREC in the late 1980s but it has now regrouped with the help of women to form an effective organisation). When women are asked why they allow men to take over they say 'It is our upbringing to defer to men. We know they are not as effective as us but what can you do?' This attitude is close to the deference and subservience which is exhibited by Bangladeshi women, whose major formal organisation in Tower Hamlets is a creation of the Greater London Council equal opportunity policy and was formed after male youths had politicised themselves. From what I can gather, the pattern of Somali women initiating political groups is not a reflection of what occurs in Somalia.

Somali women's subservience to men may also be a recognition that should they publicly be seen to be successful the men will wreck their achievements in order to remain dominant. The Somali community appears to throw away opportunities rather than risk upsetting cliques, or allowing one group to be seen to have initiative and leadership. Thus several groups within the community worked for six months to organise a Somali week of cultural and information exchange. A faction in the community, perhaps through jealousy, used violence to force the organisers to abandon the project at the last minute, to the detriment of the whole community.

Both Bangladeshi and Somali traditional societies are patrilineal and adhere to Muslim law with regard to marriage, dowry and divorce. Both groups of women are expected to live amongst their husband's kin, and both are expected to defer to their husbands privately and publicly. In both societies domestic violence[11] is regulated rather than prohibited and in Somali society is used as a ritualised expression of male dominance.[11] A Somali husband is expected to beat his wife on her wedding night with a ritual whip. The first few weeks of her marriage are thus extremely painful. Somali women are also fully circumcised, with clitoris and vulva excised. A woman is re-cut on her wedding night to allow penetration, although within Somali folklore it is considered a tribute to male virility if a husband can penetrate his wife without her being recut (Lewis 1960: 29). I have been told that girls are deliberately circumcised later than boys so that they will always remember the pain. Every Somali woman I have spoken to says that she remembers the pain as if it was yesterday. Although, since 1985

11. The evidence of domestic violence in the Bangladeshi community comes from con- fidential interviews. I cannot supply statistics as to the level but it is undeniable that the women themselves perceive it as a problem. A refuge for Asian females fleeing from domestic violence is being set up by the community. Regulation rather than prohibition of violence can be compared to the situation in the United Kingdom where the use of domestic violence is prohibited but where there is poor control when the prohibition is broken.

female circumcision has been illegal in the United Kingdom the law is circumvented as girls are taken abroad for circumcision. Female circumcision in Somalia is almost universal and protests about it mainly come from educated Somali males such as doctors. In the United Kingdom it is the Somali women who are leading the protest and trying to dissuade mothers from taking their daughters out of the country for circumcision. Female circumcision is a pharaonic and not a Koranic custom and the women explain its function as being equivalent to purdah among Bangladeshi women.

In Bangladesh, women's access to sex is controlled by keeping men and women physically separate within the village and the home. In Somali nomadic society this physical separation is not possible so sex is made physically impossible prior to marriage. Physical pleasure is severely reduced by circumcision, moreover, and so diminishes sexual desire after marriage.

The terms of a Bangladeshi marriage contract, *nikah nama,* make interesting reading. The first term states the dower, then the amount to be deferred until death or divorce. Next come the number of times a women is entitled to visit her relatives and whether she is entitled to have them visit her. The final clause which is not always included is a promise not to 'torture' her. I have asked whether torture in translation means 'beat', but understand that it either means a very severe beating or something worse. In theory, both Bangladeshi and Somali women can return to their own kin if they are mistreated in their marriages, though for Somalis divorce cannot be obtained on grounds of cruelty, only on failure to maintain a wife and children, (Lewis, 1960: 34) .

I feel sure that the acceptable levels of violence within a marriage, and the communities' or woman's ability to control unacceptable levels, is a major factor in the mental health of the wife. In fact a Somali woman will leave a violent marriage, either by walking out or by behaving in a way calculated to force her husband to. A Somali woman after marriage remains both emotionally and jurally linked to her own lineage and it would be inconceivable for a man to prevent her seeing her kin. Her kin remain partially liable for her misdeeds, however, and if she were to commit murder, both her husband and her own lineage would contribute blood money to the offended lineage, (Lewis 1960: 31). Sons are all important to a Somali wife, since her linkage with her husband's lineage is through her sons. Sons are expected to protect their mothers.

For Bangladeshi women divorce or separation are rarely realistic options. A divorced or separated wife would be ostracised by her community and culturally unable to take the necessary steps to ensure her own economic survival. Theoretically, a woman's male relatives are supposed to protect her but in practice in the majority of cases the only method of controlling violence is to wait for one's sons to grow up and protect one.

Conclusion

In conclusion, it appears that control over one's own life is a major element in the mental health of anyone, male or female, and that a major factor in controlling one's own life is being able to choose who you live with and when to terminate a marriage. The cultural factors which make divorce a realistic option for Somali women, that is to say their linguistic skills, the acceptability of their meeting and working with the host community and the support they receive from their own community both emotionally and practically, are some factors which lead to the apparent positive adaptability of Somali women. Also as the men begin to dominate Somali groups in the United Kingdom I wonder whether women will retain the 'political initiative' of the community. Already they may be beginning to return to public marginalisation. Public community events are ostensibly organised by coalitions of men and women with men taking the higher profile. It will be interesting to see whether the current influx of Somalis leads to 'ghettoisation' and a breakdown in the communities' own methods of initiating women to their new life in England. Already knowledge of the atrocities committed against relatives in the civil war and the delay in bringing relatives to the United Kingdom has led to a sharp increase in the number of 'depressed' women coming to me.

References

Carey, S. and Shukor, A., 1985 'A Profile of the Bangladeshi Community in East London', *New Community* vol. 12, no.3

Direr, S., 1983 'An Investigation of the Effects of Dislocation on the Somali Community living in Tower Hamlets', unpublished Diploma of Higher Education dissertation

Lewis, I. M., 1960 *Marriage and the Family in Northern Somaliland*, East African Studies no. 15, London: Kegan Paul and Trench Trubrer & Co.

—1961 *A Pastoral Democracy*, London: Oxford University Press

Lewis, I.M., 1981 *Somali Culture, History and Social Institutions*, London: SEPS

6

Identities Constructed and Reconstructed: Representations of Asian Women[1] in Britain

Parminder Bhachu

Introduction

On the whole, white feminists stress oppression by the patriarchy, the imposition of purdah, the control exercised by their men and capitalist producers in the economy, and the constraints of their cultural values. Non-white socialist feminists (Brah 1987 and 1988, Parmar 1984 and 1988, Amos and Parmar 1984, Carby 1984, Foster-Carter 1987 and 1988, Bhagavani and Coulson 1986), have reacted against these constructions and pointed to their ethnocentrism, the lack of understanding of the race and class dimensions of the lives of Asian and black women, the diversity of their experiences in the diaspora (Parmar 1989) and the heterogeneity of their populations in Britain (Brah 1987). A number of anthropologists (mostly white and women) writing on these issues in Britain and the United States have come under fire for representing the cultural values of Asian women as oppressive without taking account of them as active agents. Countering such representations, black feminists have pointed to the militancy of Asian women, particularly salient in Britain through their organisation of strikes, to show that

1. The categories of Asians and Asian women in Britain refer to South Asians predominantly from the Indian subcontinent and from the overseas Indian communities – the Indian diaspora – it also includes British Asians who were born and brought up in Britain. Thus, these categories have a British-specificity. I am not referring here to the Asian Americans – the Japanese, the Chinese, the Koreans, the Filipinos, etc. – who are categorised as Asians in the United States, as opposed to the East Indians from India and Pakistan. It should be borne in mind that these labels constitute 'contested terrain' and are continuously negotiated. However, the themes discussed in this chapter concerning British Asian women of Sikh origin are much more widely applicable to the conceptualisation of the cultural locations of Asian women in general in the academic literature and in the media, of both sides of the Atlantic.

this is not a new phenomenon (Trivedi 1984) in the subcontinent and Britain.[2] This militancy is further manifested in the present in the struggles and resistances in which British Asians women are engaged against racism and imperialism on both the economic and political fronts.[3] Despite this, representations of these women as politically inactive, shy and powerless are common and persist.

Asian and black women represent a range of class perspectives and political opinions. The socialist feminist perspective, is one amongst others, expressed in writings by Asian women increasingly involved in the production of knowledge about their own communities. Their productions emanate from their involvement in a range of audio-visual media, local government departments, and political organisations and from the black feminist press. Indigenous scholars, more centrally placed in the academy (Brah 1987 and 1988, Altorki and El Sohl 1988) are also reacting against negative and sometimes simplistic constructions of their real (and indeed, sometimes imagined) communities and cultural values by outsider agencies. Their protests are against the stereotypes of Asian women, who are presented as victims unable to exercise any control over their lives and the cultural locations in which they are situated. Their 'ethnic' cultural values are represented as repressive – traits they must accept – rather than as values they continuously adapt, choose to accept, reproduce, modify, recreate and elaborate according to the circumstances in which they are situated.

The assumption in large sections of the literature is that the ethnic group enforces its ethnicity, or rather facets of it that are presented as fixed, rather than as fluid structures that change over time and space.[4]

2. For example, Mrs Bhikaji Cama, was a radical political activist in student politics in London and Paris in the early 1900s, and later in the 'Quit India' movement to oust the British from India.

3. Their organisational abilities and powers of political organisation are patently obvious from their involvement in industrial disputes such as, for example, the strikes at Imperial Typewriters (1974), Grunwick Photo Printing (1976), Chix Bubble Gum Factory (1980), etc. Their political struggles include their demonstrations against virginity tests that especially affected Asian women from the subcontinent, their fights against discriminatory legislation, domestic violence and anti-deportation and family-unification campaigns. Recently, a group of 'Asian Women Against Fundamentalism' received enormous media attention for their counter demonstrations against Muslim fundamentalists and in showing their support for Salman Rushdie.

4. This applies equally to colonial discourses (Bhabha 1983, Spivak 1985), and to the race and ethnic relations literature in Britain, except for some recent literature on black peer/youth cultures Gilroy (1987), James (1986), Back (1988 and 1993) and their language and music forms (Hewitt 1986 and 1989a, Rampton 1989, Jones 1988). The literature on young Asian girls and women is not developed at all and deals almost entirely with the unchanging cultures imposed on them by their 'ethnic' apparatus and kinship groups, in which they are portrayed as passive recipients unbounded by their British class and subcultural locations.

There is little perception of Asian women as active negotiators of the cultural values that they choose to accept, and the lifestyles to which they subscribe, or of their roles as innovators and originators of newer and newer cultural forms, which take from their 'ethnic' traditions and which are continuously reformulated through the filters of their British class and local cultures. Their role as cultural entrepreneurs who are actively engaging with their cultural frameworks, whilst continuously transforming them, is one that is largely absent both from the majority of the literature and from commonsense sensibilities. It is to this important role of cultural reproduction by British Asian women that I want to turn. I will focus in particular on the impact of the economic on the cultural, and on the formulation of identities which are responsive to the local cultures in which they are situated. I want to explore this variation through an examination of one facet of their culture – the dowry system – which reflects their British consumption styles and class locations and which has been commoditised and elaborated in Britain. First, however, some background on the economic and cultural locations of Asian women in Britain.

Asian Women's Economic Activity: Past and Present

Asian women have always occupied and currently occupy a cross-section of the class hierarchy, and this is reflected in their cultural and consumption styles. The class locations and the cultural systems that Asian women occupy are much more complex than is obvious from the literature which focuses on working-class women. The complexity of Asian women's class locations is not new. It has existed for as long as the Indian presence in Britain; from aristocrats like Princess Victoria Gouramma of the Coorgs, Maharanee Jinda Kaur (see Lady Login's *Recollections and Diaries 1820–1904*), to Indian wives of British men in the eighteenth and nineteenth centuries (Ballhatchet 1980), the ayahs who were housed in the East End, and women servants (for example, slave girls employed as ladies' maids) in the service of the East India Company employees in Britain from the mid-seventeenth century onwards (Visram 1986).

As well as Indian women situated at the top, middle and bottom of the class hierarchy, there were also a number of Indian women students. The most well known in the nineteenth century was Cornelia Sorabji, who was one of the earliest practising women barristers and who later became a renowned social reformer and a prolific writer.[5]   Noor Inayat Khan was among the first forty WAAF women to be trained for intelligence work in occupied France in the Second World War. She was a secret agent based in Paris as a wireless operator and was also involved in more dangerous missions in other parts of France. She was awarded the Croix de Guerre with a Gold Star and the George Cross posthumously, after being captured by the Gestapo and executed in Dachau in 1944 (Fuller Overton 1952). Whilst her story has appeared in popular soap operas on television – based around her code name Madeleine – she has always been portrayed as a white woman of English and French parentage, thus obscuring her Asianness. In the 1930s, there were over 100 Indian women studying for medicine, law and education degrees in British universities (Visram 1986), some of whom stayed on in Britain. At this period, the famous Hollywood actress Merle Oberon, whose career initially took off in Britain was at her peak winning the most prestigious acting roles. She was the illegitimate child of a Eurasian plantation owner in India and a poor Indian woman who brought her up in Calcutta, before sending her to Britain as an adult (Higham and Moseley 1983). Thus, the presence of Asian women both outside and within working-class sectors is not new in Britain: it is rooted in the past.

My purpose in referring to the above women is not so much to counter the hegemonic construction of them as 'passive/docile/conflicted/dominated by oppressive traditions and men' – that is, the models that have so much currency in representations of Asian women

---

5. She was the first woman ever in Britain to have been awarded a law degree by a British University - Somerville Hall, Oxford, in 1889.

6. This focus on the negative dimensions, rather what are considered to be so, can also be discerned from Asian women's writing including that which is commissioned from them by the feminist publishing houses which tend to publish works that either fit 'the passive/victim' stereotype of the 'between and betwixt identity crisis/cultural confrontational/desire to return to homeland' models. Asian women find it easier to find publishers, if they fit their writings into these models (see Sharanjeet Shan's *In My Own Name* (1986), and Lena Dhingra's *Amritvela* (1988), and Farida Karodia's *Daughters of the Twilight* (1986), all published by The Women's Press). There is tacit encouragement for this type of writings. Afro-Caribbean and American black women, on the other hand, have a wider range of representations in the publications produced by these presses and by other media, though, there again, the danger of projecting them too frequently as superwomen/super macho/supersexed/bullying their men' variety of women persists. Nonetheless, a number of writings are constructed on models of them as strong and capable women – as 'rounded' and multidimensional human beings (e.g. Maya Angelou 1970, 1974 and 1985, Toni Morrison 1985, Lucille Clifton 1985). However, it is interesting to note that in the majority of cases, their writings have already been published in the United States before being reproduced in Britain.

and in the conceptualisation of their lifestyles[6] – but to point to the historical roots of the heterogeneity of their experiences and positions, which is further manifested in Britain in the 1990s in a whole range of economic and cultural spheres. I do *not* want to deflect attention from the predominantly working-class locations of Asian women to focus on prominent and successful Indian women, because I think this is patronising. There is a tendency among minority/indigenous/ethnic scholars to refer endlessly, to the economic and educational success stories and to famous individuals of the communities to which they belong in defensive protest at the deficient models, and to present a positive alternative picture.[7] However, I do want to emphasise the variety of their experiences and point to the complexity of the different niches they occupy both now and in the past. This is reflected in their current labour market profile and their active engagement with the economy, which has a strong impact on their cultural reproduction.

The Current Labour Market Profile

I would like briefly to refer to the labour market profile of Asian women to show that, contrary to the stereotype, they actively engage with the British economy. In certain cases they have a higher economic activity rates than indigenous white women.

A higher proportion of Afro-Caribbean and non-Muslim women including Sikh women were in the labour market in full time employment in the mid- and late 1980s and 1990s, than economically active white women. Of women between twenty-five and forty-four years of age, 66 per cent of white indigenous origin are economically active as are 77 per cent of West Indian origin, 62 per cent of Indian origin, and only 17 per cent of Pakistani/Bangladeshi origin. This latter rather low figure does not capture the paid homework/homesewing done by Muslim women: they are more economically active than this recorded figure reflects (Brah 1987: 41). East African Asian women, have a higher rate, at 69 per cent, than both indigenous white women and Indian and Pakistani/Bangladeshi women from the subcontinent (Labour Force Survey 1984 as reported in the Employment Gazette, December 1985). These figures change only slightly for the Labour Force Survey 1985 (reported in the Employment Gazette, January 1987) which was the last

7. See anthropologist Micaela di Leonardo's critique of this for the Italian Americans in the United States (1984: 22). Gayatri Spivak also crises the desire to represent black positively: 'But the idea of always portraying blacks or women or whatever the minority is in a positive light is, in the long run, deeply insulting' (1988: 86).

one to examine the category of East African Asians separately – 67 per cent for indigenous women, 75 per cent for West Indian women, 58 per cent for Indian women, 17 per cent for Pakistani/Bangladeshi women and 67 per cent for East African Asian women.

The differences between white and Asian representation in the managerial and professional group are slight, in fact, proportionately the same in the case of East African Asian women at 7 per cent for white women, 7 per cent for African Asian women, 6 per cent for Asian women and 1 per cent for West Indian women (Brown's PSI survey 1984: 198). As Sheila Allen (1987: 182) points out 'the difference in types of jobs and earnings found among black and white women are much less than those found among men. There are proportionately almost as many Asian women in professional, employer or management sectors (6 per cent) as white women (7 per cent) and the percentage of white women in *unskilled jobs* (11 per cent) is *higher* than either West Indian (7 per cent) or Asian women (2 per cent)' (my emphasis). The implications of this greater overlap between women's earnings and jobs, is that their expenditure patterns are also more likely to share a common ground – regardless of ethnicity and class – than that of the men, who are much more unequally distributed.

The differences in the number of economically active women (and men) who are in full-time employment are more considerable in the South East than anywhere else in the country (Employment Gazette 1988). The south-east in general is characterised by very high rates of economic activity and lower unemployment rates, a situation applicable to blacks and whites alike.[8] There are also many more Asian women in the south east in white collar/clerical and managerial/professional jobs than anywhere else, though, in comparison to the past, the amount of waged employment for Indian women in the Midlands was increasing in the late 1980s, filling in the jobs created by the mushrooming 'anorak industry', the rapid growth of clothing manufacturing sectors. There are significant regional differences in the economic niches and the employment opportunities of Asian women.

8. Over half the Indian population (54 per cent) and three-fifths of the East African Asian population is based in the south east of Britain (especially in London), in comparison to 31 per cent of whites. Nearly half of the ethnic minority labour force lives in London (Employment Gazette 1987: 18), an area (in common with the South East in general) characterised by the greatest amount of economic activity and least amount of unemployment for them (Employment Gazette 1988: 175). There are very significant differences between London and the south east and the rest of the few, though major, urban centres that Asians are settled in.

It should by now be clear that the labour market profile of Asian women is much more complex than is generally understood. They are more widely distributed in a range of economic niches and employment structures than I have actually outlined here. Their occupational profile is, therefore, determined by local economies and the opportunity structures in them. However, I want to reiterate that this should not detract from their predominantly working class location – though it should equally be emphasised that they are also present in a number of non-working class sectors, and that they have had different histories of participation in the labour market, prior to settlement in Britain. For example, the higher rate of economic activity amongst East African Asian women in Britain is related to their urban experiences in formal employment sectors in Africa, in comparison to the rural background of the majority of the directly migrant women from the subcontinent, and also to the continuation of the employment trends established prior to migration from metropolitan Africa to metropolitan Britain. The number of Asian female employees in Kenya had risen from 600 in 1948, to 3,750 in 1962, then comprising 10 per cent of the total Asian labour force in that country (Ghai 1965: 95). By 1967, this had risen to 18 per cent (Ghai 1970). This period coincides with the most intense amount of Asian migration to Britain from Africa after the full impact of the Africanisation policies on them in the mid-1960s.

Commoditised Consumption and Cultural Patterns

The varied economic profile of Asian women is reflected in their different positions in the class hierarchy and their various cultural and regional locations in Britain especially in the late 1980s and early 1990s, a period which has the highest number of British born or British raised women. This regionalism is reflected in their patterns of consumption and in the cultural styles that they adopt, even though, patterns that emerge from London are the most influential because they are products of the dominant minority community. The wealth generated through their own relationship with the labour market is deployed and expended in accordance with their sub-class styles and related consumption values.

Similarly, Asian women's identities and patterns of consumption grow out of their regional and class locations, and then from particular niches within the large metropolis. London Asian women identify themselves differently from those in Northern Ireland and Scotland

and according to the class positions that they occupy. This is not because there is no common 'ethnic' cultural base, but because younger Asian women emerge out of the particular localities in which they have been raised and from the particular class cultures to which they have been socialised (Mac an Ghaill 1988: 110, 138). Whole facets of the existence of Asian women are subject to and determined by common economic, class and regionally specific forces that impact on white British women as much as on Asian women, regardless of their various ethnicities. For example, Asian women in Birmingham are at one with the local 'Brummie' culture in their expenditure choices and in the construction of their identities, just as London Asian women living in Camden/Hampstead are Camdenian/Hampsteadian in their modes of operation, in their interpretation of their wealth, their clothes, the symbols important to the definition of their identities and styles, etc. In all these areas, Yuppie/Bluppie (young upwardly-mobile professional/black upwardly-mobile professional) Asian women share the symbolic and material culture of that sub-class.

In what follows, I am presenting only a brief summary of the escalation of the dowry system since migration to Britain, not so much to detail the process of elaboration within it (see Bhachu 1985, 1986 and 1988), but to point to the significant inflation within it of those spheres that directly concern the brides themselves. This elaboration of the dowry system is just one facet of the cultural and religious effervescence that has taken place amongst the Sikhs in the settled phases of the 1980s and 1990s in Britain (See Bhachu 1988, 1991 and 1993).

Dowries consisted of minimal items both for the bride and her affinal kin in the earlier phases in the late 1950s and 1960s. However, in the past two decades, they have escalated and also have been highly commoditised. The three components of the *daaj* -the elaborate traditional garments and some 'Western' clothes, household goods including luxury consumer items and gold ornaments in the form of sets - that are designated specifically for the bride herself and the fourth component of affinal gifts for the groom and his close kinsmen and women are always adhered to rigidly for caste endogamous East African marriages. Hence, the structure of the *daaj* has not changed over time, even though, there have been internal changes in the items presented reflecting the move to urban Britain, and also in their designation reflecting structural changes in the organisation of the household and the various power relations within it (which have favoured the brides in the 1970s and 1980s), as result of both migration and the impact of economic forces.

British dowries, for example, have escalated in number from eleven to twenty-one clothing items in the 1950s and 1960s in Africa, to twenty-one clothing items in Africa and Britain, to anything from twenty-one to fifty-one clothing items in the 1970s and 1980s. Some of these are very high quality silk saris and prestigious designer clothes from leading European and Bombay-based Indian designers, accompanied by expensive Gucci, Bally (Swiss rather than British), Zapata and other prestigious-name shoes and bags, especially in the case of the high earning professional brides. The 'standard' East African Sikh *daaj* is always presented comprising twenty-one clothing items and a whole range of accompanying accessories and prestigious consumer items for the bride. This norm persists in Britain, regardless of the prestige and standing of families involved, or that of the brides and grooms themselves providing the marriages are endogamous to the 'East African Sikhs'. It is also common to present twenty-one items in the Punjab among middle/upper middle ranking families.

However, even though a twenty-one-item daaj constitutes the 'British/American/East African Sikh' pattern, there are major qualitative differences in its content, according to the earning powers of the brides themselves. A bride who has not earned in her own right before marriage, invariably has a basic twenty-one-item *daaj,* in comparison to the earning brides whose *daajs* are much more elaborate and voluminous. The latter *daajs* include not only higher quality garments and personal accessories but also a vaster range of consumer durables – china sets, silver cutlery, electronic music equipment, exclusive linen etc. – that the brides have themselves purchased from their own earnings and which they themselves are likely to utilise and also to control.

Much more than the mid-1970s *daajs,* the 1980s and early 1990s *daajs* are particularly reflective of the British sub-cultural/regional styles, especially in the interpretation of not only the 'traditional' garments/goods/gifts, but also of their class-encoded consumption patterns. So that there are *daajs* that are Sloane Rangerish[9] in their interpretation – reflecting the exclusive 'London SW 1,3,5,/Knightsbridge/Sloane Square' locale consumption patterns of some of the high earning and professional brides, just as there are prestigious 'Designer Ethnic/European' *daajs,* the middle/lower middle class

9. By 'Sloane Rangerish', I mean the styles that emanate from the Sloane Ranger set, which are/were powerfully popularised by the 'Super Sloane', Princess Diana. There are 'Asianised' and 'Punjabised' versions of Sloane Ranger fashion trends. This is particularly obvious from the interpretation of their 'ethnic garments' such as the Punjabi suit (worn by a cross-section of North Indian women including the Sikh women), which is put together using Sloane Ranger fashion accessories and in the Sloane Ranger style.

'Oxford Street Marks and Spencerish/mass produced-departmental store' types, working class 'London East Ender' types, provincial 'Liverpudlian Sikh' and, from Manchester, the 'Mancunian types', etc. Different regional styles are quite clearly discernable. For example, a Midlands *daaj* is interpreted differently from those of London brides of an equivalent class group, despite the similarity in the content of the *daajs* and the persistence of the external framework – its three main spheres for the bride and fourth component for the affines. These regional patterns are also obvious from the marriage circuits – an informal metropolitan hypergamy – which operate in Britain. London girls tend not to marry outside London and the south east. If they are married out, in a majority of cases they move back to London to set up a nuclear residence within a couple of years of marriage. This is not a new phenomenon. In East Africa, Nairobi girls tended not to marry men from outside the capital, whether from Dar-es-Salaam or other small-town Ugandan and Tanzanian Sikh men, who were considered to be more orthodox and less socially skilled – *paindoos* – in comparison to the Nairobi-wallahs. Similarly, in India, metropolitan women from the larger cities, such as Delhi and Bombay, often prefer not to marry men from small-town provincial families.

By focusing on a cultural trait, I have tried to show that the *daajs* presented to and manufactured by young Sikh women are influenced by and responsive to class and regional trends, being products of particular consumption patterns which encode whole facets of their lifestyles that shift continuously. Just as the *daajs* are *ethnically assertive* in content, so they are assertive of the sub-class and cultural positions of British Sikh women. All this applies equally to the identities negotiated and generated by British Asians. These, too, have their specificities. They are multifaceted and activated differently according to the various contexts. They are products of particular periods and symbolic and material economies. They are governed by the same range of forces that determine the commoditisation of their consumption.

Appropriation and Transformation of British Asian Identities and Cultures

The assumptions in the British literature are that the crucial determinants of Asian identities are the nurturing forces of a homeland culture, which (at least in the early stages of settlement) provides cultural reinforcement in Britain; the maintenance of ethnic boundaries through the exclusionary forces of racism, confrontations that are said to lead to the identities of resistance and defiance, and the desire of migrant/settler/British Asians to emulate or aspire to particular 'white' class cultures and their symbols. There is a great deal of emphasis on boundary maintenance and on the perpetuation of what are presented as conscious, clearly worked out, homogeneous and fixed cultural values. Importance is attached to the impact of rejecting racism and discrimination as the fundamental forces in structuring the identities and experiences of British Asians and blacks. In all this, ethnicity is presented as something that has fixed components and symbols and is considered to be the primary agent controlling and generating the various identities of Asians. Indeed, all of these are important social mechanisms in structuring their lives and determining their life chances.

However, my concern is that there are a number of other forces that are equally important in framing their experiences, especially in the 1990s when most British Asian women are products of local and regional cultures and specific class niches in Britain. With a developed and rapidly growing population of British raised and British born Asians, some of the commonly used concepts to capture the cultural locations of British Asian women need to be revised to take account of the complexity of their British cultural locations. This is all the more imperative because their presence in different class and regional cultures, and economic niches in Britain produces a variation in their experiences. The way in which they define themselves is an outcome of these experiences. London Sikh women are as much Londoners – products of the various sub-cultures in the capital – as they are Jat or Ramagarhia Sikhs depending on their caste affliations. The professional and occupational niches they occupy bring into focus other identities that are representative of their different economic locations.

This multifaceted nature of the identities and ethnic experiences of Asian women is, of course, not exclusive to Britain. The early pioneer Punjabi Sikh women in California, situated within a predominantly Mexican milieu, were influenced by Mexican cultural styles in the interpretation of certain facets of their lives. The close connections of their men with Mexicans, often through marriages with Mexican women (Leonard 1991), lead to social networks and relationships which sometimes involved *'compadrazgo'* relations (La Brack 1982a, 1982b, La Brack and Leonard 1984). Such social interaction gave them some familiarity with Mexican cultures. These (few) Spanish-speaking Punjabi Sikh women in specific areas in California have retained some facets of these local cultures that influenced them. In the 1960s and 1970s, the local Sikh community reconstituted (La Brack

1982a, La Brack and Leonard 1984, Leonard 1989), leading to a dramatic growth of the directly migrant Punjabi Sikh population. The direct migrants have instituted more traditionally based 'Punjabi Sikh' cultural and religious patterns. The 1980s and 1990s have produced many more overtly 'ethnic' Sikh women and also the highly 'Americanised Californian Sikhs'. In contrast, the experiences of Swahili-speaking East African Sikh women, born and raised in culturally and religiously conservative and comparatively large communities in Africa that remained socially aloof from both the blacks and whites in Africa (I refer here to the women mostly), are very different. These strongly 'traditional' Sikh women, who have always retained their outward 'ethnic symbols', such as the Punjabi suit and saris, and other Sikh and Hindu religious symbols, and so forth are products of an easier climate. Their ethnicity could flourish and be expressed, overtly buttressed by the presence of many other Asians and also by their cultural base which was maintained by contracting rigidly caste endogamous marriages. Thus, the hostility faced by Californian Sikh women whose expression of their ethnic cultural symbols – the wearing of a Punjabi suit – was greeting by the opprobrium of the dominant white population, was non-existent for African Sikh women who were situated in a more friendly environment.

Thus, identities are *contextualised* and not stable, despite a common core of key fundamental religious and cultural values that constitute their cultural roots. They shift according to the forces that operate on them. In the case of the Sikhs, these are not just products of confrontation and rejection,[10] but emerge out of vibrant and changing cultures in which young Asians are situated in Britain and over which they have genuine *unselfconscious* command (Hewitt 1989: 46). They result not from conscious emulation of particular subcultures, or necessarily through the politics of confrontation, but through their natural familiarity with particular British economies and with their symbolic and material cultures. From these they appropriate, transform and reproduce both unselfconsciously and also strategically.

This appropriation and transformation also exists at a national level. The appropriation of black music styles into the mainstream markets and the impact of black cultures beyond their own groups in Britain has already been in progress for a number of years, and been commented upon (Hall 1989, Gilroy 1987, Jones 1988, Back 1988 and

10. Although the immediate post-1984 period did produce defiant identities in response to external threats, as could be observed from the appropriation of 'warrior Sikh' symbols by young Sikhs - saffron turbans and *dupattas* and *kirpans*.

1989). The commoditisation of 'Asianness and Asian Experiences' has begun, starting in the late 1980s and early 1990s.[11] For Asians, these trends are observable from among other things, fashion design which has been (for example Katherine Hamnett's 1989 summer collection) strongly Indian in its interpretation of 'Indian' women's clothes for the Western markets, the growing presence of Hindi-speaking Indians in television advertisements for the Indian foodstuffs and the further availability of Asian food at high-class food counters.

A consequence of this uptake by the mainstream media is that a number of these processes are empowering for Asians (if they can exercise control over the images produced of them), and are not only generating and negotiating for them at a local and national level, but also strategically interpreting them for the wider public by entering these arenas of knowledge and image production. I refer here to the role of Asians as constructors and interpreters of facets of their own cultural systems, identities, communities, etc. for public consumption. These include the ethnic media-wallahs, the Hampstead/West Hampstead/Camden set in London and the Moseley set in Birmingham (representing the trendy areas in which people from the media industry reside), a rapidly mushrooming community of producers and directors and ethnic commentators who comment on their productions.[12] Of course, social scientists are also involved in these processes.

A further theme also related to these commoditising processes is that there is in Britain, a growing interest in the female Asian experience. This process is obvious in the recent publications and commissioning of books, programmes and films on Asian women. Gita Metha's book *Raj* (1989) on Indian women in the time of the Raj deals with the theme of the resistance set up by Indian women to the cultures and symbols of the colonisers. They forced their menfolk to remove their public 'uniforms of slavery' and don Indian clothes in their presence in domestic territories – Metha on 'Bandung File' 18 July 1989. Film director Gurinder K. Chadda's award winning film set to Bhangra and Bangla music, *'I am British but...'*, released in August 1989 deals with the local identities of young British Asians and their own classifications of their positions and affiliations in different regions in Britain.

11. These processes have been described by Leonardo (1984) for American Italians. For example, images of Italian women as plumpish 'Pizza-Baking' mothers surrounded by warm, loving families around happy dinner tables abound, even though they are to be found in different class niches and regional economies in the United States.

12. See Parminder Dhillon's (1988) analysis of British Asian experiences on film and Preeti Manuel's IBA report (1984) on representation of black people in television drama.

She was commissioned to make another film on the cultural scene of Asian women. Television producer Behrose Gandhy produced a series of nine programmes for Channel 4 on issues of common concern to Asians and Asian women. These were transmitted on Saturday evenings in early 1990. Zerbanoo Gifford, a Liberal politician, recently published a book commissioned by publishers Unwin Hyman on successful Asian women. Nearly all of the women of whom I speak are British Asians involved in countering negative constructions of them through their own productions of images of Asian women. They are actively engaged in representing the female Asian experiences in Britain and also in formulating their own continuously changing identities *very strategically* for wider consumption.[13]

Such media expertise was also demonstrated by the Asian 'Women Against Fundamentalism', in actively putting their point of view across rapidly in a range of media – 'Heart of the Matter' BBC 1, 'Bandung File' Channel 4, a full page in the *Guardian* newspaper, *Spare Rib,* etc. – all in the period of a month. These trends are taking place not only because of the upsurge of popular interest in the British Asian experience, but also because of the platforms for which these women have fought: the right to represent British Asian women and to document their lives, their *(hi)*stories and cultures in their own ways and from their own sensibilities and experiences.

Conclusion

There is a 'normalized absence' in the literature, which views Asian ethnic and class cultural traits in terms of a 'pathologized presence' (Phoenix 1987: 51). These are presented as fixed and as enforced upon Asian women without their input and choice. For example, dowries and purdah are nearly always constructed as oppressive. Arab women anthropologists (Altorki and El Sohl 1988) have questioned the negative representations of the latter institution, pointing to Arab women's own choices in accepting the parameters of their cultures. This is especially the case in certain facets of Arab society, in which the men are dependent on their women – who are considered from a Western perspective as highly controlled 'purdahed and secluded' – in forming and cementing powerful social links that are crucial to them for effective economic production. Arab anthropologist Altorki states that:

13. Note film director Gurinder Chadda's studied, eye-catching personal style and identity - 'City Limits' 20 August 1989, and film publicity blurb - designed specifically for media consumption. She is wearing Union Jack Socks, Doc Martin shoes, and embroidered Indian skirt, with a *duppatta* thrown sideways and holds a Bulldog on a leash.

the very segregation of the sexes that prevents women gaining access to information and authority in the wider society creates the conditions for their far-reaching control over a man's destiny insofar as it is linked to his marriage... Despite the subtlety and informality characterizing the relevant information indeed enables them to determine the decisions that are nominally the prerogative of men...Thus, the idea of the unquestioned supremacy of men and the complete subservience of women in Saudi Arabian society is reduced to a myth. (1988: 64-5)

Other indigenous anthropologists and sociologists (especially those either born or raised in the West and who are Western-educated) have argued a similar stance, pointing to the empowerment of women through their experiences within their communities and with 'ethnic' cultural forms, even though these are presented by outsider agencies involved in their construction as pathological and oppressive. There is criticism of the lack of reference to the mitigating circumstances that these women are able to generate, and which may actually exist in the social structures they occupy. This type of perspective is clear from the recent works of black American anthropologist Deborah King (1988), my own work (Bhachu 1986 and 1988), Arab anthropologist Camillia El Sohl (1988), Lebanese anthropologist Saud Joseph (1988), Yugoslav sociologist Mirjana Morokvasic (1984 and 1988), Italian American anthropologist Micaela di Leonardo (1984), and a growing group of Chinese, Hispanic, African and other 'Women of Colour' social scientists in the United States and Britain, who are now themselves, as women, actively involved in the production of knowledge about their own communities. These are precisely some of the scholars who are also questioning the constructions of 'Asian/Minority/Eastern European/Muslim/'Third World' women based on the 'powerless/passive/static model', which fails to take account of the transformative powers of Asian women in generating, and in manufacturing their cultural systems. These, often simplistic, models deny their roles as the cultural entrepreneurs they are.

References

Allen, S., 1987 'Gender, Race and Class in the 1980s', in C. Husband (ed.), *'Race' in Britain: Continuity and Change*. London: Hutchinson
Altorki, S., 1988 'At Home in the Field', in S. Altorki and C. El Sohl (eds), *Arab Women in the Field: Studying Your Own Society*, Syracuse, New York: Syracuse University Press, pp. 49–68
Altorki, S. and El Sohl C., 1988 *Arab Women in the Field: Studying Your Own Society* Syracuse, New York: Syracuse University Press

Amos V. and Parmar P., 1984 'Challenging Imperial Feminism', *Feminist Review* no.17, pp.3–19

Angelou, M. 1970 *I Know Why The Caged Bird Sings* New York: Random House

—1974 *Gather Together in My Name*, New York: Random House

—1985 'Shades and Slashes of Light' in M. Evans (ed.), *Black Women Writers: Arguments and Interviews* London and Sydney: Pluto Press

Back, L., 1988 'Coughing up Fire: Sound-Systems in South East London', in *New Formations: Identities*, no.5, pp.141–52

—1993 'Race, Identity and Nation within an Adolescent community in South London', in *New Community* no. 19(2)

Ballhatchet, K.A., 1980 *Race, Sex and Class Under the Raj Imperial Attitudes and Policies and their Critics, 1793–1905*. London: Weidenfeld and Nicolson

Banerji, S. and Baumann, G., 1989' *Bhangra* in Britain 1984–1988. Fusion and Professionalization in a Genre of South Asian Dance Music', in P. Oliver (ed.) *Black Music in Britain*, Milton Keynes: The Open University Press

Barber, A., 1985 'Ethnic Origin and Economic Status', *Employment Gazette*, pp. 467–477 December

Bhabha, H., 1983 'The Other Question: Homi Bhabha Reconsiders the Stereotype and Colonial Discourse', *Screen* nos.24–6, pp.18–37

Bhachu, Parminder, 1985 *Twice Migrants: East African Sikh Settlers in Britain*, London and New York: Tavistock

—1986 'Work, Marriage and Dowry among East African Sikh Women in United Kingdom', in R. J. Simon and C. B. Brettell (eds), *International Migration: The Female Experience*, Totowa, New Jersey: Rowman and Allanheld

—1988 '*Apni Marzi Kardhi*. Home and Work: Sikh Women in Britain', in S. Westwood and P. Bhachu (eds) *Enterprising Women: Ethnicity, Economy and Gender Relations* London: Routledge

—1991 'Ethnicity Constructed and Reconstructed: The Role of Sikh Women in Cultural Elaboration and Educational Processes in Britain', *Gender and Education*, vol.1, no.3

—1993 'Twice and Direct Migrant Sikhs: Caste, Class and Identity in Pre- and Post-984 Britain', in I. Light and P. Bhachu (eds) *Immigration and Entrepreneurship: Culture, Capital and Ethnic Networks*, Transactions Publishers' Rutgers University Press, New Jersey

Bhagavani, K.-K. and Coulson, M., 1986 'Transforming Socialist-Feminism: The Challenge of Racism', *Feminist Review*, no.23, pp.81–92

Brah, A., 1987 'Women of South Asian Origin in Britain: Issues and Concerns', *South Asia*, vol.7, no.1, pp.39–53

—1988 Extended Review of G. Weiner *Gender and the Politics of Schooling* and M. Arnot *Gender Under Scrutiny* (1987) *British Journal of Sociology of Education.* vol.9, no.1

Brown, C., 1984 *Black and White Britain: The Third PSI Survey*, London: Heinemann

Carby, H., 1984 'White Woman Listen! Black Feminism and the Boundaries of Sisterhood', in Centre for Contemporary Cultural Studies, University of Birmingham, *The Empire Strikes Back: Race and Racism in '70's Britain*, London: Hutchinson, pp.212–35

Clifton, L., 1984 'A Simple Language', in M. Evans (ed.) *Black Women Writers* London and Sydney: Pluto Press

Dhillon-Kashyap, P., 1988 'Locating the Asian Experience', *Screen*, vol.29, no.4, pp.120–6

Dhingra, L., 1988 *Amritvela*, London: The Women's Press

—1988a 'Gender, Class and Origin: Aspects of Role during Fieldwork in Arab Society': in S. Altorki and C. El-Sohl (eds), *Arab Women in the Field*, Syracuse, New York: Syracuse University Press

Employment Gazette, 1987 *Ethnic Origin and Economic Status* January: 18–29
Employment Gazette, 1988 *Ethnic Origin and the Labour Market* March: 164–77
Foster-Carter, O., 1987 'Ethnicity: The Fourth Burden of Black Women Political
    Action', *Critical Social Policy* no.20, pp.46–56
——1988 'Black Women: White Feminism in Britain', *Sage Race Relations Abstracts*
    no.13, p. 1
Fuller Overton, J., 1952 *Madeleine: The Story of Noor Inayat Khan*, London: Victor
    Gollancz
George, M., 1989 'Continental Drift', *New Statesman and Society* 8 September, pp.26–7
Ghai, Y., (2nd Edition) 1970 *Portrait of a Minority: Asians in East Africa*, 2nd edn,
    Nairobi: Oxford University Press, reissue of 1965 edition
Gilroy, P., 1987 *There Ain't No Black in The Union Jack: The Cultural Politics of Race
    and Nation.* Hutchinson: London
Hall, S., 1989 'Minimal Selves', *Identity Documents*: 6 ICA, pp.44–6
Harris, H., 1972 'Black Woman and Work: The Body Politics', *Stage 1*, London,
    pp.166–74
Hewitt, R., 1986 *White Talk Black Talk: Inter-Racial Friendship and Communication
    Amongst Adolescents.* Cambridge University Press: Cambridge
——1989a. 'Youth, Race and Language: Deconstructing Ethnicity?', paper given at the
    Conference on the *Sociology of Youth and Childhood*, Phillips University, Marburg,
    West Germany. 14–15 November 1989
——1989b 'A Sociolinguistic View of Urban Adolescent Relations', paper presented at the
    Conference on *Everyday Life, Cultural Production and Race*, Institute of Cultural
    Sociology, University of Copenhagen, 27–28 April 1989
Higham, C. and Moseley, R., 1983 *Merle: A Biography of Merle Oberon.* Kent: New
    English Library
James, W., 1986 'A Long Way from Home: On Black Identity in Britain', *Immigrants
    and Minorities*, vol.5, no.3
Jones, S., 1988 *Black Culture, White Youth: The Reggae Tradition from JA to UK*,
    Macmillan Education, Basingstoke and London
Joseph, S., 1988 'Feminization, Familism, Self and Politics: Research as a Mughtaribhi',
    in S. Altorki and C. El-Solh, *Arab Women in the Field: Studying Your Own Society*,
    Syracuse, New York: Syracuse University Press
Karodia, F., 1986 *Daughters of the Twilight*, London: The Women's Press
Khan, R., 1987 *Down the Road Worlds Away.* London: Virago Upstarts
King, D. K., 1988 'Multiple Jeopardy, Multiple Consciousness: The Context of a Black
    Feminist Ideology', *Journal of Women in Culture and Society*, vol.14, no.1, pp.42–72
La Brack, B., 1982a 'Immigration Law and the Revitalization Process: The Case of
    California Sikhs', *Population Review*, vol.25, nos.1 and 2, pp.59–66
——1982b' Occupational Specializaiton Among Rural California Sikhs: The Interplay of
    Culture and Economics', *Amerasia*, vol.9, no.2, pp.29–56
La Brack, B. and Leonard, K., 1984 'Conflict and Compatability in Punjabi-Mexican
    Immigrant Families in Rurla California 1915-1965', *Journal of Marriage and the
    Family*, vol.46, no. 3
Leonard, K., 1982 'Marriage and Family Life Among Early Asian and Indian
    Immigrants', *Population Review*, vol. 25, nos. 1 and 2, pp.67–75
——1989 'Pioneer Voices: Reflections on Race, Religion and Ethnicity'. in G. Barrier
    and V. Dusenbury (eds), *The Sikh Diaspora*, New Delhi: Manohar Publishers
——1991 *Making Ethnic Choices: California's Punjabi Mexican Americans*, Philadelphia:
    Temple University Press
Leonardo M., Di., 1984 *Varieties of Ethnic Experience: Kinship, Class and Gender
    Among California Italian Americans.* Cornell University Press: Ithaca and London
Login, D. E., 1904(?) *Lady Logins Recollections: Court Life and Camp Life 1820
    1904*, reissued 1985, New Delhi: Rima Publishing House

Mac An Ghaill, M., 1988 *Young, Gifted and Black*, Milton Keynes: Open University Press

Mama, A., 1984 'Black Women, the Economic Crisis and the British State', *Feminist Review*, vol.17, pp.21–35

Manuel, P., 1984 *The Representation of Black People in British Television Drama*. Report for the Independent Broadcasting Authority

Mirza, H., 1987 'The Dilemma of Socialist Feminism: A Case for Black Feminism', *Feminist Review*, vol. 22, Spring

Mitter, S., 1986 'Industrial Reconstructuring and Manufacturing Homework: Immigrant Women in the U.K. Clothing Industry', *Capital and Class*, vol. 27, Winter, pp.37–8

Morokvasic, M., 1984 'Birds of a Passage Are Also Women', *International Migration Review,*. vol.18, no.4

—1988 *Minority and Immigrant Women in Self-Employment Business in France, Great Britain, Italy, Portugal and Federal Republic of Germany: Motivation, Situation and Recommendations for Action*. Research report presented to the Commission of European Communities, Bureau for Employment and Equal Opportunities for Women

Morrison, T., 1985 'Rootedness: The Ancestor as Foundation', in M. Evans (ed.) *Black Women Writers*, London and Sydney: Pluto Press

Parmar, P., 1984 'Gender, Race and Class: Asian Women in Resistance', in CCCS *The Empire Strikes Back: Race and Racism in '70's Britain*, London:Hutchinson, pp.236 75

—1988 'Gender, Race and Power: The Challenge of Youth Work Practice', in P. Cohen and H. S. Bains (eds) *Multi-Racist Britain*, Basingstoke and London: Macmillan Education, pp.197–210

—1989 'Other Kinds of Dreams', *Feminist Review*, vol. 31, pp. 55–65 Spring

Phoenix, A., 1987 'Theories of Gender and Black Families', in G. Weiner and M. Arnot (eds) *Gender Under Scrutiny*, London: Hutchinson, pp.50–63

Rampton, B. H., 1989a 'Evaluations of Black Language Crossing and the Local Sociocultural Order', *Adolescence and Language Use*, Working Paper 3, Sociological Research Unit, Institute of Education, University of London

—1989b 'Perceptions of inter-racial Panjabi Use within and Adolescent Peer Group', *Adolescence and Language Use*, Working Paper 4, Sociological Research Unit, Institute of Education, University of London

Robinson, V., 1988 'The New Indian Middle Class in Britain', *Ethnic and Racial Studies*, vol. 11, no. 4

Sahgal, G., 1989 'Fundamentalism on the Rise', *Spare Rib*, no.202, pp.6–7, June

Shan, S., 1986 *In My Own Name* London: The Women's Press

Spivak, C. G., 1985 'The Rani of Sirmur', in F. Barker *et al. Europe and its Others*, Proceedings of the Essex University Sociology of Literature Conference, pp.128–51

—1988 'In Praise of "Sammy and Rosie Get Laid"', *Critical Quarterly*, vol.13, no. 2, pp.80-8

Trivedi, P., 1984 'Asian Women in the Making of History', *Feminist Review*, vol.17, pp.37–50

Taylor, H., 1983 'Sexism and Racism: Partners in Oppression', *Cassoe* Newsletter May-June 1983, pp.5–8

Visram, R., 1986 *Ayahs, Lascars and Princes. The Story of Indians in Britain 1700–1947*, London: Pluto Press

Warrier, S., 1988 'Marriage, Maternity and Female Economic Activity', in S. Westwood and P. Bhachu, (eds), *Enterprising Women: Ethnicity, Economy and Gender Relations*, London: Routledge

Westwood, S., 1984 *All Day Every Day: Factory and Family in the Making of Women's Lives*, London and Sydney: Pluto Press
——1988 'Workers and Wives: Continuities and Discontinuities in the Lives of Gujarati Women', in S. Westwood and P. Bhachu (eds) *Enterprising Women: Ethnicity, Economy and Gender Relations*, London: Routledge
Westwood, S. and Bhachu, P., 1988 'Images and Realities', *New Society* 6 May 1988, pp.20–2

7

International and Internal Migration: The Changing Identity of Catholic and Hindu Women in Goa[1]

Stella Mascarenhas-Keyes

Introduction

A large number of studies in the last few decades have looked at migration within and from Third World countries. These studies, however, have a number of limitations. First of all, they focus on the rural migration of peasants and the landless in search of casual unskilled and semi-skilled jobs in the modern and informal urban sector. In this chapter, the perspective is broadened to include rural-urban migration for non-manual work and the effects of regular salaries and superannuation benefits on the household, and particularly on the lives of women.

A second limitation is the lack of adequate consideration of gender issues and the predominant emphasis on male migration. Although there have been some attempts recently to redress this situation (Youssef et al 1979; Fawcett et al. 1984; Singh 1984; Morokvasic 1983, 1985) the emphasis, however, has been on the individual migration of unaccompanied females for wage labour. Associational migration of females is widespread and, as I shall show in this chapter, there are significant effects on womens' lives in a situation where their production activities are secondary to their reproduction activities.

Finally, while the inter-relationship between different patterns of migration has been explored to a limited extent (for example, Watson 1975; Castles and Kossack 1973), the relationship between different

1. The research on which this chapter is based was supported by a United Kingdom Social Science Research council studentship from 1978-81. I am grateful to Dr Sue Wright and Shaun Keyes for helpful comments on earlier drafts of this chapter.

categories of female migrants remains unexamined. In this chapter I shall attempt to redress this balance by analysing migration patterns within and from Goa, with a particular emphasis on the processes which have led to changes in the socio-economic role and hence the identity of two categories of women.

Goa has developed into a migration-oriented society (Philpott 1968) over the course of the twentieth century, and the historical context in which this has occurred is discussed in the first part of this chapter. Goa's two major ethnic groups, Catholics and Hindus,[2] have been involved in different patterns of migration; the first, international migration from rural Goa to urban India and overseas,[3] largely characteristic of Catholics, while the second pattern of internal, rural-rural migration within Goa, is largely characteristic of Hindus. As I demonstrate in this paper, these two patterns of migration have become intimately linked.

Against this background the chapter will discuss the changes in the identity of Catholic and Hindu women, particularly those who are married, with respect to their role as carers of children, as housewives and agriculturalists. The chapter ends by exploring the inter-relationship between the two categories of women and highlighting possible future trends.

The material on which this chapter is based is drawn from the village I shall here call Amora, where anthropological fieldwork was conducted from 1979-81. The village is situated in the coastal part of Goa and had a de facto population of 2,800 distributed into 687 households. It comprised roughly equal proportions of Catholic and Hindu Goans, as well as a few tribal Kunbis. The majority of Catholics were Brahmins (68%), the rest mainly Sudra, with ancestral links to Amora. By contrast, the majority of immigrant Hindus were Sudra, who together with the Kunbis had come from Pednem and Salsette regions respectively in Goa to work for the Catholics. Large numbers of Hindus settled in Amora from around 1950. The Catholic population

2. There is a small number of Catholics of tribal origin, called Kunbis and Gauddas,who some believe were the original inhabitants of Goa. The term 'Catholic', used in this chapter, does not include the tribals. Similarly, there is a large number of immigrant Hindus (about 30 per cent of the total population of Goa according to the 1981 census) who are not indigenous to Goa. They are not included when reference is made to Hindus in this chapter.

3. Since Goa was a Portuguese enclave within India for 450 years, the term 'international migration' is used here to refer to migration from Goa to elsewhere in India as well as overseas. Although the change in political status in 1961 makes migration from Goa to Maharashtra and neighbouring areas, inter-regional migration, the term 'international migration' is still employed because such migration is a continuation of a tradition that began when the current regional boundaries were national boundaries.

of the village was over-represented by females and old (forty-five years and older) persons. Nuclear households predominated, mainly through choice.[4] Catholic females outnumbered males by three to two, the unbalanced sex ratio being partly accounted for by male migration. Roughly a third of the total number of 282 Catholic households are headed by women: wives, widows and unmarried women of various ages (Mascarenhas-Keyes 1990a: 110). Each Catholic household was responsible for its own land rights, usually to *communidade* land.[5]

With few exceptions, every Catholic household in Amora received either substantial cash incomes from current migrants or superannuation benefits from returnees. The Hindus earned their livelihood mainly through farming, domestic labour and construction work. In 1980, there were 286 households of Pednem Hindus. These households usually comprised the nuclear unit as this was the unit that migrated or was established if marriage occurred after migration.

Background

Goa is a tiny region of 3,700 square kilometres situated on the west coast of India. It was under Portuguese rule for 450 years until 1961, when, following its liberation, it was incorporated into the Indian Union. Under colonial rule, the establishment of two distinct ethnic groups was favoured (Boxer 1969: 305; Cunha 1961). According to the 1981 census, approximately a one-third of the indigenous population of 1,007,749 are Roman Catholic; Hindus account for 63 per cent with Muslims making up almost all the remainder. A small proportion of the population are tribal Kunbis or Gauddas, who are either Catholic or Hindu. Apart from the indigenous population of Goa, there are a number of immigrants from other regions of India, mainly the Ghats and Kerala, who came to work in Goa after its liberation. The Catholics are the descendants of the sixteenth- and seventeenth-century converts (D'Costa 1965). They were and still are concentrated in

4. Catholic married couples ideally prefer to set up a nuclear household in a separate house, on, or as soon as economically possible after, marriage. Remittances from international migration enabled many couples to realise this ideal.

5. A large proportion of land, particularly in the coastal regions, belonged to the *communidade*. It was owned, until some recent changes in land reform, by the male *gauncares*, the male descendants of the original settlers of the village. In some villages, like Amora, they are exclusively Brahmin, in others Chardos (more or less equivalent to Kshatriyas), and in a few, a combination of castes. Such land was not for sale and usufructuary rights were allocated to villages through periodic auctions (for further details on the *commu- nidades* see Xavier 1852, Azavedo 1890, the report of the Goa Land Reforms Commission 1964, Almeida 1967, de Souza 1979, Pereira 1981).

the coastal areas of Goa. The Hindus live mainly in the hinterland but over the course of this century large numbers have migrated to the coastal villages and towns.

Under colonial rule the economy of Goa underwent a number of changes which contributed to the adoption of a bourgeois life style by a minority, while the Goan masses remained impoverished (Gomes 1862, Fernandes 1940, Cunha 1961). This contributed, directly and indirectly to international and internal migration. The changes can be briefly summarised as follows. First, Goa became the administrative, trading and ecclesiastical headquarters of the Portuguese Estado da India which covered a vast geographical area from Africa to the Far East (Boxer 1969, de Souza 1979). As a result, military expeditions and missionary activities outside Goa were financed by revenue from custom duties and heavy taxation of the local population (Rodriques 1977, Harrison 1975: 340). Furthermore, a large amount of state revenue was spent throughout colonial rule on salaries and benefits for the large secular and religious bureaucracy rather than being distributed across the population (Fernandes 1924: 26, Cunha 1961, Techno-economic survey of Goa, Daman and Diu 1964: 161, de Souza 1979: 171).

Secondly, there were multiple changes made to the land ownership patterns, tenure relationships and usufructuary rights which contributed to the overall decline in agricultural productivity. These changes were detrimental to the majority of Goans, particularly Catholics.[6] The problems were compounded by the rising population rate (Gonçalves 1906: 158).[7] As a result, rice, the staple food, was imported into Goa throughout colonial rule (Gracias 1950: 600). Thirdly, data available for the nineteenth up to the mid-twentieth century indicates that imports of a variety of consumer items led to a considerable negative balance of payments (Gonçalves 1906: 122–3, Fernandes 1939: 5-6, 1940: 10-12).

6. The *communidades* were adversely affected by the appropriation of a portion of communal land by the Portuguese mainly in the sixteenth and seventeenth centuries (de Souza 1979: 71–4) and from the nineteenth century by state interference in the customary code of practice which, *inter alia*, changed the prevailing norms governing access to usufructuary land rights (Pereira 1981, Report of the Goa Land Reforms Commission 1964). Private ownership became more widespread. The introduction of the Portuguese Civil Code in 1867 led to considerable fragmentation of private land and contributed to the decline in agricultural productivity. Since a greater proportion of land in the areas where the Catholics lived belonged to the *communidades*, and since the Portuguese Civil code was directly applicable to Catholics and optional for Hindus, Catholics were more severely affected by the economic changes.

7. The population statistics, available only for the coastal areas of Bardez, Salsette and Ilhas (now Tiswadi) and for the period 1776–1900, indicate that the population doubled during that period.

Apart from economic changes, sociocultural changes occurred, these being most evident among the Catholics partly as a result of government policy highlighting the changes as they affected that group (Mascarenhas-Keyes 1987: 64-9, 94–144). I shall briefly summarise the ones most relevant to this chapter. Western education, mainly under the aegis of the Catholic Church, was actively promoted. Portuguese became the official language and was used as the medium of instruction in many schools and in tertiary institutions. In view of the high status it enjoyed at the expense of marginalising the local vernaculars of Konkani and Marati, it came to be used as a first language in the homes of the Catholic elite, thus paving the way for the incursion of other foreign, Western languages (Mascarenhas-Keyes 1989). While the Hindus retained their traditions (Saxena 1974), the Catholics became characterised by cultural syncretism. This was manifested, for instance, in the adoption of Portuguese surnames, use of Western dress, consumption of beef, pork and alcohol, incorporation of Western culinary practices, and familiarity with Western instruments and music. Social stratification in terms of caste continued to exist among Catholics, although in an attenuated form (Da Costa 1977, Mascarenhas-Keyes 1987: 125-34). Ascribed status came to be complemented by achieved status as new avenues for wealth accumulation, education and employment opened up.

With regard to women, colonialism initiated a number of changes which may be briefly noted. First of all, celibacy became an acceptable state as women were encouraged to become nuns (and men to become priests). Thus the concept of remaining single was introduced to Catholics and undoubtedly is a contributing factor in accounting for the large number who remain unmarried or marry late (Srivastava 1977, Panandiker and Chaudhuri 1983). Secondly, Catholic females had increased access, compared to Hindu females, to primary and secondary education (Menezes Braganza 1923). Thirdly, there were employment opportunities for educated women in the bureaucracy and educational system. While such employment was not extensive, it introduced the idea that women could be involved in production activities outside the home and farm. Fourthly, Catholic women were given better property rights (Derrett 1965), and in the 1867 Civil Code, were given equal rights to men. Thus the overall status of Catholic women under colonial rule improved in comparison to that of Hindu women in Goa and the rest of womanhood in India, although initially only a limited number were able to take advantage of this.

In the post-colonial period, various attempts have been made with varying success to improve Goa's economy and infrastructure through development programmes encouraging industrialisation, commercialisation and tourism (De Sousa 1978, Newman 1984). English replaced Portuguese as the official language, and the development of Konkani and Marati has been encouraged. The educational system has expanded at all levels, and, in common with the rest of India, attempts have been made to improve the socio-economic position of lower castes, tribal people and women.

International Migration

The persistent adverse economic conditions under colonial rule affected various sectors of the Goan population in different ways and, from the mid-nineteenth century onwards, large numbers resorted to migration to improve their circumstances. The majority of migrants, both Catholic and Hindu, migrated to cities and towns within India (which then included Pakistan). The development of increasing job opportunities worldwide also led to substantial migration overseas. While Catholics took advantage of these opportunities, only a handful of Hindus went abroad. International migration is, therefore, more characteristic of Catholics and I shall now focus on them.

The reproduction of international migration over the course of the twentieth century progressively encompassed a greater cross-section of the Catholic population (Da Costa 1956, Pinto 1960, Nelson 1971, Kuper 1973, D'Souza 1975, Khan 1980, Ifeka 1985b, Mascarenhas-Keyes 1986). Catholics took up jobs in various cities of India, Pakistan and East Africa as well as on local and transatlantic ships such as those of the BI and P & O lines. Thus they engaged in rural-urban migration. From the middle of the twentieth century secondary urban-urban migration to the West occurred mainly from East Africa (Mascarenhas-Keyes 1979).

There are important gender differences in the pattern of migration. Both in the past and at present, independent Catholic migration has been predominantly male, with most men migrating before marriage and continuing with their jobs outside Goa after marriage. In places where permanent settlement was not desired or possible, return migration generally coincided with the employees mandatory retirement (Mascarenhas-Keyes 1988a).

As regards Catholic women, three main patterns can be identified. First, independent migration of unattached females. Such females, invariably adult, generally of low caste, have migrated to work as domestic servants and ayahs for families in India (Mehta 1960) and more recently in the Gulf. A small contingent comprise upper-caste women who migrated to work as teachers and office staff, usually because they had become the sole breadwinner owing to the death or desertion of their husbands or fathers. Unmarried women who joined the convent to become nuns went to various locations.

Secondly, there is associational migration of women. Since the probability of Catholic women marrying migrants is high, wives expect and are expected to be mobile. Many adult women have accompanied or joined their husbands abroad, at or some time after marriage. In some cases, they have remained with him for the duration of his job or for a lifetime, while others returned at the end of his contract or on his retirement. Even when wives have joined migrant husbands, a period of conjugal separation has been inevitable for many, because of the tremendous emphasis placed on the education of children and the concomitant necessity of ensuring access to appropriate facilities (Mascarenhas-Keyes 1990a:111–13).

Thirdly, for some, there is habitual residence in Goa. Some wives only join their migrant husbands for short periods of time on holidays, if this is possible. The higher cost of living, and actual or perceived adverse environmental factors in the host country, often deters associational migration. In cases where men work in bachelor status jobs, on ships or in the Middle East, wives have been prohibited from accompanying husbands. Wives and children rarely accompany migrants who obtain short-term contracts, particularly abroad, because the temporary uprooting of the family is expensive, inconvenient and, in particular, is disruptive to the childrens' education.

Many of the village resident wives of migrant men in 1980 had, however, spent all or part of their childhood outside Goa with their migrant parents. Some returned as children or teenagers when their fathers retired, but the majority returned to Goa prematurely when their fathers lost their jobs and prospects of permanent settlement in East Africa after independence (Kuper 1975, Mascarenhas-Keyes 1986).

Complementing the geographical dispersal of Catholics has been the development of occupational diversity. The cultural attributes of Catholics facilitated job acquisition as males of all castes were able to obtain long term jobs in India and on passenger ships as cooks, butlers, waiters and musicians (D'Souza 1975, Pinto 1960). Such jobs continued to be taken up by succeeding generations of migrants, particularly by those who were less educated. However, during the course of this century, Catholics, particulary the upper castes, have become increasingly characterised by an inter-generational orientation towards men aspiring for long-term, well-paid, salaried employment with promotional prospects and superannuation, preferably outside Goa. Indeed, international migration has increasingly become an inevitability for a large number of Catholics, particularly the educated with bourgeois aspirations. There is little likelihood that a small region like Goa with limited potential for urbanisation and development of a tertiary sector can provide sufficient and well paid salaried non-manual jobs to meet their demands. Consequently, both occupational mobility and geographical mobility have become intimately linked, with consequences for the identity of women which I shall discuss shortly. International migration has in turn partially contributed to internal migration in Goa, as we shall now see.

Internal Migration

There has been considerable internal migration in Goa during the course of the twentieth century. Three factors are responsible for this: first, the development of mining from the 1950s onwards; secondly, the expansion of tourism from the 1970s onwards, and thirdly, international migration.

International migration has led to rural-rural internal migration and it is on this pattern that I shall focus now. To understand this inter-relationship, a diachronic perspective needs to be adopted. Initially, increased labour needs were met by Amora Catholic lower castes who took advantage of the new employment opportunities in the village to improve their socio-economic position. They were keen to emulate the upper castes and in due course they also became characterised by inter-generational occupational and geographical mobility. Consequently, the supply of labour within the village gradually declined and the demand, which continued to rise, was met by the immigration of Kunbis and Hindus from elsewhere in Goa.

The tribal Kunbis came from Salsette in south Goa. They initially came in work gangs, remaining in the villages for a short period of time. These gangs were usually made up of men, and occasionally of women if there was employment available for them. The increased opportunities for continuous and long term male and female employment in Amora and neighbouring villages led to many of them migrating for settlement into these areas. It appears that the first Kunbis settled in

Amora around the 1930s. In 1980, they accounted for 15 per cent of the village population.

The Hindus originated mainly from Pednem in the northern hinterland of Goa where agricultural work is the main occupation, but where the agrarian land is not very fertile. Furthermore, there were very few opportunities for earning additional income. The Hindus earned their livelihood in Pednem through agricultural work. Few of them owned any land and those who did only had very small plots, considerably less than an acre. Consequently, most were employed by a small number of land owners. Both women and men worked as agricultural labourers. When the demand for labour in Amora and neighbouring villages arose, Pednem Hindus were keen to capitalise on it and through chain migration, large numbers eventually settled there. By 1980, 38 households had land rights, mainly usufructuary rights to private Catholic owned land or *communidade* land. Hence, with few exceptions, the Pednem Hindus worked as labourers for Catholics. The women provided domestic as well as agricultural labour. Their employment as household servants was a new phenomenon for them as they were not similarly engaged in Pednem. In addition, entrepreneurial trends were apparent. There were 154 enterprises, all run by Hindus and Kunbis. These took the form of vegetable selling, fishing, artisan work and milk production. Throughout the 1980s and early 1990s, many Hindus have taken advantage of government schemes that have provided easier accessibility to land for residential purposes and financial support schemes to enhance home ownership. Prior to this, Hindus were dependent on Catholics for accommodation that took the form either of outhouses in the compound or a part of the main residential house which was vacant because the owner and his family were living outside Goa.

The Effect of Migration on Catholic and Hindu Women

There are three main areas in which identity changes are most prominent. These are expressed in the role of women as carers, homemakers and agriculturalists. I shall examine these roles separately for both categories of women.

Care of Children

Women have caring responsibilities primarily for their children and secondarily for their aged parents or parents-in-law. In this section I focus predominantly on the role of women as carers of children. Married women, both Catholic and Hindu, expect and are expected to have children soon after marriage and this is a normal pattern, apart from cases of infertility.

CATHOLIC WOMEN

The concept of motherhood has undergone considerable changes in the context of international migration. These changes are closely aligned with a strong commitment, on the part of both husband and wife, to the relative subjugation of self interest and a correlatively predominant focus on 'children and their future'. Such 'child-centred' marriages imply, for instance, that the independent employment of wives and the care of the elderly are of secondary importance, to be accommodated so long as the primary objective is fulfilled.

Children became one of the major foci for the investment of remittances. The continuing availability of employment, particularly white-collar jobs in the former British India and British East Africa, together with the limited investment channels in Goa, has spurred parental aspirations for their children and encouraged the education of all children, with priority for males, at least up to the secondary standard. Within the new global economic context, of which Catholics saw themselves as a part, the identity of women, and particularly their role as mothers changed. This is epitomised by the notion of progressive motherhood (see also Mascarenhas-Keyes 1990a), a concept which derives from the commitment of Catholics, particularly the educated upper castes, to 'progress' (an oft-used word). The ideas about 'progress' have been strongly influenced by Western capitalist thought, partly as a legacy of colonialism. Inherent in the concept is its dynamic element, in that various aspects of mothering have been changed and refined in response to varying circumstances.

Women see themselves as having not only reproductive and nurturing functions but also additional responsibilities particularly with respect to the education of children. In order to pursue progressive motherhood effectively, women realise that they require various skills and attributes. Progressive mothers regard themselves as relatively cosmopolitan and receptive to the advantages of modern vocational education. Furthermore, they also see themselves as potentially geographically mobile so that they can increase the access of their children to appropriate educational facilities. Skills include familiarity with English, in order to provide the same linguistic environment as the non-vernacular schools their children attend, as well as an ability to help children develop the good handwriting, spelling and numeracy which are a prerequisite to white collar jobs.

Progressive mothers must be able to relate to the temporal demands and discipline of the academic cycle and schoolday routine. They have to create free time not to pursue additional leisure activities but for the diligent supervision of childrens' homework. Progressive mothers see themselves as having to relate to professional persons, such as teachers, who are also concerned with their childrens' educational progress. They perceive a need to make effective use of psychological techniques in order to sustain children's interest and diligence in school work. Such mothers feel that they should meet the expectation that children be suitably attired for school, not the fields, and eat the varied, non-vegetarian diet that is expected to stimulate the development of 'brain' rather than 'brawn'. They see themselves as keen advocates of primary health care as a means of preventing children from succumbing to even minor ailments which might require absences from school and possibly lead to poor examination performances.

Progressive mothers believe in their indispensability and do not willingly relegate the long term care of their children to others such as kin, affines, friends or servants (see also Caplan 1978: 110, Sharma 1980: 129), and experience constant anxiety about how adequately they themselves are fulfilling their role. Apart from self-evaluation, there is on-going, critical evaluation by husbands, teachers, peers and seniors. Good school performance and the appropriate social and moral behaviour of their children reinforces the woman's concept of herself as a progressive mother.

HINDU WOMEN

The maternal role of Hindu women in Amora has also been affected, first by the change in household composition, and secondly by exposure to an environment which places considerable emphasis on education. In Pednem, most households comprised the extended family and consequently there were other adult women, such as the mother-in-law and sisters-in-law who helped to care for the children on a day-to-day basis. In the absence of these women, other kin and neighbours living in the villages played this role.

In Amora, the mother had to assume full time care of her children as migration usually involved only the nuclear unit, the other members of the extended family remaining behind. Older siblings helped to look after the younger ones when their mother was out working. Since the

Hindus had to take up accommodation in Amora wherever they could, and this depended on what was made available to them by the Catholics, kin were usually dispersed throughout the village. Furthermore, since migrant kin and affines were usually young people with families, the number of free adult women available to help mothers look after their children was either nil or negligible. Consequently, Hindu mothers saw themselves, to a greater extent than they did in Pednem, as having the sole responsibility for the day-to-day care of their children.

From the environmental angle, in Amora, Hindus were exposed to a cultural ethos which highly favoured formal Western education. Not only is there better provision there, but the quality of the education is considerably higher than in Pednem as there are superior amenities and better qualified teachers. Furthermore, in comparison to Pednem, a variety of tertiary educational facilities exist in the nearby town, which are within easy commuting distance. Hindus were aware of the use to which education has been put by the Catholics to advance their socio-economic position.

However, Hindus did not consider international migration, and particularly long-term international migration, which is characteristic of Catholics, as an option they would pursue. They did not consider it appropriate for husbands to leave their wives behind in order to work outside Goa. Furthermore, the Hindus are far more firmly rooted in Goa, and hence in India, than the Catholics, because of their minimal exposure to the Portuguese Lusitanisation processes.[8] They consider it unthinkable to spend most of one's life, or even a lifetime, away from the motherland. They do not regard living in Amora as living in an alien place as it is part of Goa and only a short bus journey, of about two hours, back to their home village. Consequently, unlike the Amora Catholic mothers, the Hindu mothers have not seen themselves as oriented towards the social reproduction of migrant labour. Their aspirations for their children have been limited to their employment prospects in Goa.

The three major fields of potential employment are agriculture, construction and technical work. Ideally, Hindus have preferred their children to work on their own land rather than take regular employment as

8. The colonial attempts to Lusitanise (i.e. make Portuguese) was most intense in the first 200 years of Portuguese rule. During this period only the three coastal areas of Bardez, Salsette and Ilhas (which included Murmogoa) were under Portuguese rule, the remaining areas, including Pednem being gradually annexed towards the latter part of the eighteenth century.

agricultural or domestic casual labour. In a few cases, their children have been successful in doing this, as exemplified by the son of one of the first settlers who, with the help of a government agricultural loan, bought a water pump and has a very profitable vegetable farm. Furthermore, since there seemed to be continuous employment available for masons and builders, Hindu parents were keen for their sons to learn these trades. The supply of construction work has tended to remain continuously high because international migrants want residential homes built, the tourist industry requires new hotels and the government is improving the country's infrastructure. The establishment of a number of government and private small-scale industries both in the village and in the vicinity that offer a regular wage for semi skilled and skilled work, has attracted the Hindus. A few young men and one or two young women have been successful in obtaining such work. However, since employers have invariably given preference to those with secondary education even if not directly relevant to the job, Hindu mothers, as well as fathers, have tried to encourage their children, particularly sons, to study.

However, they have been faced with various dilemmas. First of all, they were unable to relate to their childrens' studies because they were illiterate. Secondly, their homes did not have basic amenities, such as electric light, to provide an opportunity for night study. Thirdly, they sometimes had to delay their child's attendance at school during the day, or even for a number of days, because their labour was necessary for farm work. Fourthly, they did not have sufficient disposable cash to buy school books and other necessary materials.

The main change for Hindu women has been that they have a greater share in the day-to-day care of their children than they had before migrating.

Women as Homemakers

CATHOLIC WOMEN

Catholic women continue to perceive themselves as homemakers. However, the influx of remittances from international migration into Amora has had two important implications for Catholic women. First of all, the quantity of housework has increased and women expect and are expected to maintain higher standards commensurate with their improved socio-economic conditions. Secondly, womens' perception of themselves as responsible for the physical nurturing of their family has taken on additional dimensions because of the dietary changes made possible by the increase in disposable income.

The building of large, brick, residential houses to replace the mud huts was one of the channels into which international migrants invested money. Ideally, new homes were to house the nuclear unit. They had a number of rooms, with windows and cemented floors, furniture and exclusive or shared use of a well adjoining the house. Since the house is a tangible symbol that the international migrant has 'made it', it is not surprising that owners took great pride in their homes. They were keen to maintain their fabric and external appearance, often damaged by heavy monsoon rains. In the absence of husbands, wives took responsibility for the maintenance of the fabric of the house. When necessary, they commissioned repair work and recruited and supervised the workers.

Modernisation of the interior has been a gradual process dependent on cash resources. It has included the introduction of indoor flush toilets, electric water pumps, paraffin and gas cooking stoves, fridges, electric mixers and kettles. However, only a few homes have such a range of amenities and therefore the manual drawing of water, fetching of firewood, sweeping and swabbing of the floor, manual grinding of spices and foodstuffs continue to be important components of the wide repertoire of housework tasks. Women have been very keen to keep the house neat and tidy not only because they are houseproud but also because visitors often 'drop in' unexpectedly. An untidy house elicits critical comment and reflects unfavourably on their identity as housewives.

Another aspect of housework that has increased is the laundering of clothes. Families of international migrants pay great attention to being properly attired, particularly when they enter the public domain as dress is a visible sign that the family has 'come up'. Children have to be neatly dressed for school, church, visiting relatives and recreational activities. The washing of clothes is a long, arduous process requiring water to be drawn from the well, heated on a wood fire and then vigorously used to scrub the clothes. Clothes of good quality, often purchased outside Goa and used on special occasions, need delicate handling when laundered, which is more time consuming. Clean clothes are ironed with a charcoal iron which has to be frequently replenished with heated coals.

The increase in disposable income through international migration has had an impact on a woman's role in the nurturing of her family. It has enabled a Catholic family to eat a more varied diet that is perceived as being nutritionally superior as it complemented the staple diet of rice and fish curry with greater amounts of expensive items such as meat. Specifically, the effect of remittances has been to increase the amount of time required for shopping, preparation and cooking.

Shopping in the town, which is more time consuming, has been preferred because of the wide choice, lower price and better quality of products. Although a few homes have fridges where food can be stored, their reliability is uncertain because of the erratic electricity supply. Similarly, although some households have electric grinders and mixers, their habitual use cannot be relied upon because of the erratic electricity supply. Furthermore, because they do not grind spices to the required consistency, they are resorted to only when manual grinding is not possible. Cooking is a long process, particularly the preparation of meat dishes which have been greatly influenced by Portuguese culinary methods (Mascarenhas-Keyes 1988b).

The extent to which Catholic women themselves have engaged in housework and cooking has varied along a continuum. On the one hand their involvement has been minimal because a full-time servant does everything. This is most common among elderly widowed women with substantial incomes living alone. At the other end of the continuum are women who do everything themselves. These women are usually from poorer households that cannot afford any paid help. Between the two ends are Catholic women who, like many Indian urban women (Sengupta 1960: 192, Mehta 1960: 58, Vatuk 1972: 28), engage labour on a regular or intermittent basis to perform a range of tasks normally done by a housewife.

While the increased household income has enabled Catholic women to obtain help to undertake the drudgeries of housework, it has also increased the amount of such work. Furthermore, women still bear ultimate responsibility for all housework. Thus some of their time is spent on supervising the work of servants and where this has not been done adequately, they do it themselves. Since houses are situated very close to each other, neighbours are keenly aware of the conditions of the home and even the daily menu. The relative lack of privacy creates a degree of pressure on women to maintain high standards of housework. The employment of labour to partially or completely undertake housework has led to women seeing themselves, ideally, as supervisors of labour.

HINDU WOMEN

Hindu women in Amora, unlike those in Pednem, have the sole responsibility for all housework because they live in nuclear units. However, they often called on the help of female children. Apart from a small number of Hindus who in the last few years have built or bought their own brick homes, most continue to live in the mud huts or outhouses belonging to Catholics. Such accommodation is equivalent or smaller than that to which they were used in Pednem, and consequently the overall quantity of housework has been relatively similar.

The role of Hindu women as nurturers of their families has changed to a limited extent. The Pednem Hindus are not vegetarians and meat (lamb and chicken) can be consumed on two days of the week. However, because meat is expensive, it is eaten infrequently, usually on ceremonial occasions. The staple diet of rice, fish curry and vegetables is eaten daily as it was in Pednem. Hence the amount of time involved in cooking and associated activities has remained unchanged. However, since Hindus now lived in nuclear households as compared to their life in an extended family in Pednem, the responsibility for cooking lies entirely with the only adult woman in the house. Often, of course, young female children are pressed into service and they help with cooking part of the meal. The major change for the Hindu women has been that they now help another category of women, the Catholics, to better discharge their responsibility as homemakers, a point to which I shall return later.

Women and Production Activities

The identity and role of Catholic and Hindu women with respect to production activities has changed a great deal as we shall now see.

Land was the major economic resource through which Catholics and Hindus earned their living prior to migration. In Amora one crop of paddy has been cultivated, using the monsoon rains. A second crop has been grown if there has been easy access to water from the river or wells. Pulses and vegetables have also been grown. Most households have one or more fruit bearing trees. In Pednem, as the land was less fertile paddy was not extensively grown, but was supplemented by the cultivation of other cereals such as *ragi* and *pakod* (Almeida 1967).

The involvement of women in production activities related to their position in the status hierarchy. Women belonging to households with a lot of land and income from employment in the formal sector, have not engaged in productive labour outside the household as labourers have been hired. Women and children from families with smaller amounts of land have undertaken a range of farming activities, particularly during the busy periods of planting and harvesting. The reciprocal exchange of labour has been common in such families during periods of peak activities. Women from poor households have undertaken paid agricultural work throughout the year. Women have also traditionally been involved in the distribution of surplus production to be sold on a wholesale or retail basis in the village or in the vicinity. The rearing of farm animals is not widespread in Goa. Most households have reared chickens and, in Amora, Catholic households reared one or more pigs to clear the nightsoil from the 'pig' toilets.

Against this background, the changed position of Catholic and Hindu women will be examined.

CATHOLIC WOMEN

Catholic women have increasingly come to regard it as not fitting for them to be involved in farm work. The availability of immigrant labour and the financial resources in Catholic homes to pay for their hire has facilitated the trend towards withdrawing from farm work.

Although households were in receipt of remittances, they continued to retain existing land rights, to *communidade* and/or private land. With the help of remittances, private land has been purchased, but since this has been in very short supply in their village, very few households have substantially increased their holdings. The retention and/or augmentation of land rights has occurred for two main reasons. First, it was because possession of land rights has remained a status symbol, albeit a lesser one than in the past. Secondly, it provided some security, in case changes in the global political economy threaten employment outside Goa.

Since a variety of residence patterns have been pursued by international migrants and their families, particularly over the course of the twentieth century, a range of tenurial relationships evolved. These relationships were affected by post-liberation agrarian reforms, which lead to some households losing or surrendering all land rights.[9]

In 1980, half the Catholic households in Amora had rights to agrarian land, and since government policy did not permit these to remain fallow, the land was cultivated. Agricultural land holdings per

9. The relevant legislation was the Agricultural Tenancy Act, 1964 and Land to the Tiller Act, 1976. Those Catholics who were outside Goa or not in a position to defend their case, lost their rights. The legislation affected not only Catholics but all individual and corporate land owners.

Catholic household ranged from half a hectare to nil and hence some households relied entirely on remittances while others had more than one source of income.

The management of the household farm increasingly became the responsibility of women in the absence of men through migration or death. The involvement of Catholic women in agricultural activities has ranged along a continuum. On the one hand, women have remained fully involved in the activities which have been traditionally regarded as 'women's work'. Women falling into this category have been very few: those belonging to households with a recent onset of migration, lack of substantial earnings, or limited prospect of the breadwinner obtaining long term employment outside Goa. With the exception of a few Brahmin households most of the households in this category belonged to the Sudra caste. At the other end of the continuum have been women who have withdrawn completely. Most of these women have come from households with no land rights because they had either surrendered or lost them in the preceding decade or so. The remainder have been women with holdings who have elected not to do farmwork, but to function in a management capacity, hiring and supervising labour. Between the two ends of the continuum, women have been engaged in a range of production activities, sharing the labour with paid help. The general principle underlying shared work is that activities which are physically arduous and/or time consuming have been done by hired labour.

The involvement of women in agricultural activities was a dynamic one. Women have shifted to different positions along the continuum from one year to the next. These shifts have been affected by various factors, such as the proportion of cash income to the Catholic household budget, and the assurance of its relative permanency; pregnancy; household size; the number of dependent school and college children (an especial consideration); ill health; and migration to join husbands or to accompany children to a more appropriate educational site.

Apart from practical considerations, the attitude to manual work has changed. Catholic women have increasingly begun to regard themselves as not suited for such work. There are a number of reasons for this. First, as such work has come to be regarded as low status, women, particularly of the upper caste, have wished to preserve their self-esteem and reduce their vulnerability to scorn and ridicule by others. Secondly, those who had not undertaken such work or were only minimally involved when they were children and adolescents because they were at school have refrained from such work 'because we are not used to it'. Thirdly, commitment by younger women to the time consuming progressive motherhood has taken precedence over work in the fields. Fourthly, older women who had done fieldwork when younger and would traditionally have continued to do some farmwork, have come to regard old age as a time for rest and relaxation, for tending aches and pains and not for working in the fields.

A few married, and most single, women who have withdrawn completely from agriculture have worked as teachers, clerks and secretaries. Such withdrawal commenced in childhood because of their parents' stress on education.

HINDU WOMEN

For Hindu women, migration to Amora has led to a fundamental change in identity. They increasingly began to regard themselves as marketable labour and relatively more independent and autonomous than when they were in Pednem. This identity change was premised on their greatly improved economic position which derived from three areas.

First of all, they have had greater opportunities for working as agricultural labourers than they had in Pednem. Secondly, and more importantly, women (as well as men) have had greater opportunities for acquiring land rights and thus perceiving themselves as potential owners. In the case of paddy land, the land rights have usually taken the form of unofficial leases to *communidade* land. These leases have often officially been in the name of Catholics, some of whom have died, or have migrated or have been living in Amora, but have withdrawn from farming (Mascarenhas-Keyes 1990b). Thirdly, Hindu women have also had access to vegetable plots, usually leasing them at a nominal rent on a seasonal basis. Since the return on vegetable cultivation has been high, and the land in Amora yields a good crop, they have been able to earn substantial amounts of money from the sale of vegetables. Those who have been unable to obtain land to lease, have bought fresh vegetables wholesale from the Catholics and then sold them at considerable profit on a retail basis in the nearby market town. They have capitalised on similar opportunities to buy fruit wholesale from Catholics. Thus they have experienced a substantial increase in their personal income and this has reduced their economic dependence on their husbands.

Inter-Relationship Between Catholic and Hindu Women

One of the major impacts of migration which has affected both categories of women relates to their new relationship as employer/employee.
The existence of a large number of independent households has led to a
greater number of individually negotiated labour arrangements. This relationship has created different dilemmas for each category of women.

For most Catholic women, the role of employer has been a new one,
made possible by their improved socio-economic circumstances. A few
who had lived outside Goa had engaged a domestic servant, but no one
had employed agricultural labour since they had lived in urban environments. For the Hindu women, it has been a novel situation for each of
them to be working for a different employer. In Pednem, since a large
proportion of the land was privately owned by one or a small number
of men, large clusters of women were employed by one person or, in
any case, were accountable, on a day-to-day basis, to a male supervisor.
In Amora then there has been a far greater degree of individuation.

There have been two systems through which the employer/employee
relationship has been initiated, both of which were still evident in
1980. The first was a form of 'tied labour' whereby the workers lived
in accommodation provided by the owner and have been a permanent
source of labour to fulfil agricultural and domestic needs. This system,
which had been traditionally followed by elite families, was taken up
by the nouveau riche Catholic migrant families.

Tied labour provided security for both employer and employees, the
former being assured of having workers when needed and the latter
being guaranteed continuous employment and accommodation. Under
the tied labour system, employees benefited from the patronage of the
employer in the form of small cash loans, the donation of old clothes
and left over food and, in cases of emergency, such as death or serious
illness, cash gifts or loans. For the Hindus it ensured that there was always someone with financial and other resources who could be turned
to in case of need. For the Catholic women this system ensured that
the employees were more compliant and obliging for fear of losing
their accommodation and the more general patronage provided.
Moreover, if they decided to migrate, whether on a short-term or long
term basis, they had a readily available, known and trusted caretaker
for the house and fields.

This system, which was popular in the colonial period, became less
so after legislation introduced in 1964, 1975 and 1976 was regarded

by employers as disproportionately disadvantaging them.[10] Consequently, the number of Catholics who used this system declined and they began to favour the second system.

The second system involved the casual hire of labour and led to the proletarianisation of workers. The proletarianisation of workers had important implications for the relationship between Catholic and Hindu women. For the Catholics, the second system created a number of problems. First of all, Catholics had to actively seek labour, particularly during peak agricultural periods when there was great demand. This process was helped, to some extent, by the fact that ties of loyalty and previous experience of working for a particular employer led to many workers returning to provide the same agricultural service to the family year after year. Such core workers were supplemented with other workers. Secondly, the sharing of labour created conflicts between employers. Domestic servants sometimes arrived late at the second and subsequent houses. This delay was imputed to the selfishness of other employers who gave the servant more work to do than was possible in the time available. Thirdly, shared labour meant that privacy was often violated as servants disclosed intimate details of their domestic life which could be used for malicious intent or to serve the prurient interest of others.

Fourthly, there was conflict related to remuneration. There was a constant demand for female workers throughout the year but at peak times, demand was very high, such as when paddy is harvested. The demand for domestic workers was high during Christmas and when migrant men and their families returned to the village on holiday. The competition for workers raised wage levels. The absence of a previously agreed rate by employers meant that each household set its own rate. This led to disagreements between Catholic households as they accused each other of poaching workers by offering better terms.

For the Hindus, the second system had a number of advantages. First, the demand for labour enabled Hindu women to work for a number of different employers, taking advantage of opportunities whenever and wherever they arose. Sometimes these were one off assignments, but more often they were on-going, particularly in the case of part time domestic work. Hindus were also able to change employers if their employment conditions were not suitable. Unsatisfactory employers soon earned reputations for being mean or difficult to work

10. The land legislation referred to above and the Mundkar Act 1975 which gave occupancy rights to those currently living in accommodation they did not own were considered by employers to be detrimental to their interests.

for, and in time of demand, they found it difficult to recruit staff. Equally, employees earned good or bad reputations which affected their employment prospects.

Secondly, since the Hindus knew that they were in demand, they had been able to improve their bargaining position. Payment was a combination of goods and cash, although there were increasing demands by workers to be paid entirely in cash. This demand was based on the knowledge that Catholic households have cash incomes from remittances. However, the Catholic employers preferred to pay in kind as far as possible. This was because they had greater surpluses of paddy as their consumption of rice had decreased, both with the adoption of a more varied diet and because fine grain, white rice, which they preferred, could be obtained cheaply in the shops. Thus, payment in kind ensured for them ready disposal of their surpluses, while for the Hindus it usually meant them being involved in redistribution of extra produce for which they had no use.

While the first generation of Hindu female migrants to Amora saw themselves as employees of Catholics, there were indications in 1980 that the second generation of females was trying to move away from this identity. There were three main factors which were responsible. First of all, as noted earlier, there were better educational provisions and a more positive evaluation of education in Amora than in Pednem. Although many children who attended school also worked part time in the fields they were increasingly beginning to regard such work with contempt and to aspire to better jobs. Secondly, there were greater opportunities for occupational diversification in Amora. For instance, a tailoring class was set up to equip young women with marketable skills which could be put to use in the village and the nearby town which was frequented by foreign tourists and better off indigenous shoppers. Thirdly, in the post-colonial ethos of egalitarianism, and with the promulgation of legislation to foster this, the idea of playing a subservient role to Catholics has increasingly been regarded with distaste.

The aim of the new generation of Hindu women is household self sufficiency, whereby any fieldwork and housework they do will be for themselves and their families and friends on a reciprocal basis. Alternatively any productive activities they are engaged in should not be of a servile nature, but should have a degree of status because they require formal education or vocational training, and the ability to work in a modern non-agrarian economy. For many females, however, it is inevitable that they will have to carry on as their parents have done because they have failed to acquire the relevant skills and resources.

Conclusion

In this chapter I have tried to demonstrate the shifts in the identity of two categories of women that have occurred as a result of migration. These shifts have been facilitated through the availability of increased economic resources drawn from an urban economy outside of Goa and used within a rural context. These resources have enabled Catholic women to see themselves, ideally, as progressive mothers, optional carers of the elderly, as being unsuited to farmwork and better suited as managers of agricultural and domestic labour. For Hindu women, it has led to an increased perception of themselves as marketable employees, able to earn a substantial income and acquire a greater degree of independence and autonomy.

References

Almeida, J.C., 1967 *Aspects of Agricultural Activity in Goa, Daman & Diu*, Panaji: Government Printing Press

Azavedo, A.E. D'Almeida, 1890 *As Comunidades de Goa*, Lisbon

Baden-Powell, B.H. 1900 'The villages in Goa in the Early 16th Century', *Journal of the Royal Asiatic Society*, art XI, pp. 262–91.

Boxer, C.R., 1969 *The Portuguese Seaborne Empire 1415–1825*, London: Hutchinson

Caplan, P., 1978 'Women's Organisations in Madras City' in P. Caplan and J. Bujra (eds), *Women United, Women Divided*, London: Tavistock

Castles, S. and Kossack G. 1973 *Immigrant Workers and the Class Structure in Western Europe*, London: Oxford University Press

Cunha, T.B., 1961 *Goa's Freedom Struggle: selected writings by T.B. Cunha*, Bombay

D'Costa, A., 1965 *The Christianisation of the Goa Islands*, Bombay

Da Costa, A., 1977 'Caste Stratification Among the Roman Catholics of Goa', *Man in India*, vol. 57, no. 4, pp. 283–92

Da Costa, P.J. Peregino, 1956 *A Expansao do goes pelo Mundo*, Goa

Derrett, J.D.M., 1965 *Hindu Law in Goa: A Contact Between Natural, Roman and Hindu Laws*, Stuttgart: Ferdinand Euke Verlag

D'Souza, B.G., 1975 *Goan Society in Transition*, Bombay: Bombay University Press

De Sousa, D., 1978 'The Role of the Catholic Church in Goa's Development' *Religion and Society*, vol. 25, no. 2, pp. 13–32

De Souza, T.R., 1979 *Mediaeval Goa: a Socio-Economic History*, New Delhi: Concept

Fawcett, J.T., Khoo, S., and Smith, P.C., 1984 *Women in the Cities of Asia: Migration and Urban Adaptation*, Boulder, Colorado: Westview Press

Fernandes, A.C., 1924 'The Demographic Problem in Goa', *Boletim do Instituto Vasco da Gama*, Goa: Bastora

—1939 'Conferencia', *Boletim do Instituto Vasco da Gama*, Goa, Bastora

—1940 'A Renovacao Economica de India Portuguesa', *Boletim do Instituto Vasco da Gama*, Goa: Bastora

Fieldhouse, D.K., 1966 *The Colonial Empires: A Comparative Survey from the 18th Century*, London: Weidenfeld & Nicolson

Gomes, F.L., 1862 *A Liberdade de Terra e a Economica Rural da India Portuguesa*, Lisbon

Goncalves, J., 1906 *Problemas Demographicos Da Populacao Goeza*, Goa: Casa Luso Franceza

Gracias, J.B.A., 1950 *Historia Economico-Financeira da India Portuguesa (1910 to 1947)*, Lisbon: AGC

Harrison, J.B., 1975 'The Portuguese' in A. L. Basham (ed.), *A Cultural History of India*, Oxford: Clarendon Press

Ifeka, C., 1985 'Hierarchical Woman: Towards Re-thinking Woman's Role in Development in India', unpublished paper

Khan Haward, R., 1980 'An Urban Minority: The Goan Christian community in Karachi' in K. A. Ballhatchet and J. Harrison (eds), *The City in South Asia: Pre-Modern and Modern*, London: Curzon Press

Kuper, J., 1973 'The Goan Community in Kampala', unpublished PhD thesis, University of London

—1975 'The Goan Community in Kampala', in M. Twaddle (ed.) *Expulsion of a Minority: Essays on Ugandan Asians*, London: Athlone Press

Mascarenhas-Keyes, S., 1979 *Goans in London: Portrait of a Catholic Asian Community*, London: Goan Association (UK)

— 1986 'Death Notices and Dispersal: International Migration among Catholic Goans', in J. Eades (ed.), *Migrants, Workers and the Social Order*, London: Tavistock

— 1987 'Migration and the International Catholic Goan Community', unpublished PhD thesis, University of London

— 1988a 'Modernisation and the status of aged Catholic International returners in Goa', paper presented at the Association of Social Anthropologists Conference: The Social Construction of Youth, Maturation and Ageing, London

— 1988b 'Sorpotael and Feni: the role of food in Catholic Goan ethnic identity', paper presented in the Oxford University seminar series Food and Ethnic Identity, forth-coming in Webber, J. and Mach, Z. (eds) *Food and Ethnic Identity,* Oxford: Berg

— 1989 'Language and Diaspora: The significance of Konkani and English among Catholic Goan women migrants', paper presented at the Oxford Conference on Women and Second Languages, forthcoming in P. Burton, K. Dyson and S. Ardener (eds), *Bilingual Women: Anthropological Approaches to Second Language Use*, Oxford: Berg

— 1990a 'Migration, Progressive Motherhood and female autonomy: Catholic women in Goa', in L. Dube and R. Palriwala (eds), *Structures and Strategies: Women, Work and Family in Asia*, New Delhi: Sage

— 1990b 'International Migration: its development, reproduction and economic impact on Goa up to 1961' in T.R. de Souza (ed.), *Goa through the Ages* Vol 11. *An Economic History, Goa:* Goa University Press

Mehta, A.B., 1960 *The Domestic Servant Class*, Bombay: Popular Book Depot

Menezes Braganza L. de 1923 'A Educacao e Ensino na India Portuguesa', in *A Inida Portuguesa*, vol. 11, pp. 18-70, Nova Goa: Imprensa Nacional

Morokvasic, M., 1983 'Women in Migration: Beyond the Reductionist Outlook', in A. Phizackerlea (ed.), *One Way Ticket: Migration and Female Labour*, London: Routledge & Kegan Paul

— 1985 'Birds of Passage Are Also Women', *International Migration Review*, vol. 18, no 4

Nelson, D., 1971 'Caste and Club: A Study of Goan Politics in Nairobi', unpublished PhD thesis, University of Nairobi

Newman, R.S., 1984 'Goa: The Transformation of a Region', *Pacific Affairs*, vol. 57, no. 3, pp. 429–49

Panandiker, V.A. and Chauduri, P.N., 1983 *Demographic Transition in Goa: Its Policy Implications*, New Delhi: Uppal Publishing House

Pereira, R. Gomes, 1981 *Goa, Vol. 11: Gaunkari: The Old Village Associations*, Goa: Panaji

Philpott, A., 1968 'Remittance Obligations: Social Networks and Choice among Monserratian Migrants in Britain', *Man*, vol. 3, no 3, pp. 465–476.

Pinto, J., 1960 *Goan Emigration*, Goa: Saligao

Report of the Goa Land Reforms Commission 1964, Goa: Government Printing Press

Rodriques, L.A., 1977 *The Portuguese Army of India*, Goa

Saxena, R.N., 1974 *Goa: Into the Mainstream*, New Delhi: Abinar

Sengupta, P., 1960 *Women Workers in India*, Bombay: Asia Pubishing House

Sharma, U.M., 1980 *Women, Work and Property in North West India*, London: Tavistock

Singh, A.M. 1984 'Rural-To-Urban Migration of Women in India: Patterns and Implications', in J.T. Fawcett, S. Khoo and P.C. Smith (eds), *Women in the Cities of Asia: Migration and Urban Adaptation*, Boulder, Colorado: Westview Press

Srivastava, H., 1977 'Marriage Among the Christians of Goa. A Study Based on Parish Registers' *The Indian Economic and Social History Review*, vol. 14, no. 2, pp. 247-54

Techno-Economic Survey of Goa, Daman & Diu, 1964 Delhi: National Council for Applied Economic Research

Thadani, V.N. and Todaro, M.P., 1984 'Female Migration: A conceptual Framework', in J.T. Fawcett, S. Khoo and P. C. Smith (eds), *Women in the Cities of Asia: Migration and Urban Adaptation*, Boulder, Colorado: Westview Press

Torrie, J.S. da Fonseca, 1898 *Estatistica da India Portuguesa*, Nova Goa: Imprensa Nacional

Xavier, F.N., 1852 *Bosquejo da Historias das communidades de Goa*, Nova Goa

Vatuk, S., 1972 *Kinship and Urbanisation; White Collar Migrants in North India*, Berkeley: University of California Press

Watson, J.L., 1975 *Emigration and the Chinese Lineage: The Mans in Hong Kong*, Berkeley: University of California Press

Youssef, N.H., Buvinic, M. and Kudat, A., 1979 *Women in Migration: A Third World Focus*, Washington DC: International Center for Research on Women

8

Vietnamese Refugees in Hong Kong: Behaviour and Control

Linda   Hitchcox

This chapter discusses the complementary and alternative roles of Vietnamese women, pointing out that the traditional image of the subservient female living within the tight controls of a patriarchal society is the public aspect of a multi-layered interaction between Vietnamese men and women (see also Indra 1987). The traditional image receives overt support within the Hong Kong detention centre where the idea of 'refugee' or 'asylum seeker' denotes helplessness and dependency in the minds of the authorities. In a situation where compliance and obedience are administrative objectives, women are less likely than men to feel their identities are being threatened. However, at the same time, their vulnerability is increased in relation to male residents. The frustrations arising from a similar sense of helplessness encourage some men actively to seek to re-establish some sense of power and control within the under-life of the detention centre. Women, by their physical weakness, are very vulnerable in such a situation.

The fieldwork to which this paper refers was conducted during April, May and June 1990 in nine detention centres in Hong Kong. Thirty-five women contributed formal interviews. Many more informal discussions were held with other female asylum seekers as part of a two-year project, in progress, to examine migration and aid intervention in Vietnam.

Introduction

Traditionally, in Vietnam, the Confucian rule of *Tong* or 'Three Submissions' was adapted as a guideline by which the woman should conduct her life. As an unmarried girl she was to submit herself to her father's wishes, as a married woman to those of her husband and as a

145

widow and mother she should defer to her son. The maintenance of these principles received support from the practice of ancestor worship, which assumes that the perpetuation of the lineage and the family heritage depends on having a male heir who can perform the ceremonial duties. Many proverbs and sayings testify to the weakness of women, their helplessness and lack of intelligence as, for example, 'Women with their weak legs and soft hands, have no strength to work for a living; they only talk.'

Women, because of their weakness, are also believed to be particularly vulnerable to the chances of fate. The following saying also emphasises that a woman's existence is likely to be undistinguished: 'A woman is like a drop of rain, no one knows whether it will fall in to a well or a bucket.' Sentiments of this kind echo throughout much early Vietnamese writing, including the immensely popular epic poem of Kieu by Nguyen Du, written in the early nineteenth century. The poet also acknowledges that the fate of women is harsh and 'from ages out of mind has spared none' (Huynh Sanh Thong 1983).

In practice, images of women that emphasise their subservience and inadequacy tend to be ideal, male perceptions that fit awkwardly into the historical accounts of the bravery and sacrifice of legendary figures such as the Trung sisters, who successfully led resistance against Chinese invaders in the first century AD. Similarly, the legend that describes the origin of the Vietnamese nation tells of a partnership between Lac Long Quan and his wife Au Co. They divided their sons between them when they agreed to rule independent territories, but at the same time also promised that they would always provide each other with mutual co-operation and support.

Possibly, such discrepancies may be understood as the intrusion of Chinese culture into an existing Vietnamese tradition that included greater respect for the contribution of women (Hodgkin 1981: 67, Woodside 1971). Almost certainly, perceiving the gap between the ideal and the real situation helped to fuel outspoken attacks on the attitudes of men, written by women in the form of folksong and poem. The feminist poet Ho Xuan Huong, writing in the late eighteenth and early nineteenth centuries, is especially appreciated for her sexual imagery and scathing attacks on men.

> Where are you hurrying to, you bunch of dull-witted creatures? Come here and let your elder sister teach you how to compose poetry. (trans. Nha-Trang Cong Huyen Ton Nu Thi 1969: 210)

Folk songs, too, portray an active awareness on the part of women of their own worth compared to the faults of men as extracts from the same volume show:

> Listen to me! Do not marry a student who lies down after each meal on his long back, good only for wasting fabric.
> In the icy cold climate of winter, he simply lies there waiting to spend the thirty-six coins I earned transplanting rice.

Also:

> Coming from a literate family, I have unfortunately married a dull-witted man.
> Just as the golden dragon feels it disagreeable to bathe in a pond of muddy water,
> A wise one like me is annoyed living with a stupid one like him.

(ibid: 212)

As part of the ideal of the subservient woman there traditionally existed a recognition of her equal rights before the law (pre-eighteenth century), as long as she performed her duties as a good wife (Vassal 1910). These duties included near total control of the household if she was a first wife. She was also responsible for the planting out of the young rice seedlings and for the marketing of all the produce of the household. Today, as elsewhere in Southeast Asia, women are accepted as being particularly skilful at marketing; the bargaining of goods is still generally left to them by their husbands (Pelzer White 1988: 174). From the fifteenth to the beginning of the nineteenth century, women had a right to their own property and an equal share in inheritance, even claiming the entire sum if there was no male heir (Nguyen Khac Vien 1987: 76). Nevertheless, it is clear that the authority of women related closely to the private sphere of the well-being of home and family; they traditionally played little part in the ordering of village affairs.

The French colonial period in Vietnam, because of its opposition to Chinese influence, tended to open up opportunities for women, particularly in regard to education, at the same time as it instituted a system of repression on the Vietnamese nation as a whole. The struggle for liberation recognised that the contribution of women was essential if success was to be achieved. Opposition leaders such as Phan Boi Chau (1867–1940) spoke out against the rule of *Tong*. Within the Indochinese Communist Party, the Women's Union formed a rallying point for the active participation of women in the political life of the country. In North Vietnam, during the resistance against the French and later against the Americans, women participated fully in their wartime roles, either by undertaking combat duties if necessary, or taking charge of family and business affairs during the absence of sons or husbands. The thirty to forty years of conflict since the 1950s have probably been the most important factor in changing the lives of women in Vietnam, eroding entrenched attitudes, opening up new careers and access to education denied to previous generations. After 1975, the right to such opportunities was encoded in Articles 63 and 64 of the Constitution of the Socialist Republic of Vietnam. Nevertheless, as is universally the case, the gap between the ideal and reality remains clearcut. Vietnamese women continue to be politically weak, and are very vulnerable to rising unemployment and economic instability, the situation prevailing in Vietnam in the early 1990s.

This brief overview gives a general indication of the kinds of circumstance and tradition likely to have shaped the attitudes of women in Vietnam, with the proviso that any generalisations about this diverse and rapidly changing society should be treated with caution. In the following section I explore the situation of those Vietnamese women who decide to leave Vietnam, and experience the traumatic effects of forced migration and detention.

Migration from Vietnam Since 1975

In the thirty-five formal interviews conducted with women in the detention centres of Hong Kong, only two out of the group of twenty married women stated that they had no clear reasons of their own for leaving Vietnam; they had followed their husbands who had made the decision to go (see Camus-Jacques 1989: 150). The remainder were able to give clear accounts of why they had left, sometimes linked to their husband's background when they had suffered the consequences of their partner's actions, but more often drawn specifically from their own experience. In three cases, women had been attracted to their husbands because of a common experience of living outside the law and the necessity of making an escape. In one report the liaison had been made en route.

A sustained migration of large numbers of Vietnamese is not surprising in view of the extraordinary difficulties through which Vietnam has passed. The unification and division of countries under radical or totalitarian regimes usually causes dislocation and unrest among the population. In Vietnam, it may be many years before the incongruities resulting from the divisions of colonialism and war are healed, particularly if the country remains in diplomatic isolation and consequently, in a necessarily defensive position.

In the urgent search for national unity it is commonly the case for the leaders of newly-established nation states to be deeply suspicious of those within society who, for political, ethnic, social or other reasons do not appear to fit the nationally-prescribed programme. The pressures arising from the imperative to conform are likely to force people to leave, especially if it is legally extremely difficult to leave the country for any reason.

Government employment, the right to work at a professional post, to carry identity papers, apply for further education, or move from a district may be decided with reference to the person's grandparents and parents. Connections to the French regime, land ownership or any anti-communist activity result in access being denied to skilled work or further education. Of the female sample interviewed, 14 per cent gave this reason. One such woman, from a French landowning family, had been allowed to attend training as a teacher on payment of raised fees, but had had constant difficulties with her employers thereafter. The uneasy situation came to a climax when she refused to teach a particular political issue she regarded as not being true. She was removed from her post and put under surveillance until she eventually found a way of leaving Vietnam.

Likewise, religious practice attracts discrimination, ranging from consistent oppression to outright persecution. One young Catholic woman from the South, whose family had connections to the pre-1975 regime, attempted to run Sunday classes for children. She refused to discontinue these when brought before the authorities and was sent to a re-education camp. There she spent two years in forced labour until her health completely broke down and she was hospitalised. She managed to escape from the hospital and went into hiding until she was able to leave Vietnam.

Membership of an ethnic minority (11 per cent of the sample), such as the Hoa or the Nung associated with pre-1975 or 1979 political events in Vietnam, may also be interpreted as suspicious by the authorities. In 1979, the property of many ethnic Chinese was confiscated. Not all wanted or were able to leave the country at that time. Two of the ethnic Chinese women in the sample reported that they had made a number of attempts to escape before they succeeded in reaching Hong Kong. Another woman was a Vietnamese but she had been a headmistress in a Chinese school. She was removed from her post and not allowed to teach elsewhere.

The Vietnam Government is now faced with a massive task of unification which means not only the reworking of the social fabric of society and securing its political loyalty, but the development of a ruined economy and infrastructure, in the face of long-standing isolation from the Western international community. Vietnamese who are considering the possibility of leaving, appraise their future situation, and that of their children against this background of chaos and hardship. Moreover, it appears from interviews that the perception of Northerners in particular, was that the outlook was one of increasing instability with a government less and less in control.

Such reactions are reasonably predictable, in the light of our knowledge from other countries about short-term public responses to social and economic restructuration. Since 1987, there has been a period of remarkable economic change in Vietnam with the restructuring of the money supply and the development of a multi-layered economic system. Inflation declined from an estimated 300-700 per cent in 1987 to double figures in 1989. This has been achieved by a centrally-ordered policy of monetary restraint, a principle feature of which has been very high interest rates (of the order of 100 per cent).

During this period, both entrepreneural opportunities and constraints were created, which, in the short term, have tended to exacerbate a general loss of confidence. Circumstances of rapid economic change tend to encourage migration because of the immediate de-stabilising effects which are created in the economy (see also Bach 1989). One of the most important negative features was the high cost of servicing loans, due to the raised interest rates. It became increasingly difficult for the industrial and state sectors to service themselves for production, and as a result were unable to pay salaries over a long period (many months in the coal industry), and unemployment grew. Six of the interviewed women had lost their jobs due to the introduction of competitive enterprise. At the same time, rising food prices, previously heavily subsidised, also increased hardship.

All the women interviewed reported being based in urban areas, but such a response often hid a complicated history of frequent movement, particularly in the period immediately prior to the escape. Very few had professional skills (2 per cent) or government employment (14 per cent). Twenty-one of the women had spent some period of their lives farming either in their home villages or else after removal to new economic zones or collectives. From this experience they could report on the daily realities of subsistence farming where the labour of women is essential for the survival of the family and is the lot of the majority of women in Vietnam. All had experienced increasing drudgery which had, if anything, rather worsened in latter years. Although general statements about the reasons are difficult to make because of the diversity of their circumstances, relocation to virgin territory, changes in collective organisation with the contracting out of some agricultural tasks, few resources and infertile soils were commonly mentioned.

Grinding poverty or persistent discrimination are not the only reasons why people may decide to go. The decision may also possibly be a response to a sudden crisis and its consequences: for example, what were described by four women as false accusations followed by a prison term; in two cases, persistent criminal activity and imminent arrest, otherwise the husband deserting from the army, or else, protesting in vain against the actions of an employer and subsequent persecution. After such events it became impossible for the family to remain in the country. Hence, they decided to leave, even though the majority of them knew they would probably have a difficult time in Hong Kong. As mentioned earlier, women were unlikely to blindly follow their husbands from Vietnam, unless they themselves also had good reasons for departure. In the two cases linked to criminal behaviour of the gangland type, it appeared that the operations of the women had been closely linked to their husband's activities which probably means that the decision was collaborative.

Whatever the reasons for leaving, they were very unlikely to be whimsical and were usually the result of a complicated process, involving the family, immediate circumstances, perceived future prospects, perceptions of threat and intolerable oppression, economic and/or political. Once the decision was made, women in particular entered an inevitably politicised phase of their lives whereby they had placed themselves, intentionally or not, in open opposition to the government, by deciding to become asylum seekers. For single women the decision is especially perilous and requires considerable endurance, stamina and determination to successfully carry out an escape.

The Journey

The journey from Vietnam is a hazardous enterprise for women. Dangers from pirate activity on the routes to Thailand and Malaysia are well-known (see Camus-Jacques 1989: 146, Callaway 1987: 322), but the route to Hong Kong can be equally perilous. The story of one eighteen-year-old girl illustrates common difficulties. I begin with her account of her background, which provides the context of her later experiences.

I grew up in a family with very good and strict traditions. My father worked on a local newspaper and my mother spent all her time with her husband and children as do many women in Vietnam.

When I was six or seven, the conflict broke out with China and my mother was sent away from us. I don't really know why. Father and the family had a really hard time - better not to ask.

Then I remember after three years, my mother came home. The police told my father and we all cried so much. When my mother came, I stood there because I didn't recognise her. They told me that she had gone for forced labour. She came to me and held me and I recognised at that moment that she was my mother. We were so happy that we all cried again, but I was afraid too because I did not know what might happen next.

My mother was so sick that my eldest brother stayed home to help her. He was not allowed to study because of our background. So we continued with my mother earning a little money from tailoring and from keeping pigs in the house.

One day my grandmother died and my father and I made the long journey so that we could go to my grandmother's grave. While I was staying in the village I found out for the first time that I had been baptised a Catholic and my religious name was Maria.

After I returned home I continued with school in the same way. Mother was very weak and she still had to report to the police twice a week. I finished school and was successful in getting a place on a vocational training course for nursing. But when I was there I soon got in to difficulties. One day I was on the platform and used the microphone. I criticised the way the school was run. I was called to the director and told that I would be punished if it ever happened again. But I could not stop when I found that money held by the authorities was missing and I wrote about this in the student magazine. I also refused to study political education. The director dismissed me from the school.

Next day the police arrested me. They held me for three days and questioned me over and over again. On the third day, three men came in to my cell and they did things to me and attacked me so that I did not know what was happening and I was crying out in pain for my feeling and my experience. I only wanted to die. The next day they came for me to take me to hospital, a mental hospital, because I was shouting so much.

When I came there, I was very, very weak but I also knew that it was my only chance. I had no choice, I had to escape. I went by foot to the home of a friend about twenty kilometres away. I told him the story and he hid me for two days and then we went to another place where I had to hide for one week. He had a friend who organised for me to leave the country.

I went by boat from Hai Phong, but we were unlucky. The boat broke down and we landed on this small island. There, I met other fishermen. I had no money, I had no choice, I had to agree that I would give to the brother of the boat master and he gave me a forged marriage certificate.

We sailed along the coast of China, sometimes begging, sometimes stealing. At one place the boat broke down and a group of us stayed with an old woman. She let us sleep in the kitchen by the stove and there was a sixteen-year-old boy. I don't know if he could forget that night. I could not forget it and I wanted to run in to the sea and kill myself.

I arrived in Green Island [Hong Kong] and there, I had to say that the man was my husband and the boy was my brother. It was not my husband and it was not my brother.

Now I am very sad because I lied in Green Island. I wait in this detention centre and I know that nobody can share my feelings. Nobody can understand me because they all have enough suffering. Many nights I can not sleep and I think of suicide. Sometimes I hear [others] crying and I try to ignore them and likely it is the same for them when they hear me.

This story is retold as described because it portrays fairly typical difficulties and horrors experienced by single women when making their escape. More important, from the informant's point of view, was the reason for deciding for the first time to relate the story. This decision was not taken out of a sense of self-pity or helplessness, but in order that I should properly understand why she had had to leave Vietnam and her determination to persevere until she had arrived in a first asylum country. While aware of discrimination against her family, events directed at herself had turned her from activist to prisoner and then to fugitive in the space of a few months. She had become politicised beyond her eighteen years and was willing to undergo intense personal shame (by sharing her secret) in order to tell me of her belief in the injustice of her government.

The Detention Centres of Hong Kong

The present system of detention centres in Hong Kong is a response to the major influx of arrivals who entered Hong Kong in 1988 and 1989. The movement also provoked a long-envisaged policy change whereby the pre-June 1988 camp population kept their existing refugee status and were moved in to controlled open centres. The policy thereafter, was to deter as many new arrivals as possible from entering Hong Kong by imposing (1) screening for refugee status on new arrivals, in accordance with internationally recognised migration practice, and (2) restrictive conditions of detention on those waiting to be screened or who had been rejected. A voluntary repatriation programme is run by UNHCR, encouraging people to return home if they have been screened out.

The detention centres are high-security holding camps, consisting of concrete yards, high barbed wire fences dividing the yards into separate pens and Nissen-type buildings for accommodation and services. Space is very limited, each resident having a bedspace and a few yards of recreation area. The capacity of the camps range from 2,000 to 24,000 people adding up to a total population of approximately 43,000. Agency offices provide specific services social work, medical clinics and education. A few recreational activities are available, but for many hours a day inmates have nothing with which to occupy themselves. Inactivity and boredom increase the daily tensions created by uncertainty about the future and the constraints and over-crowding of camp life.

Men, denied their ordinary role of breadwinner, become listless and frustrated, while the younger ones seek self-esteem in gang brotherhood and acts of defiance against the administration. Women and children are physically vulnerable in a community where traditional values are slowly collapsing and being replaced by outsider control. Added to this debilitating sense of lack of power or authority over their own lives are the ordinary difficulties of daily living.

Insecurity and Protection in the Camps

Because of the volatile atmosphere in the centres, controlling the population is a major concern of the management. The problem is tackled by demanding passivity and obedience from the Vietnamese community. This authoritarian approach does not prevent regular outbreaks of violence as the majority of the detainees feel that they are living in a hopeless, demoralising situation and have little to lose by rebelling from time to time. Residents are being encouraged by the administration to improve security within their own community, but poor communication between management and managed makes such co-operation extremely difficult to organise. Locked gates and gatekeepers in the larger camps, such as High Island and Whitehead, increase the problems of collaboration. If asylum seekers wish to leave a compound for any reason, they must approach the gate with a written request in Vietnamese, and convey their errand to a Cantonese-speaking guard. He may or may not allow them to pass. Informing on troublemakers is particularly difficult for those asylum seekers who are threatened by them. It is possible to write a letter to the authorities, but many are afraid of committing pen to paper, when they are not sure who will read what they write and in what circumstances. Passing through the gates without disclosing the reason for doing so, or in order to make an appointment is extremely difficult. It is an act of courage to make oneself 'stick out from the crowd', perhaps by approaching the commandant, particularly when an interpreter usually has to be found. There is also the worry that if the information is revealed, the friends of the accused individual will always find means of exacting retribution.

One group of women, living together in a single women's hut in one of the island detention centres, became alarmed by the activities and repeated threats of gangleaders. Gang activity, led by criminals is fairly common in all the camps and poses a constant and pressing problem for the majority of the camp population. On this occasion, the women locked the door of their dormitory each night for four months and stayed up on guard. Eventually, the hut representative met with the staff and asked for more protection from these threats and the daily problems created by drugs, fights and robberies. In some trepidation, she and another woman also gave the names of two of the gang leaders to the authorities, hoping they would be immediately arrested. Instead, the management put six guards around the hut, which meant that every resident in the detention centre instantly became aware that complaints had been made. The women felt so exposed and afraid that they did not dare even go out of the hut to the latrines. They asked for the 'protection' to cease. The next stage of response by the administration was to interview the two women again, a procedure that was clumsily camouflaged by calling eight additional women from other huts. Since the first hut was already known to the gangleader it was easy for them to spot the informants; one woman occupant was beaten up by the gang and later hospitalised. She told the authorities that she had fallen out of her bedspace, and there was no improvement in security for the remainder of the women. The gangleaders were not interviewed or detained, reportedly because there was too little evidence. The women could not understand why they had been questioned and the gang leaders had not.

This episode is not only important and typical of the difficulties of communication, but also conveys the ambivalent attitude to women that can underlie the basically supportive position of the authorities. Women, as the physically weaker sex were regarded as being in need of protection and, as long as they behaved in a compliant and helpless way, they usually obtained rather more consideration from the authorities than the men received. If women were interpreted as being overly demanding, in this case making frequent complaints, taking protection and then objecting to it, the management interpreted their behaviour negatively. It was either unwomanly, that is to say unseemly and strident or else due to female hysteria, also unacceptable as a distortion of ideal feminine sensitivity. Accordingly, the claims were regarded as non-serious and it was therefore necessary to closely cross-question the women to discover weaknesses in their stories.

Male detainees tended to feel that the protection of women from attack was not an important problem. One individual stated, 'there is more open sex generally because we are all so close together in the huts. Women are not really treated worse; there is just more time and opportunity'. Such attitudes from men put a constant strain on marriages with occasional complaints from women about their husbands sleeping with single girls and regular occurrences of battering of wives and children.

The root problem was agreed by women to be the under-occupation of men, who suffered from the total loss of their role as decision maker and provider for the family. They were worse off than the women in this respect because the latter at least could rely on the familiar occupations of childcare, cleaning the living space and washing, making and mending clothes. In some centres, cooking of a minimal kind was also allowed and the preparation of food could take up many hours of a women's day. In general, women were also protected from the more brutal forms of law enforcement sometimes employed by the administration, because they were more likely to be perceived not only as helpless, the stereotypical description of a refugee regardless of sex, but also as victims.

Official Perceptions of Asylum Seekers and the Feminine Stereotype

Other observers have referred to the process of reification that is inclined to equate the individual with the state of being a refugee (for example, Moussa 1988). This fallacious perception derives from the usage of a legal category, which is no more than an aspect of an individual, as a description of personal identity. The consequence is that the legal status of 'refugee' not only constrains the use of a person's abilities and talents but encourages the generalised understanding that an individual is a refugee and little else.

The stance of regarding those who are defined in political and legal terms as refugees, as, correspondingly, occupying one social niche with identical needs, outlooks and problems (especially problems), derives most directly from the sheer scale of the crises that arise and the need to gain control as efficiently and rapidly as possible. Control, accompanied by the implementation of procedure and regulations is not easily achieved by paying attention to the variability of the human condition whether in terms of gender, age talents or outlook.

If through the action of management there is the persistent tendency to develop a neutralised category of individuals named 'refugee/asylum seeker', then concomitantly the image of people so categorised will reflect the roles and objectives of that management since it is the latter which is being projected rather than the reality experienced by those who are managed.

The required responses from detainees, appropriate to a well-controlled population and favoured by management, tend to be stereotypically feminine in type. This official bias provides a corresponding degree of support to the women residents rather than their male counterparts. The management supplies order, protection, care and maintenance, but to fulfil these objectives, certainly paternalistic in their implementation, it is necessary to have not only a controlled population, but also one that is perceived from the official perspective as being permanently in a state of helplessness and dependency.

The circumstances that prevail in the detention centres of Hong Kong conspire to create and develop such attitudes; attitudes which in a generalised sense incorporate idealised virtues of Vietnamese women. As mentioned earlier, Vietnamese society is by custom patriarchal, deeply influenced by Confucian principles which make women subject to the authority of their husbands, their fathers and their sons. Within the context of such traditions and given the functions of the camp, it is easy and appropriate for the camp administrations to give to women and for women to receive from those in authority. Thus, women asylum seekers are usually able to accommodate to the role of recipient more easily than men for the sake of their families, a role which is reinforced by the continuation of domestic tasks. The confines of the camp do not entirely prevent them from fulfilling their familiar duties of home-making, cooking and child-rearing. Such stress and anxiety as they frequently experience is often related to violence within the camps but here too they are likely to rely on the administration to afford them protection. That this function may not be adequately operated does not negate the fact that their best protection often lies in the official quarter rather than with their own menfolk.

Conversely, to the camp administration, the women are the least threatening or troublesome group within the confined population. Officials expect trouble from men, especially single young men, frustrated by their inability to lead, work, organise and shoulder usual family responsibilities. Officials know that women tend to avoid violence for the sake of their children and attempt, during the normal course of their daily lives to maintain family life, thus engendering a measure of stability to an otherwise volatile population.

The effect of enforced inactivity upon the men, together with the tacit encouragement by the administration of quasi-feminine qualities, is to encourage men to participate more and more in domestic chores, particularly child-minding, the preparation of food and the washing of dishes and pans. The washing of clothes remains, whenever possible, a woman's task. Small-scale activities run by women are seen by the administration as non-threatening, being directed towards the problem of family subsistence.

Such trends relate to elements of womanhood which are familiar and acceptable both to the administration and to Vietnamese women. (The stereotype is almost universal.) An atmosphere that tends to be more supportive of an aspect of the feminine, traditional to Vietnamese, results directly from the fact that a compliant resident population is a high priority for the camp administration.

At the same time, it should be emphasised that Vietnamese women do not only behave according to such stereotypes. In Vietnam, the idealised model of the obedient wife and daughter coexists with other histories which present women as war leaders, critics, poets and satirists, and within the home, custodians of Vietnamese national identity. Recently, women refugees have suffered persecution in a similar fashion to men through prolonged imprisonment and re-education, and have risked their lives to escape in similarly dramatic circumstances. In the survey, there was no statistically significant difference between the reasons why men and women respondents had left Vietnam. The upheavals of war and the advent of communist rule have done much to challenge the stereotype of the shy, dependent and retiring female.

All this is fairly irrelevant to the objectives of the administration, which is to make detention in Hong Kong sufficiently tough to deter other Vietnamese from leaving Vietnam. Accordingly, for these and other reasons, the detention centre is a difficult and constraining environment for women. One aspect of their identity, the compliant female, is emphasised at the expense of the whole. The violence against women, I suggest, is greatly exacerbated by the detention system, arising out of the sense of powerlessness men endure. They are rendered unable to provide for and protect their families, to fulfil what they assume to be their male roles (Harrell-Bond 1986: 282).

Conclusion

Within Vietnamese society there is a well-established tradition of a complementary partnership between men and women that forms the basis of stable family life, a social unit of vital importance in Vietnamese society. The strong influences, largely of Chinese origin, that insisted on the absolute subordination of women, have been modified by colonialism and the introduction of marxist notions of social equality. When the decision to leave Vietnam was taken, women did not usually rely on their husbands, but had clear personal reasons for taking this momentous course of action. Fifteen out of the sample of thirty-five women were single and declared themselves to be entirely responsible for the decision to leave.

Once in the camps, they found themselves subject to a regime that, on the part of the authorities, denied any sense of independence, but was generally responsive to the image of the victimised woman, as long as it was also a representation that included passivity and compliance. Such an image usually invoked protection and swift retribution against men who threatened women. Paradoxically, the same regime was indirectly responsible for making the lives of women unsafe at the hands of the resident population, by rendering males largely helpless and dependent, thus exciting considerable stress in terms of how men saw themselves, their role and identity in relation to women. Such a situation encourages gang-type relations to flourish since men can regain a measure of control, albeit deviant, by embarking on criminal activities.

To sum up, it is probable that the relationship with the authorities into which most asylum seekers are thrown does not affront the dignity and identity of Vietnamese women in as direct a manner as it does that of men. Between donor and recipient, there is a shared image of femininity made evident in the practice of control by the administration and the controlled practice of Vietnamese womanhood.

References

Bach, R. L., 1989 'Transforming Socialist Emigration: Lessons from Cuba and Vietnam', Binghamton, unpublished manuscript

Callaway, H., 1987 'Women Refugees, Specific Requirements and Untapped Resources', *Third World Affairs 1987*, pp.320–329

Camus-Jacques, G., 1989 'Refugee Women: The Forgotten Majority', in G. Loescher and L. Monahan (eds), *Refugees and International Relations*, Oxford: Oxford University Press

Harrell-Bond, B.E., 1986 *Imposing Aid: Emergency Assistance for Refugees*, Oxford: Oxford University Press

Hodgkin, T., 1981 *Vietnam: The Revolutionary Path*, London: Macmillan

Huynh Sanh Thong, 1979 *The Heritage of Vietnamese Poetry*, London: Yale University Press

Indra, D., 1987 'Gender: A Key Dimension of the Refugee Experience', *Refuge*, vol.6, February

Moussa, H., 1988 'Women Refugees: Cultural Adjustment as Empowerment. Preliminary Report', unpublished report of the International Consultation on Refugee Women 15-19 November

Nguyen Khac Vien, 1987 *Vietnam A Long History*, Hanoi: Foreign Language Publishing House

Nha Trang Cong Huyen Ton Nu Thi, 1973 'The Traditional Roles of Vietnamese Women as Reflected in Oral and Written Literature', unpublished DPhil thesis for the Graduate Division of the University of Berkeley

Pelzer White, C., 1988 'Socialist Transformation of Agriculture and Gender Relations: The Vietnamese Case', in J. G. Taylor and A. Turton (eds), *Sociology of Developing Societies: Southeast Asia*, Basingstoke: Macmillan

Vassal, G.M., 1910 *On and Off Duty in Annam*, London: Heinemann

Woodside, A., 1971 *Vietnam and the Chinese Model: A Comparative Study of Vietnamese and Chinese Government in the First Half of the Nineteenth Century*, Cambridge, Massachusetts: Harvard University Press

9

Female Migration and Social Mobility: British Female Domestic Servants to South Africa, 1860–1914

Cecillie Swaisland

A major problem in any study of women is that of determining the motives for actions about which little is recorded by the actors themselves. In some historical studies the problem is compounded by the low level of literacy of many in the subject group. One of the focuses of this chapter is the history of a category of women about whom more is written than who were able to record their own feelings and experiences. The British domestic servant of the later nineteenth and early twentieth centuries was beginning to emerge from illiteracy as universal primary schooling was established, but for many writing was difficult, and the publication of memoirs quite outside their experience. Most of the information about and comments on the servants of the day came from employers and others who shared an inbuilt class bias, and often a lack of knowledge and sympathy with personal factors.

Most of those who emigrated from Britain to the colonies and the United States under the classification of 'domestic servants' in the late nineteenth and early twentieth centuries came from the lower classes. There were, however, some middle class women who emigrated as domestic servants – for reasons that will become clear. The latter have left an abundance of written material in the form of letters, journals and published reminiscences.

This chapter will examine the emigration as domestic servants of women from two major class divisions: the working or labouring classes and the middle or 'genteel' classes. Their motives for emigration and the consequences, often unforeseen, of such decisions, related in a variety of ways to social mobility, both upward and downward. Although this will be particularly underlined, it does not imply that there were not many other reasons for the extreme step of emigration.

161

Before undertaking the specific task in hand, it is necessary to look at the background against which the emigration of women from Britain took place, and also to outline briefly the history of South Africa as a receiving country for women. The emigration of single women from Britain to South Africa, of which domestic servants made up a significant part, cannot be understood except against the background of the socio-economic changes in nineteenth-century Britain as the country industrialised and urbanised; against the facts and ideologies of the great emigration movement; against the position of women in British society and against the history and cultural situation of the colonies of southern Africa.

As Britain became industrialised and urbanised and the size of the population grew, there were dramatic changes in life styles at all social levels. For the lower classes it was not only a time of opportunity in which many were able to rise into the ranks of the burgeoning middle classes, but also a time of acute deprivation and misery (Stearns 1972). Sheer economic necessity forced many individuals and families to leave the country and seek a new life overseas.

For the expanding middle classes, too, it was a time of both opportunity and uncertainty. Those with capital had to carry the risks of failure and if disaster struck there were, inevitably, repercussions in family life. Women brought up in a protected environment were particularly vulnerable and could find themselves unsupported and unprepared for supporting themselves (Delamont and Duffin 1978: 9–24). At the same time Britain was expanding her colonial empire and many men were drawn to overseas territories as soldiers, administrators, traders, adventurers and fortune-seekers. Most of those who went were young and their going placed great strains on the society they left behind. Much was made at the time of the resulting imbalance of the sexes and its effect on the social and matrimonial expectations of young women.

The Emigration Movement arose from these strains. It organised, facilitated and theorised upon the movement to the United States, Canada, Australia, New Zealand and South Africa of uncounted millions of British subjects, estimated as a larger number than the total population of Great Britain in 1801.[1] The movement gave birth to numerous ideologies and schemes which rose to a peak in the 1850s and then gradually dwindled as conditions in Britain improved and the colonies became more selective in the immigrants they were prepared to receive.

1. Wider issues of the emigration movement are discussed in *Emigration in theVictorian Age* 1973.

Most emigration was private and haphazard, which accounts for the difficulty in quantifying the exodus, but by the middle of the century emigration societies of all sizes and degrees of efficiency had sprung up to cope with every type of emigrant – families, working men, pauper children, working women including factory workers, dressmakers and milliners and domestic servants. For middle-class women there was no society until the 1860s.

The British Government was a reluctant participator, fearing always the cost of involvement, but at its peak between 1840 and 1878, the movement was regulated by the Colonial Land and Emigration Commission, set up by the Colonial Office. This body, among its other roles, was particularly concerned with improving the conditions under which unaccompanied women emigrated.[2]

The majority of the women who emigrated were wives and daughters travelling with their families or joining men who had gone on ahead. A significant minority, however, were single women leaving to escape grinding poverty or the often appalling conditions in the occupations open to them in their home country. Some of those who emigrated as domestic servants were so-called 'fallen women', such as those who had been seduced and had perhaps produced an illegitimate child. Such women sought a new start where their history was unknown. To these were added a small number of middle class women – 'distressed gentlewomen' who had fallen on hard times.

For a gentlewoman there was little alternative in the early years of the period to total dependence on male relatives or, if disaster struck, to becoming a housekeeper or governess in someone else's home, with all the incongruence of status that entailed (Peterson 1972). Later, as education and training became more widespread and efficient, their situation improved.

The position of women in Victorian England was culturally and legally circumscribed. For working class women who were obliged to work by poverty and lack of any welfare provision, life was hard and wages poor in factory, dressmaker's workroom or domestic service. For women of the 'genteel classes', a privileged and protected life in the home masked great underlying insecurity and frustration. Excluded from public affairs, inadequately educated at home or in inefficient boarding schools in the 'accomplishments' deemed necessary for a suitable marriage, legally classed as children without rights, and subjected to damaging pseudo-scientific theories on health and psycholo-

2. For a full history of the Colonial Land and Emigration Commission, see Hitchins 1931.

gy, many sought an outlet in negative behaviour such as frivolity, ostentation or invalidism (Showalter 1980: 157–81). Others reacted more positively by attempting to storm the bastions of male privilege in education and the professions and in espousing the causes of women's suffrage and legal position (Kamm 1966: 15–30). A minority sought relief in crossing the ocean to a new life in the United States or the colonies. Most damaging for middle class women was the lack of employment opportunities, a lack which was compounded by the attitudes of the day towards marriage as the only acceptable career for such women, and towards work of any kind for 'ladies'.

The women's emigration movement was a feature of the latter half of the nineteenth century. It had as its aims the alleviation of the lot of the working girl through emigration; the protection of the lives and virtue of women on emigrant ships on the long voyages across the Atlantic or round the Cape to the Antipodes; the balancing of the sexes in the United Kingdom and, in mirror image, in the colonies. From the 1860s, it sought also to provide employment outlets overseas for distressed gentlewomen for whom paid employment meant a painful loss of status and who felt it to be easier to seek work, even lower class work, in the colonies where they were not known.

From the middle of the nineteenth century there were a variety of emigration societies for women. Among the earliest was Angela Burdett-Coutts' scheme, founded in 1846, for the rehabilitation of prostitutes and their subsequent transmission to the colonies (Patterson 1953: 71, 159–61). Sidney Herbert's Fund for Promoting Female Emigration followed in 1849 with the aim of alleviating the lot of impoverished seamstresses, milliners and domestic servants (Herbert 1851). Both of these schemes were shortlived and sent only several hundred women abroad, almost all as domestic servants.

In 1862, the Female Middle Class Emigration Society was founded to help impoverished gentlewomen, especially poor governesses, to emigrate (Hammerton 1979: 125–47). This was the first of a string of societies, each of which grew out of its predecessor. The most influential society was the British Women's Emigration Association (BWEA), which operated from 1884 to 1919. It was followed by the Society for the Overseas Settlement of British Women from 1919, and the Women's Overseas Migration and Appointments Society from 1962 (Plant 1950).

Supplementing and assisting these societies were others dedicated to specific purposes. Important among them was the British Ladies Female Emigration Society, founded in 1849 to help the Colonial

Land and Emigration Commission provide matrons for the supervision, protection and education of women on emigrant ships (Ross 1882: 315). The Girls' Friendly Society and the Young Women's Christian Association concerned themselves with establishing contacts and hostels for women in the receiving countries; the Society for the Propagation of the Gospel dealt with spiritual matters and provided teachers and materials for men and women on emigrant ships while the Travellers' Aid Society and the National Vigilance Association attempted to protect women travellers, especially against the white slave traffic.[3] By the end of the century, there were also many training institutions preparing women for life in the colonies.

The hazards of unaccompanied travel were recognised early in Britain by both the authorities and the emigration societies. Notices in journals, public libraries, etc., warned women of the risks at ports of embarkation, on the voyage and on arrival. These warnings were ignored by many travellers, whether from ignorance, choice or necessity. The women's emigration societies gradually perfected a system of protected emigration under which their protégées were counselled, housed in hostels before embarkation, supervised by matrons on the voyage and placed in employment on arrival with back-up contacts and accommodation. But the numbers the societies could or would cope with was small. They were always short of funds and their selection processes rejected nine out of ten women who applied to them, on the grounds of health, reputation or unsuitability for colonial life.[4]

South Africa was always low in the order of preference for emigrants. Most popular were the United States, Canada, Australia and New Zealand, in that order. Until the discovery of minerals from 1870 onwards, South Africa was not a strongly favoured destination for men and this dictated the number of women who accompanied or followed them. For single women this was crucial as they could only hope to succeed where the demand was strong for the supportive roles of domestic and agricultural servants, governesses and later for professional women such as teachers and nurses. In a largely male exodus, the demand from the colonies for wives was also a significant feature.

The reasons for the lack of general emigration to South Africa, lay in a series of factors rooted in South African history and society.

3. The British Women's Emigration Association and her daughter organisations were deeply concerned about the moral dangers to women travellers and in 1919 co-operated with others to form the British National Association for the Prevention of the White Slave Traffic.

4. Plant 1950 covers the role of the women's emigration societies during the period under discussion.

Unlike most of the other colonial territories, southern Africa was already occupied by people of European origin when British immigration began. Land was owned by the Dutch farmers, the Boers, and there was strong resistance to what was regarded as an invasion (Davenport 1977: 22, 29-30). In Britain, information about the territory was sparse in the early years, largely owing to the low rate of immigration which restricted the flow of information along informal channels. The volume of letters, remittances, home visits and reports in journals and newspapers which was so much a feature of the New World and the Antipodes, was lacking.[5]

Such news of South Africa as reached the general public in Britain before 1870 was of economic problems, an out-dated land tenure system, an unfavourable climate for agriculture, of difficult internal travel, of border clashes with black races and of disagreements with the Boers. There was so much adverse publicity in English newspapers and journals that the rate of British emigration to the territory remained low.

Although South Africa was generally less attractive to the female emigrant than other destinations, there were certain factors that induced a steady trickle of women to settle there. A major advantage was the climate, which was recommended by doctors for the pulmonary complaints that afflicted so many Victorian and Edwardian women.[6] South Africa became known as the 'Lungs of the Empire', and, indeed, my own family emigrated there in 1930 on medical advice when my older brother showed signs of tuberculosis. Another attraction was that South Africa was not and never had been a penal colony, a fact that had caused so many problems for women migrants to Australia.[7] Yet another attraction, in an evangelising age, was the opportunity to spread the gospel in a country with a large and, in the view of the time, heathen black population.

After the discovery of diamonds in 1871 and gold in 1886, the demand for women immigrants, both as wives and employees, grew rapidly. Opportunities arose first in the more lowly manual roles and later in professional ones for governesses, teachers, nurses and doctors. During the Second Anglo-Boer War of 1899-1902, the demand

5. For a discussion of the importance of informal networks, see Erickson's work (1972) on emigration to the United States.
6. A pamphlet on health and emigration to South Africa was published in 1891 – Noble *et al. The Voyage to South Africa and Sojourn There*.
7. In 1849 the citizens of Cape Town successfully repulsed an attempt by the British Government to land convicts. The full history of the *Neptune* incident and its aftermath is recorded in Hattersley 1985.

for nurses was acute. After the war there was a strong imperialist movement to persuade British women to go out as wives and workers in order to maintain a British presence and culture.[8] How successful this was is another story.

Up to this point the external pressures brought to bear upon women to emigrate to South Africa as domestic servants have been considered. But what were the needs and aspirations of the women themselves? This must be seen against the background of domestic service in Britain, which was mainly but not entirely, a lower-class occupation. The few exceptions were middle-class women who were obliged by poverty to accept posts in other people's homes as companions, ladies' maids, housekeepers and governesses.

The task of defining domestic service is not a simple one. So many different categories were subsumed under the general title that some of the earlier censuses from 1851, did not attempt to give an overall figure but recorded the numbers in a large and diverse variety of occupations. The 1851 census gave an approximate overall figure of half a million women who could be classed as servants but broke this up into 'maids of all work' or general servants (400,000), charwomen (54,000), housekeepers (50,000), cooks (47,000), housemaids (42,000), nursemaids and ladies' maids (21,000), inn servants (20,000) and even gatekeepers (300–400) (Martineau 1859: 308). By 1901, a single figure of 1,622,000 was given, which claimed to represent a reduction of 27,000 since the 1891 census. It was admitted, however, that in 1891 daughters who helped in the home had been included but excluded ten years later (Article 5 in *Edinburgh Review,* vol.208, 1908: 367).

The position was even more obscure for those who emigrated as domestic servants. Because the decision as to who could be accepted as an immigrant was, after about 1850, dictated to the Emigration Commission by each individual colonial territory, the rules of recruitment were stringent. In order to qualify for the free or assisted passages granted by each colonial territory and needed by most emigrants, many factory workers, seamstresses or even some middle-class women such as governesses, allowed themselves to be described as domestic servants.

The class-based experiences of those who served as domestic servants differed. For those of working-class origin the status of the occu-

8. The South African Colonisation Society, a daughter organisation of the BWEA, was formed in 1902 to co-operate with the British and South African Governments in sending women to South Africa.

pation fell as the nineteenth century progressed. As early as the 1830s and 1840s employers were complaining about the poor quality of servants and of the difficulty in keeping them. At this period there was however little flight from service because of the lack of any alternative employment.

Statistical changes became more apparent later in the century when a sharp decline in the numbers of domestic servants began to be observed in census returns. Many employers blamed the emigration societies for the loss, but the societies experienced similar difficulties in recruiting enough suitable servants to satisfy the demand from the colonies, especially as many of the emigrants fled the occupation soon after arrival, when they saw opportunities to better themselves.

The decline in numbers was attributed not only to uncongenial conditions in the homes of many employers, but also to the growing availability and greater freedom in factory or shop work. Employers found it hard to believe that their comfortable homes were rejected for, as they saw it, the lower pay and harder work of the factory floor, but the flight reflected a general demand for improved status among working women.

In 1914, when the movement was well established, Ethel Colquhoun (later Mrs Tawse-Jollie) of Rhodesia wrote of the flight of the domestic servant:

> into more congenial paths and probably the greater part into the underpaid and often overworked ranks of the inferior shop-girl. The girls of the shop-keeping class ascend a step into clerical work or teaching, and the professional man's daughter usually tries for the superior grades of the same two classes of employment. It is an endless procession away from the family doorstep, and on the other side of the door lie the despised domestic duties which no one wants to do. (Colquhoun 1914: 569)

The motives for emigration of established servants are difficult to determine directly because of the paucity of reminiscences left by the women themselves. It is clear from the records of the emigration societies that very few servants from upper-class households, such as housekeepers, cooks or ladies' maids, sought to emigrate unless accompanying their employers. There was little or no incentive for them to go to South Africa as there was no chance of bettering their conditions or status in a country which had neither the traditions nor resources to reproduce the servants' halls of English upper-class homes. Most South African homes were too small and accommodation at too great a premium to allow this. Servants of this class usually stayed with their employers or, unless they married while abroad, returned to

Britain (Knightley 1905: 137-41). Among the lower ranks of servants there was also little incentive to emigrate. Instead, servants sought to improve their lot by changing employers, by marrying or by moving into other occupations as they opened up.

The majority of servants who made their own way to South Africa were either those seeking to escape from some traumatic experience such as seduction or an illegitimate birth, or those who for some misdemeanour, had been dismissed without a character reference. Women without a 'character' had great difficulty in obtaining further employment at home and hoped to succeed in a country where they were not known. There was a great deal of dissatisfaction in South Africa with women who were found to have a 'past', as it was claimed that they often proved to be poor servants (Hely-Hutchinson 1902: 77).

Such women were obliged to emigrate privately as the emigration societies were very careful in their selection of domestic servants: and knew from experience that women with any kind of unsavoury reputation would not be accepted. They feared that any failure would cast opprobrium on those who had enabled them to emigrate. The societies were often obliged, therefore, to send out women who were untrained in domestic duties, either because they came from a different class or because they were from a different occupation.

Although there is little evidence of emigration actively being sought as a means of upward mobility by working-class women except, perhaps, through marriage, the situation changed rapidly after arrival in South Africa. The new immigrants were not slow to assess the local situation and to see in it chances of betterment. The first thing noted by many was that contracts signed in Britain before departure could not readily be enforced in South Africa unless re-signed before a magistrate.[9] It was also immediately apparent that the demand for white servants outstripped the supply, making it possible for many to renege on their contracts and sell their services to a higher bidder. Many soon found that by moving inland from the coast they could command higher wages for less work. This was especially the case after the discovery of minerals, from the 1870s onwards, when, before domestic service for black people became common, the boarding houses, hotels and bars which catered for the influx of male workers were desperate for domestic help.[10]

9. The women's emigration societies of the late nineteenth and early twentieth centuries insisted on contracts being re-signed in South Africa.
10. The history of this period is covered by Van Onselen 1982.

Many of those who went unprotected to the diamond fields at Kimberley or to the gold-mining city of Johannesburg joined the ranks of the large number of prostitutes who found rich pickings in a predominantly male society. Some made fortunes but others sank to the very depths of society (Bristow 1982: 28, 204–11, Doughty 1963: 123–5).

Most importantly, the newcomers quickly recognised the value of their white skins. For the first time in their lives there was a class of people who ranked lower than themselves, and they were not slow to take advantage of it. Employers soon learned that disaster could result from mixing the races in the kitchen. Many white servants gave themselves airs and refused to undertake tasks previously taken for granted, even, in some reported cases, insisting on a small black boy pushing the perambulator for them when taking the family baby for a walk. Black servants, too, reacted strongly. At this period they were mainly male and most still retained strong ties with the tribal background in which they had recognised status. They refused to take orders from a person who was a servant like themselves and a woman into the bargain. There are many accounts of the turmoil this competition caused.[11]

The final factor that made white servants difficult to manage and maintain was that, from the moment of arrival, they were much sought after as wives by English-speaking men, among whom the imbalance of the sexes was acute. Lucie Duff-Gordon, who went to the Cape in the 1860s in the vain attempt to cure her tuberculosis, reported in her *Letters from the Cape* (1927: 114, 149) that marriage claimed many immigrants soon after arrival: 'The demand for English girls as wives is wonderful here. The nasty, cross little ugly Scotch maid has had three offers already - in one fortnight....The consumptive young girl whom I packed off to the Cape and her sister are about to be married.'

The demand for wives continued and, in 1906, led to a proposal by Barnardo's Homes to send parties of girls to South Africa. The girls would be trained as domestics until old enough to marry. After much consultation, Stuart Barnardo, who had gone to South Africa as a mining engineer, reported to his father that he did not consider the plan feasible. The main problem was the cost of keeping the girls until old enough to enter service and, in any case, he had been told by Lord Milner that, great as was the need for white servants, people 'would

11. Such incidents were frequently reported in the house journal of the BWEA and SACS – the *Imperial Colonist*.

prefer the finished article to children who needed training and maintenance until fit for service'.

Stuart Barnardo also referred to the problem of competition with the black population.

> You must remember that no matter what the social rank or position of whites in the country where they originally come from, yet as soon as they set foot in South Africa, they find themselves one step higher in the social scale owing to the native population. This, in the great number of cases, causes them to look down on them and refuse to undertake work of the kind they have previously been quite willing to do, and indeed accustomed to. (Wagner 1982: 186)

Lady Hely-Hutchinson, the wife of the Cape Governor, summed up, both to Stuart Barnardo and in writing, her view of immigrant white servants. To Barnardo she claimed that there were too many young servants coming out who were not much use until they were eighteen years old and 'when they reach that age they refuse to be servants any longer but go to the restaurants, bars etc., or marry young men who ought to have wives of a higher class'.

In 1902, she had described the emigration of domestic servants from Britain as 'a lamentable failure', even those so carefully selected by the emigration societies. Commenting on the tendency of the immigrant servant immediately to reassess her social position, she said that such women consented 'as a favour to share, never to undertake the household duties'. She frowned particularly on those whose main motive was marriage, and, in general, she described the immigrant servant as 'flighty, self-asserting, purposeless, ignorant, lazy and inefficient'. She accused the emigration societies of sending out 'individuals who are obliged for health's sake or other prohibitory reasons', to leave their native land with the result that the colony received 'common-minded girls of doubtful morals' (Hely-Hutchinson 1902: 71–87). The BWEA responded that the only women who would merit this description were those who went out without their assistance but admitted that the very careful sifting they undertook meant that the demand could not be satisfied (Cecil 1902: 683–5).

It may be concluded from this brief analysis of the emigration of working class domestics that, for such women, there was little expectation of upward mobility before leaving Britain but that, once in South Africa, the brighter prospects for betterment were rapidly assessed and advantage taken of them. There is no way of accurately quantifying this upward movement and the truth of the assertion can only be assumed from the many comments over more than half a century on the histories of the women in South Africa.

The recruitment for the colonies of middle-class women as domestics was very different from that of the lower classes. In general it may be said that the 'distressed gentlewoman' had more reason to seek emigration as a solution to her problems but, despite many brave attempts, less ability to adapt to circumstances overseas.

In nineteenth-century Britain there was a strong belief in the existence of a surplus of over one million women, many deprived of a livelihood or marriage. It was pointed out, however, by a succession of contemporary demographic commentators, that, on census evidence, certain aspects of the belief were mythical. The returns from 1851 confirmed an overall surplus of women but this was among older women, mainly widows, and not among the younger cohorts available for marriage or, as the emigration societies believed, for emigration.[12] Belief in the surplus and its consequences persisted for over seventy years, however, despite repeated denials. It was very selective, placing both the surplus and its results in the ranks of middle-class women among whom evidence of distress was all too apparent.

It is clear that the real problems for middle-class women were not primarily demographic, except perhaps in old age, but stemmed from the results of rapid social change. The first of these was the stripping of many useful roles from wives and daughters as they became symbols of the success of the new middle classes, often expressed in terms of conspicuous consumption. Added to this was the enhancement of the role of marriage as a means of increasing capital through judicious alliances.

The results of these changes were that girls were educated as adornments of wealth, in the 'accomplishments' believed to make them attractive as marriage partners. Although there is great danger in overgeneralising the effects of these changes on middle-class women, most of whom were as robust as at any other period, the effects on many were disastrous.

In the first place, such women were ill-prepared for coping with disaster, should it strike, in the form of the bankruptcy or the death of the father or other male relative on whom they were dependent. Secondly, the frivolity and ostentation in which so many had been encouraged led to a flight from matrimony among middle-class men (Greg 1862: 447-8) who could not contemplate the cost of maintaining an extravagant wife and the large family that was both customary and inevitable before

12. Examples of this debate may be found in Sala 1854 and Colquhoun 1914.

the advent of respectable contraception. It may be that some of the men in flight from matrimony found it expedient to serve abroad, but there is surprisingly little evidence that the drain of men to the colonies actually caused the plight of 'distressed gentlewomen'. Rather, the problems sprang from inadequate education and the limited opportunities for employment for those who needed to support themselves.

The evidence of distress was real enough. The emigration movement for middle-class women began in the 1860s as a result of the economic plight of the many women who presented themselves at the doors of an early feminist group in London, the 'Ladies of Langham Place', sometimes called the 'Ladies' Circle'. In an attempt to cope with the demand, Emily Faithfull founded the Victoria Printing Press and Maria Rye the Law Copying Society, both for the employment of women only. In addition, Bessie Rayner Parkes established the Society for Promoting the Employment of Women (Kamm 1966: 89–105).

When these enterprises were seen to be no more than scratching the surface of the need, the group formed the Female Middle Class Emigration Society (FMCES), to enable women, especially those with a reasonable level of education and, perhaps, some teaching skills, to emigrate as governesses. Important as this society was, it only succeeded in sending a few hundred women abroad as it was always short of funds and there was little demand from the colonies for such skills until later in the century (Hammerton 1979: 124). There was, however, a continuing demand for domestic help and the FMCES tried to ensure that all their protégées had some domestic skills. Despite this, most of the women who applied to the society were, as a result of their upbringing, helpless in these areas.

The FMCES faltered on until the mid-1880s and was then absorbed into a more vigorous organisation with wider objectives. The British Women's Emigration Association, founded in 1884, was as strongly committed to improving the lot of the distressed gentlewoman as its predecessor, but was more realistic about the needs of the colonies. It realised that no woman could succeed abroad if she had nothing to offer but her need. Two strategies were adopted: the first was to eliminate those who had none of the required educational or domestic skills by stringent selection procedures. This improved the success rate of emigrants but ensured that the numbers sent overseas remained small. The second course was to undertake the training of otherwise suitable middle class candidates in the domestic skills appropriate to colonial life - housework, cookery, laundry, horticulture and small animal husbandry. A Colonial Training Home was opened at Leaton,

Staffordshire in 1890 (and later transferred to Stoke Prior in Worcestershire), which trained many hundreds of women of whom a high proportion went to South Africa. The college survived until the First World War when lack of funds and changes in needs forced its closure (Monk 1963: 112, 117).

Why did middle-class women offer themselves for emigration? After 1860, in the early years of organised emigration for such women, the main motive appears to have been the fear of downward mobility. Letters to the FMCES from the governesses show how sensitive most were concerning their roles as ladies.[13] The ideology of the lady was at its strongest and few would dare to go against the mores of their class. The woman who did not find a marriage partner was a failure and those who were forced to demean themselves by accepting paid employment were social outcasts. Many, such as the sisters portrayed in George Gissing's *The Odd Women* (1893), accepted this and suffered. The attraction for those who accepted emigration as a solution was that, in a country where they were unknown and away from the censure of family and acquaintances, they could undertake work that would otherwise be closed to them because of the loss of status involved.

As the century advanced and the position of women improved, other motives crept in. The 'New Woman' had a more robust attitude to life and adventure, and the professional woman sought more interesting work and faster promotion than was possible in the overcrowded professions of nursing and teaching at home. But throughout the period, there were women with little education and few skills who hoped to fit into colonial households as companions, mother's helps (with or without some teaching) or lady helps.

The lady help, a woman of middle- or lower-middle-class origin who was prepared to offer her services in a domestic capacity, was a particular feature of emigration to South Africa, as she seemed to fit the needs of expatriate British families there better than in other territories. The main reasons for this were the shortage of white domestic servants coupled with the lack of accommodation in most colonial homes. It was felt to be more congenial to be served at close quarters by a woman of some education and culture than by the average immigrant servant.[14]

The shortage of accommodation was, however, a major factor in limiting the employment of white servants, and a middle-class domes-

13. Letterbooks 1 and 2 of the Female Middle Class Emigration Society are housed in the Fawcett Library, City of London Polytechnic.
14. Examples are to be found in the *Imperial Colonist*.

tic help had the additional disadvantage of needing and expecting superior housing than the traditional servant. She was also more expensive to keep - a great deal more than the black servants who were becoming available.[15]

There were opportunities for the adventurous to use their domestic skills other than for service in homes. Some women made a good living as boarding house keepers, as the proprietors of nursing homes for the tubercular women who flocked to the country in search of a cure and in other ventures where such skills could be combined with enterprise. The major obstacle to these was lack of capital, for few with any means sought emigration in the first place. Sometimes success was achieved by a few women pooling their meagre resources and investing jointly in an enterprise (Lowth 1903).

Marriage claimed many women, although what change in social status this achieved for middle-class women is difficult to determine. For most working-class servants, marriage provided an upward step, but there are many harrowing tales of middle-class women who bitterly regretted the outcome of an over-hasty marriage.

To many in Britain, the emigration of middle-class women with some domestic training was the ideal solution both for the problem of the 'surplus' in Britain and as a means of supplying the need for domestic help in South Africa. A. M. Brice wrote that 'a woman of gentle nurture would have no difficulty in finding in the colonies a society of men and women of similar antecedents, even though their work might appear to be that of a lower scale' (Brice 1901: 605).

There were many reports of successes, such as that of a girl about whom a correspondent wrote in 1905: 'a delightful girl, not a bit afraid of hard work...who had been accustomed to every luxury, up to yachting etc. at home but, evidently, is finding a life of helpfulness...a preferable one' (*Imperial Colonist* March 1905: 3). The reason for the girl undertaking such a role was not stated. Other employers were not so enthusiastic. Lady Hely-Hutchinson was no more pleased with this type of domestic help than with the traditional servant. The lady help, she wrote, 'is anxious that it shall be understood that she is a lady...She is really too delicate to undertake any but the very lightest duties and makes it plain that but for circumstances over which she has no control, she would not be found in what she considers such a benighted, outlandish and God-forsaken place' (Hely-Hutchinson 1902: 78).

15. The advantages and disadvantages of employing servants of different race and type were discussed in the report of the Commission on Assaults on Women (Government of the Union of South Africa) - UG39 1913.

The BWEA's daughter organisation, the South African Colonisation Society, founded after the Boer War, was obliged to admit that many who emigrated as lady helps were 'unemployed because unemployable, decayed gentlewomen...who have gone out to South Africa with the idea that the inefficient will prosper better than here'. The society made it clear that it only sent out adequately trained women to definite postings. They felt sure that 'in times of domestic stress, they are far more helpful as less likely to stand on their dignity than a servant would be' (*Imperial Colonist*, August 1904: 86 and May 1905: 57).

The period during which middle-class women emigrated as domestic help was a brief one – only, in reality, the years between 1890 and 1914. The First World War was a turning point for women as it provided opportunities for many to escape from proscribed roles into wider occupations and responsibilities. Improved conditions after the war made it unnecessary for women to seek new lives overseas, although professional women continued to seek advancement and a widening of their horizons by offering their skills in territories which had not yet trained enough of their own for the purpose.

Because of the problem of quantifying evidence that is largely anecdotal, it is difficult to form firm conclusions on the motives for the emigration of women of the lower- and middle-classes as domestic servants. However, the mass of such evidence has certain inferences. For the working-class domestic servant, emigration was the result of poverty and distress in the home country. There is little evidence that colonial life in general or South Africa in particular, provided a strong pull, except as an opportunity for escape. However, when such women arrived in South Africa they were quick to assess and take advantage of the situation and many were able to improve their lot or even their social status.

For the middle-class women who took the unusual step of emigrating as domestic servants, the situation was almost reversed. Although the causes of their distress lay in the home country, they were better able to assess the possible advantages of life overseas and to seek help to attain it. Many succeeded, but some failed when they proved unable to adapt to new circumstances or when South African homes were unable to accommodate them.

Marriage could provide a means of social mobility for women emigrants, but, whereas for the working-class servant it promised upward mobility in most cases, the outcome for the middle-class immigrant was more problematical.

References

Brice, A.M., 1901 'Emigration for Gentlewomen', *Nineteenth Century*, vol.49, April
Bristow, E.J., 1982 *Prostitution and Prejudice: The Jewish Fight Against White Slavery, 1870–1939*, London: Clarendon Press
Cecil, Lady A., 1902 'The Needs of South Africa: Female Emigration', *Nineteenth Century*, vol.51, April
Colquhoun, E., 1914 'The Superfluous Women', *Nineteenth Century*, vol.75, March
Commission on Assaults on Women, Report – UG39 (Union of South Africa) 1913
Davenport, T.R.H., 1977 *South Africa: A Modern History*, London: Macmillan
Delamont, S. and Duffin, L. (eds), 1978 *The Nineteenth Century Woman: Her Cultural and Physical World*, London: Croom Helm
Doughty, O., 1963, *Early Diamond Days in South Africa*, London: Longman
Duff-Gordon, Lady L., 1927 *Letters from the Cape*, Oxford: Oxford University Press
Emigration in the Victorian Age: Debates on the Issues from 19th Century Critical Journals, 1973: Gregg International Publishers
Erickson, C., 1972, *Invisible Immigrants, The Adaptation of English and Scottish Immigrants to 19th Century America*, London: Leicester University Press
Gissing, G., 1980 *The Odd Women* (1990 edn), London: Virago
Greg, W.R., 1862 'Why are Women Redundant?', *National Review*, vol.15, no.28, April
Hammerton, A.J., 1979 *Emigrant Gentlewomen: Genteel Poverty and Female Emigration 1830–1914*, London: Croom Helm
Hattersley, A.F., 1965 *The Convict Crisis and the Growth of Unity: Resistance to Transportation to South Africa, 1848–1853*, Pietermaritzburg: University of Natal Press
Hely-Hutchinson, Lady, 1902 'Female Emigration to South Africa', *Nineteenth Century*, vol.51, January
Herbert, S., 1851 *Fund for the Promotion of Female Emigration*, 1st Report, London
Hitchins, F.H., 1931 *The Colonial Land and Emigration Commission 1840–1878*, New York: University of Pennsylvania Press
Imperial Colonist (House Journal of the BWEA and SACS)
Kamm, J., 1966 *Rapiers and Battleaxes, The Women's Movement and its Aftermath*, London: Allen and Unwin
Knightley of Fawsley, Lady, 1905 'The Terms and Conditions of Domestic Service in England and South Africa', *Imperial Colonist*, no. 48, December
Lowth, A., 1903 *Women Workers in South Africa – Some Hints on Lucrative Employment*, London: Kegan Paul
Martineau, H., 1859 'Female Industry', *Edinburgh Review*, vol.109, no.222, April
Monk, V., 1963 *New Horizons: A Hundred Years of Women's Migration*, London: HMSO
Noble, J. (ed.), 1891 *The Voyage to South Africa and Sojourn There*, London
Patterson, C.B., 1953 *Angela Burdett-Coutts and the Victorians*, London: John Murray
Peterson, M.J., 1972 'The Victorian Governess: Status Incongruence in the Family and Society', in M. Vicinus *Suffer and be Still: Women in the Victorian Age*, New York: Indiana University Press
Plant, G.F., 1950 *A Survey of Voluntary Effort in Women's Empire Migration*, London: SOSBW
Ross, A., 1882 'Emigration for Women', *Macmillan's Magazine*, vol.45, February
Sala, G., 1854 'The 1851 Census', *Household Words*, vol.10, no.239, October
Showalter, E., 1980 'Victorian Women and Insanity', *Victorian Studies*, vol.23, no.2, Winter
Stearns, P.N., 1972 'Working Class Women In Britain 1880–1914', in M. Vicinus *Suffer and be Still: Women in the Victorian Age*, New York: Indiana University Press
Van Onselen, C., 1982 *Studies in the Social and Economic History of the Witwatersrand 1886–1914*, London: Longman

Vicinus, M., 1972 *Suffer and Be Still: Women in the Victorian Age*, New York: Indiana University Press

Wagner, G.M.M., 1982 *Children of the Empire: The Emigration of Orphan and Pauper Children*, London: Weidenfeld and Nicolson

10

Women Alone: Migrants from Transkei Employed in Rural Natal

Gina Buijs

This chapter is based on research which I carried out in Pondoland, southern Natal, and in Durban in 1984 and 1985, and in which I was interested in looking at women migrants from Transkei who were working in Natal.[1] The research was concerned with two selected groups of women: one was composed of agricultural workers in the sugar plantations of Natal and the other with women who managed to circumvent the draconian influx control regulations of the time and obtain both work and settled accommodation in the city. This chapter will focus on the former group.

Until the 1980s women in the Transkei (perhaps the most well-known of the bantustans in South Africa, situated on the eastern coast between the Cape and Natal provinces) were referred to, if they were mentioned at all by sociologists or anthropologists, as 'women left behind', (Mayer 1961, 1980). Migrancy was considered a predominantly male phenomenon in the rural areas of Transkei and Ciskei. However, recent statistics have shown that thousands of women leave Transkei each year to work elsewhere in South Africa. In this chapter I will be looking at the motives of some of these women in leaving their rural homes; their reasons for choosing a particular form of employment; the role played by kin and friends in initially finding work; the peripheral presence of men in their lives and a consequent reliance on other women, often fellow workers, for support and friendship.

Bozzoli (1983: 146) notes that in considering the role of black women in South Africa, two forms of struggle need to be identified. These are (1) the struggle within the domestic system and (2) the struggle between the domestic sphere and the capitalist one. She writes: 'it is not only that "domestic struggles" are the key to unravel-

1. The research on which this chapter is based was funded by a grant from the New Staff Research Fund of the University of Natal.

179

ling the evolving subordination of women. It is also that they provide a crucial dimension to our understanding of a whole variety of other factors, ranging from the composition of the labour force to the form of the state.' Bozzoli considers that her use of the term 'domestic struggle' concerns the extent to which the domestic sphere is the site of labour, income and property relations.

Wendy Izzard, writing on female migrants in Botswana (1985: 259), notes that students of migration have been faced with the challenge of articulating the particular and the general, of integrating the factors relevant at the level of individual migrants with the broad social, economic and political structures of the regions in which the migrant is involved. She says that there have been two major approaches to studying migration: first in terms of the migrant as a unit of analysis and secondly in terms of absenteeism. She rejects the former as tending to consider migrants apart from the wider familial group to which they belong and prefers to consider migration within a familial context and as a process rather than an event, one which has emphasised the contribution of mobility to the developmental cycle of the household. The term 'household' is itself fraught with complication and Izzard prefers to use the term 'household strategy' as developed by Gulbrandsen (1977), according to whom 'household' is implied in the wider sense of a familial group which may comprise several residentially separate sub-units.

Recent research on women migrants has emanated mainly from Botswana (Izzard 1985, Peters 1983) and Lesotho (Kimble 1982), and although there is a considerable body of literature dealing with migration in South Africa, there is little mention of women as migrants, as opposed to studies dealing specifically with town or city dwelling women who, at one time, may have migrated (cf. Jacky Cock on domestic servants: Cock 1980). However, figures produced for the Institute for Management and Development Studies at the University of Transkei in 1984 showed a total of 50,476 external female migrants compared to 349,026 external male migrants; the figure for women is about 14.5 per cent of that for men. The report from which these figures have been drawn notes that most of these women were employed in domestic service and were working close to the Transkei border, in Natal or East London. Other occupations with a large proportion of female migrants included nursing and manual labour. The report notes that since the majority of these migrants are unmarried, remitting at least a portion of their wages to their rural homes in Transkei, and working in domestic service, 'this trend contradicts the traditional idea of most female migrants migrating to follow husbands – there is little doubt that female migrants play a significant part in the migrant labour system, albeit illegally' (1984: 10).

This last phrase reflects the statistic that official (legal) work contracts were made out for 352,000 migrants from Transkei in 1982, of whom an estimated 95 per cent were male and 5 per cent female. The stumbling block for both men and women in obtaining legal employment outside Transkei since 1976 has been that before they leave the territory they are obliged to obtain a travel document, and in order to work they must obtain special permits specifying the type of employment offered to them and the name of the employer. These are known as 'attestation certificates' and cost R2 per annum. I was able to consult the records of the magistrate's office in the town of Lusikisiki in Pondoland, the largest tribal area of Transkei, for January 1984, which showed that in that month 1,109 men and 2 women signed contracts which allowed them to work outside Transkei. In February that year 947 men and 1 woman signed contracts. The magistrate explained to me that these women were nurses, professional workers whose services were in demand. He commented that it was well known that many women did leave the area to work in South Africa without having either travel documents or attestation certificates. These women left on buses which followed routes where there was no border post. The attitude of the magistrate appeared to be 'how can we stop them?' The fact that so few women leave Transkei legally to seek work may have contributed to the impression that few women do, in fact, migrate.

The women I interviewed were, with two exceptions, living in an area of Kwa Zulu on the Natal South Coast, and the majority were, or had been, employed by a large local sugar company as casual agricultural labourers to do weeding and cane planting in the fields. My sample was a small one (n = 22) and makes no claim to be statistically significant and since I was conducting the research personally and had neither the time nor the means to take a random sample the results can only be suggestive.

The history of the employment of Pondo men on the sugar estates of Natal goes back to the beginning of the twentieth century. It was in this period that the remaining Indian indentured labourers completed their terms of indenture and Africans were employed to fill their places. Beinart (1982: 143), writing about the pre-war period, records that:

the major change in patterns of migrancy was the shift by substantial numbers of workers especially from the coastal districts of Eastern Pondoland
and Port St. Johns to the sugar fields of Natal...by 1936, out of a total of
30,000 migrants from Pondoland districts, some 19,000 (60-65%) still
worked in the Rand mines and perhaps 5,000 to 7,000 (around 20%) on the
Natal sugar estates.

Beinart comments that, while wages on the sugar estates were lower
than in the mines, contracts were shorter, usually for six months, and
thus workers could spend longer periods at home, even if they migrated yearly. The estates were also more accessible than the reef mines,
most workers coming from the coastal districts of Lusikisiki, Bizana,
Port St. Johns and Flagstaff. Agricultural recruitment was apparently
subject to less stringent controls than mining recruitment. There were
men who had been rejected by the mines on health grounds who were
employed by the estates. There were also reports that some recruiters
rounded up groups of under age youths on trucks and carried them
back to Natal without passes or contracts. Conditions for workers on
the estates at this time were known to be poor. 'Members of the
Pondoland General Council at the Council session in June 1930 spoke
very strongly of the unsatisfactory state of affairs prevailing' wrote
Monica Hunter (1979: 109). Beinart comments that 'there are sugges-
tions in the evidence that it was particularly men from poorer families,
more heavily indebted to traders, with more regular need for male
labour at home, with fewer options on the labour market, who migrated to Natal' (1982: 146).

While neither Beinart nor Monica Hunter mention women migrants
from Pondoland in this pre-war period, and I have been unable to ascertain with any certainty when women first began to arrive to work in
the cane fields in Natal, I was able to interview one woman who said
that it had been twenty years since she was forced to migrate to earn
cash. Sarah G. lives at Grosvenor on the Pondoland coast. She said
that she left her home to go and work on the estate of a white sugar
farmer near Umzinto in southern Natal to earn cash because her father
was in debt and she was his eldest child. Agricultural work was the
only type of wage labour available to Sarah as she had no education.
She worked on the white farm for four years for R1.20 a day. While
Sarah said she found the work in the cane fields hard, she claimed that
she could not have found alternative means of making money, by, for
instance, beer brewing or hawking. Sarah has four children from a liaison with a Zulu man whom she met while working in Natal. She has
not been back to Natal since her initial period of work there and she

said that now her four children are working (although two do not support her) she is in the process of building her own house near to that of
her father. Her father, a local headman, earns a small income caretak-
ing some cottages at Grosvenor. For Sarah, migration was a temporary
measure to settle her father's debt; it was not, as for most of the other
women interviewed, a matter of survival.

Before looking at why women are nowadays compelled to leave
Transkei, it is necessary to say something about the work that they do
in the cane fields and the conditions under which they work.
Agricultural work in the cane fields consists of two main types. First,
there is cane cutting which is done by hand using sharp knives. In
South Africa this is considered a particularly strenuous occupation and
is exclusively male. The cane cutters are almost all Pondo men.
Secondly, there is cane weeding and planting. These tasks are traditionally done by women, although a man may apply for a position as a
weeder while waiting to be taken on as a cane cutter. Weeders may be
Zulu or Pondo women, although, in conformity with then current influx
control regulations, company officials I spoke to maintained that Pondo
women were no longer employed and that all the women workers were
Zulu. Management maintained that such Pondo women as were in the
fields were not employees but were there simply to assist their menfolk
(husbands or boyfriends) to stack the cane in bundles, and therefore to
allow the men to complete their daily tasks more speedily and to earn
more money. The cane cutters have to cut a certain amount of cane daily and are paid a bonus for subsequent bundles cut.

It was soon evident to me, however, that a large number of Pondo
women were employed on the estate. I was allowed access to the register at the estate labour office on which casual or *togt* workers names
were recorded.[2] While the register gives no indication of the sex of the
worker as such but does record the district of origin, it appeared from
a cursory inspection that approximately half of the casual workers
came from Pondoland and very few of these, judging by the names,
were men. A company official stated that, in January 1984, there were
834 casual or *togt* workers employed on the whole estate (which I
shall call Sebenzi), and all of these were women. Before 1976, when

2. *Togt* is a word meaning day worker or day labourer which has come into use in
South Africa from Dutch *togt*: of or pertaining to casual or day labour, from Dutch *togt*,
a march or tour (see J. Branford *A Dictionary of South African English*, Oxford: Oxford
University Press, 1980, p.301). Influx control regulations did not apply to *togt* workers
since they did not sign contracts and were not regarded as employees in the same sense
as those who did sign contracts with employers.

restrictions were placed on the movement of all people in and out of Transkei, women from Pondoland were recruited by white run agencies and signed contracts to come and work on the estates in the same manner as male cane cutters.

One such woman was Mayishe M., aged approximately forty, from Ngqeleni district in Transkei. Mayishe said she had left her husband sixteen years before when he 'went mad', and took her two children away from her husband's home with her. She first found employment in a local shop in the district but was only paid R3 per month and given some food. Mayishe said this amount was not enough to feed her children and herself. Then she heard from local women about the opportunities for *togt* labour in the cane fields at Sebenzi. These particular women had already completed contracts at Sebenzi and had been recruited by a white run agency in Transkei. When Mayishe accepted her first contract sixteen years before I spoke to her she was paid two shillings and sixpence per day, working, she claimed, from 6.00 a.m. to 4.00 p.m., weeding the cane fields. In practice today no set hours are prescribed and the women work from sunrise until they have completed the piece of work or task set for the day. This appeared, from my observation, to be between 2.00 p.m. and 3.30 p.m. When Mayishe first began to work at Sebenzi the women *togt* labourers were housed in compounds specially set aside for them on various estate sections. They also received food in the form of rations and medical attention in addition to their wages, as did the male cane cutters.

The so-called 'independence' conferred on Transkei in 1976 meant that women like Mayishe could no longer legally migrate to work and conditions on the estates became much harsher for those who were willing to be employed as *togt* or casual labourers. No provision is made for food or housing for the women labourers by the company, they receive only sorghum beer during the day's work. Medical attention is confined to those injured on duty. In 1984 a day's wage for weeding was R2.60.[3]

Mayishe M., having been forced to leave the company compound at Sebenzi by the new company regulations, now rents a small plot of land for R6 per month from a black cane farmer, in a piece of KwaZulu adjacent to the cane fields at Sebenzi. On this scrap of land she has built a shack, which she shares with her Pondo boyfriend. He is a cane cutter, formerly employed by the company, but who was retrenched and now works for a black cane farmer. Mayishe said that, despite the new regulations, which have made her lot harder, she was

3. In 1984 one rand was approximately equivalent to 30 British pence.

pleased to be able to have paid work and to be independent. She said she has no intention of stopping work. She sends money back to Transkei to pay for her children's school fees and she also has a 'small patch of land' at her mother's brother's homestead, where, she said, she hopes eventually to build a house. Her eldest son, now twenty-one, left school at the end of 1983 having completed primary grades, and has gone to Johannesburg to look for work in the mines. Mayishe said that she had not heard from him since his departure, and she indicated that while she hoped he would help her to build a home in Transkei there was no way she could be sure of this. She implied that boyfriends were no more to be depended on than sons, because when asked if she would like to marry her current boyfriend she said 'what for?' and made it clear that she wanted to keep her independence. Henrietta Moore (1988: 95) writes: 'gender relations and in particular, conflict between men and women are central to any understanding of why women migrate, and of how and why women experience changing social and economic pressures differently from men.'

The feelings of Mayishe about the unreliability of men in general, and the necessity for women to look after themselves, were echoed in other interviews. Like Mayishe, Nomacana D., who was born near Flagstaff and was thirty-three years old at the time of the interview, is illiterate. The eldest of eight children, she said her family was too poor to be able to educate her, but three of her sisters attended primary school. Nomacana said she decided to migrate to the cane fields after about two years of marriage (when she was about fifteen) as the result of frequent quarrels with her husband. She has one son from the marriage, who lives with her husband in Transkei, and whom she sees when she visits her natal home. She admitted that her last visit home took place two years previously, but said she intended going again in July 1984 'for a small rest'. Nomacana said she would stay at her natal home for about a month but could not afford to stay longer 'as there is no money there'. While such casual work as the women do is supposed to be seasonal, in fact there is a steady demand throughout the year for weeding, and the women can expect to be employed for approximately nine months out of every twelve.

Nomacana's father had died, but her mother was still alive and living in Transkei. Nomacana said she sends her R30 every second month. Like Mayishe, Nomacana lives in a shack in the nearby area of KwaZulu with her boyfriend. She said that this man does support her, but she was obviously uneasy about depending on this support: she said that while she does not like weeding because she thinks the work is 'too hard' she has to continue for she has no other secure source of income. Nomacana stressed that she was not interested in marrying her boyfriend, (even if she had been able to, which she was not as the bridewealth or *lobola* which her husband had given to her family at marriage had not been repaid). Nomacana said she was 'tired of my husband and tired of marriage'.

Stichter notes that generally in Africa 'unhappy marriages are an important cause of migration and often this involves escaping polygamy' (1985: 151). Some married women reported that they were forced to migrate when their husbands threw them out of the marital home. Gumuza M. from Lusikisiki said: 'that's why I'm here'. Her husband had two wives, of whom Gumuza was the senior. However, the junior wife was younger and more favoured, so Gumuza left. She said her husband refused to support her: 'he wouldn't give me anything. I came here to get some money. I had no clothes at home, nothing.' Out of her earnings of approximately R60 per month, Gumuza sends R40 home to support her aged mother and her daughter who is at school; with the rest, she says 'I must buy something to eat.' Gumuza was one of the women interviewed who lived in an old barracks, formerly inhabited by Indian workers, in a remote part of Sebenzi. The women were allowed to stay there rent free by a sympathetic white section manager who had taken pity on them.

The increasing impoverishment of the bantustans has meant that women like Gumuza have lost the security provided by former kin networks and relationships. In 1936 Monica Hunter described a class of Pondo women 'who dislike the labour and restrictions of a wife, refuse to stay at any *umzi* [homestead]...and run home to live as *amadikazi*' (1979: 207). She describes an *idikazi* as 'any woman living temporarily or permanently with her own people, who has been or who is married, or has had a child. A widow who has returned to her home, a woman who has permanently left her husband and a girl who has never married but had children at home, all are *amadikazi*.' She comments that the 'class of *amadikazi* in Pondoland is very large and practically every man who is married has his special friend among them. While some are "any man's woman", there are also respectable middle-aged women who have been forced to leave their *umzi* because they were "smelt out" [accused of witchcraft], or, most frequently, because *udaliwe yindoda* [my husband tired of me]' (1979: 207). There would thus seem to be a long tradition in Pondoland (not replicated, apparently, in other areas of Transkei (C.W. Manona, personal communication)) of women refusing to put up with unsatisfactory relation-

ships with men and returning to their natal homes. However, while it
appears that in the past a woman's lineage kin were usually able and
willing to accept her back and that such households could support extra members, this no longer appears to be the case today, as the situation of Nogubona S. makes clear.

Nogubona comes from a 'red' (traditional) family in the Bizana district of Pondoland. She said that her husband was from a very poor
family and that both his parents had already died when she had married him about fifteen years previously. She had four children, the eldest eleven years old. For the last three years her husband, who
worked as a cane cutter in Natal, had failed to visit her or to send any
money to support her or her children. She heard from local women at
Bizana that he was living with a woman in Durban. Because her husband's parents, to whom she would traditionally have first turned for
help, had died, Nogubona said she took her children to her own home
and then came to Sebenzi to look for work. Unfortunately, two years
before I spoke to her Nogubona's father told her he could not afford to
support her children any longer. The children had neither clothes nor
food. Nogubona said her father felt that she and her children were not
his responsibility; he was old and could not cope any longer.
Nogubona's father was a polygynist; Nogubona and her sister were the
children of the junior wife, while the senior wife had three sons. It is
noteworthy that no offers of help were forthcoming from any of these
kin and in general no respondent mentioned assistance from brothers
and very few from sons, although mother's brothers and father's
brothers did provide help on occasions.

Nogubona's story supports Henrietta Moore's point that 'changes in
kinship systems and in the organisation of agricultural production have
meant that many poorer women have lost the security provided by former kin networks and relationships' (1988: 63). While subsistence
agriculture in Transkei could support a rural population adequately, it
was possible for women to be accepted back into their natal patrilin-
eages if their marriages broke down. Karen Sacks (1979) makes an
important observation about the status of women in what she calls
'non-class' societies which is based partly on the previously
favourable position of *amadikazi*.

Sacks identifies two modes of production in non-class societies: a
communal mode and a kin corporate mode. In the second type kin
groups collectively control the means of production, and women's status varies according to whether they are defined primarily as sisters, in
which case they are considered to be members of the controlling kin

group, or wives, whose rights are derived through marriage into a controlling kin group rather than their relationship to their own (natal) kin group. The point of Sacks' argument is that where women are able to exercise their rights as sisters their status is improved in comparison to those societies where the rights are more narrowly defined as those of wife. Sacks writes:

> I do not think I do much violence to the data by interpreting sister in situations of corporate patrilineages to mean one who is an owner, a decision maker among others of the corporation, and a person who controls her own sexuality. By contrast a wife is a subordinate in much the same way Engels asserted for the family based on private property. (Sacks 1979: 110, quoted in Moore 1988: 34)

Sometimes a husband's lineage kin may try to care for a widow and her children but they are not always able to do this. Emma S.'s husband died three years before the interview, leaving her with three children. At first her husband's brothers had looked after the children, but by 1984 these kin had also died and Emma decided to come to Sebenzi to work 'because there was no money coming in'. The husband of Emma's newly married daughter had paid three cattle as part *lobola,* but these had died in the drought prevailing in Transkei. In this case (and some others) it was the *mother* who was away working while the daughter was able to remain at home. Influx control regulations in South Africa have meant that even elderly women are unable to retire to their homes and depend on the support of their daughters as the daughters are not legally allowed to obtain employment outside the bantustan. The situation for women migrants in South Africa is thus to an extent different than elsewhere (where Izzard, for instance, reports that 'several authors have noted that the phenomenon of return in old age is just as marked for women as for men' (Izzard 1985: 278)).

The death of senior agnatic or affinal kin quite clearly restricted the number of people to whom most of my respondents could turn for help. A large number of children also presented a problem, since kin could only be expected to care for one or two. Masingelele M. is also a widow. Aged about thirty-five, her parents and siblings had all died some time ago and her husband had died five years previously of a chest ailment, leaving her with six children. Masingelele said she was forced to look for work to keep her children alive, and friends at home in Port St. Johns had told her about the plantation at Sebenzi. Masingelele had four of her children living with her at Sebenzi and two living at her husband's home. Half her earnings are sent back to Transkei each month to support her children there, and a daughter living with her at Sebenzi earns R20 per month as a shop assistant in a small town nearby.

Apart from the women who had been, or were still, married, approximately half the women interviewed had never married, but had mostly had children. Izzard (1985) comments that the likelihood of a woman marrying in southern Africa today must be considered in the light of the declining marriage rate. She points out that Schapera and Roberts have noted the significant growth in the proportion of Tswana women who remained unmarried in one ward in Mochudi village, from 23 per cent in 1934 to 55 per cent in 1973. She suggests that this proportion can be correlated with a rise in the proportion of unmarried mothers, and notes that Molenaar found in 1978 that 60 per cent of all children in one ward in Kanye village were born to unmarried mothers, compared to the 8 per cent found by Schapera in 1938 (1985: 267, 268). Kaufman (in Lesthaeghe 1989) shows that these statistics are not unusual for South Africa where the rate of adult women remaining unmarried (50 per cent in some areas) appears to be considerably higher than for the rest of the continent.

Many women said that it was in order to support their children that they had come to work at Sebenzi as casual labourers. Edna Bay comments 'African women stressed that while motherhood is all important, work in the sense of income generating activity is very much an essential and expected part of life – African women do not choose to work or to have children, they work *because* they have children' (1982: 5). Lombulelo Z. has two young children. Her boyfriend, the father of the children, does not want to marry her but he does contribute R30 each month towards the support of the children. Lombulelo used to live with her children at her father's homestead in Transkei, assisting in his fields, until the year before we spoke, when her mother died. Then, she said, her father 'got another woman', and began to treat his children badly, beating them so that she was forced to come to Natal and look for work. Although she said that she found weeding the cane fields hard, and quite different from working in her father's fields at home, she said that she does not intend to stop as she does not see any other way of getting an income. She has one younger brother employed in the mines, and two younger ones who live at home who 'would like to work but they can't get identity documents', she said, meaning that they are unable to leave Transkei without identification. It appears likely in Lombulelo's case that her father's household was simply unable to sustain so many adults and children, and that she and her children were the immediate casualties.

Schoolgirl pregnancies, in which the father of the child refused to support or even acknowledge paternity, were another common cause of women being forced to seek paid employment away from Transkei. Nomvuyo M. went to school to Standard Four (primary education ends at Standard Five), but was forced to leave school when she found that she was pregnant. Her boyfriend denied responsibility, he 'threw me away', as she put it, refused to pay the traditional damages to her family, and left the district. Nomvuyo's child is now nine months old. When her father died in 1972 Nomvuyo stayed on at her natal homestead under the guardianship of her elder brother who inherited the land and cattle, but, Nomvuyo said, 'my brother has his own children, he didn't want to support a baby'. Nomvuyo came to Sebenzi with her baby, whom she leaves in the care of a child minder while she works. She pays this woman R12 a month and said: 'I get less money now but I'm forced to pay her this'.

In extreme cases, some women were left with no close kin at all. Thandela S., aged nineteen, said that she was first forced to look for work as a casual labourer when her father, a cane cutter, stopped sending money to her mother and herself in Transkei. She had no siblings. 'There was no money at home and we were starving,' she said. Four years previously her father had died and her mother had also died recently, whereupon her father's fields were allocated to someone else by the local headman. Thandela's only link with kin is that she has been told that she can stay at the home of a mother's brother if she does visit Transkei. Thandela lives alone in a squatter's shack. She did have a boyfriend, but he has returned to his home in Transkei which is in a different district to her own. Thandela said she did send money to her mother when she was alive, but does not remit now as she has no dependents.

It appears, then, that for a majority of these women, migration was necessary to stay alive. In most cases they had dependent children, and were either widowed, unmarried or had been deserted by their husbands. In some cases they were the only support of elderly mothers and in one case of a grandmother. Most of the women found their way to Sebenzi because they had friends or kin in their home areas of Transkei who had worked or were currently employed on the estate. In most cases without formal education, they felt, no doubt correctly, that they would be unable to obtain paid employment elsewhere. Several did say that they would have preferred to take on domestic work, but influx control regulations prevented them from being registered as domestic servants at the local labour offices.

While men sometimes played a role in the women's search for work by providing them with the address of an estate, few men appeared able or willing to provide any substantial assistance to their female kin or to their dependants. In most cases the women maintained that male kin who would formerly have been expected to care for them had died, absconded, or were unable to obtain jobs themselves. In other instances women had been physically beaten or abused by husbands or fathers.

A few women I interviewed at Sebenzi had managed to escape from manual labour, and employment in the informal sector is one alternative which women sometimes prefer to *togt* labour. Busiswe N. is twenty-four and comes from Port St. Johns. Her father, who has died, had two wives, and Busiswe said that after her father's death her mother absconded and all contact with her was lost. When Busisiwe became pregnant she said she decided to leave home (possibly through shame) and come to work at Sebenzi. Busiswe said she disliked weeding the cane fields and decided to brew and sell sorghum beer instead. She said she buys sorghum and yeast to the value of R20 per month and makes R60 profit on her sales. Busiswe said she has both Pondo and Zulu male customers who come to buy beer from her on their way home from work. She indicated that she was not really happy with her way of life at Sebenzi: selling beer was not respectable, and her male customers tended to be noisy. She said she would like any other sort of job – except weeding. She would also like to marry the father of her child, a mineworker who comes from the same district of Transkei as she does, but 'he isn't interested in marriage'. Beer brewing is associated with prostitution, and although I did not ask about this illegal form of employment, company officials alleged that it was common practice among female casual labourers.

Women who came to the area before 1976, and who had the benefit of even a few years of formal education, were sometimes able to avoid the fate of becoming agricultural labourers by entering domestic service. Gladys S. attended a mission school at Buntingville where she passed Standard Five. When she left school she was able to find a job as a domestic with a white family at Port St. Johns. She left this job after two months because the wages were too low. She commented that payment was only R10 in Transkei whereas it would be R30 in Natal for the same job. Gladys decided to go to the Sebenzi area because she had friends working there. On arrival she found herself a job as a domestic, and, after working for ten years as a domestic and a further four as a shop assistant (as which she doubled her wages), Gladys married a local Zulu man. The marriage arrangements were taken care of by her husband's family, and *lobola* of nine head of cattle and money was paid. Gladys now lives with her husband and their two small daughters at her father-in-law's homestead in KwaZulu. She is now no longer a shop assistant but self-employed, sewing dresses and aprons, which she sells locally. Gladys says she earns about R300 per month and helps to support her extended family. As her husband is employed as an office messenger by the sugar company and also earns several hundred rands per month, compared to the *togt* workers, Gladys is well off. She admitted as much when she said that she felt more at home now in KwaZulu than she had done in Transkei, life, she said was 'much better here, because there is more money around'.

Conclusion

My findings appear to support the conclusion of Eleanor Preston-Whyte (1978: 162) that: 'migration is often motivated by absolute necessity which arises from the fact that migrant women have no man able or willing to support them in the country'. Nevertheless, it is not clear that it is mainly 'Christian women who are faced with this type of crisis, for...women from traditionalist backgrounds are largely cushioned from such problems by their membership of an on-going and cohesive family unit'. The case histories mentioned here would appear to show that, even in traditionalist homesteads, resources are simply inadequate to support a deserted or widowed brother's wife or unmarried daughter with several children. Pauline Peters comments that: 'it is possible to discern certain points of vulnerability in developmental cycles, when, given particular economic conditions a developmental phase of disadvantage or failure can feed into an exacerbating spiral and thence into the longer-term intergenerational reproduction of disadvantage' (1983: 117). Spiegel (1986: 256), writing about a Transkeian village, says: 'it would appear that the increase in female employment...may be related to a tightening up of the possibilities for reciprocal help in the village because of a lack of adequate resources for extra-household distribution, and to a growing incidence of childbirth among young unmarried women'.

In support of Preston-Whyte's contention, conventional marriage was seen as unacceptable to many of the women interviewed, who seemed to think that they would manage their lives and those of their children more successfully without a legal husband. The absence of a husband meant that these women could take lovers who were often able to contribute something towards the support of the women or their children, yet they were under no obligation to these men and were able to make their own decisions as to how to spend their wages and where to board their children. The independence that being single conferred on a woman was highly valued by many. Only one or two single girls who were heartily sick of manual labour and considered it demeaning, would have preferred to be married instead.

Lack of formal education or of previous work experience meant that casual agricultural work was the only option for most of these women in obtaining paid employment. Most informants had had either kin or friends who had previously worked in the cane fields at Sebenzi. There are few opportunities for agricultural work in Transkei itself, apart from the tea estates at Magwa, so that women who want to work are forced to look further afield. The estate at Sebenzi was relatively near Pondoland, a journey of between three and five hours by bus, and the women were willing to accept the harsh conditions attached to *togt* labour in return for a secure income.

Nattrass (1983: 9) refers to the 'impoverished African rural sector in which the major characteristics are those of rural degradation and un-der-development. This sector's ability to support its resident popula-tion has declined steadily over the past half century and with the pre-sent tendencies there seems little hope of reversing this trend'. She comments on the uneven spatial distribution of economic resources in South Africa over the past century, so that most economic activity is concentrated around major urban areas. At the same time, institutions designed to segregate races and control the movement of black people made it impossible for blacks to move into urban areas as families: 'it became increasingly difficult for such people to participate in the modern economy in any capacity other than that of a farm labourer or as a member of the migrant work force' (1983: 11).

Migrant women from Transkei are thus forced into the position of leaving behind children and other kin in order to earn cash to support them. Legislation governing the so-called independent states effective-ly prevents these women from applying for better paid jobs in factories in cities, and, despite relaxation in influx control regulations within the republic, in 1990 these restrictions were still in effect. Instead, the women are relegated to the domain of agricultural work where they are more vulnerable to abuse and exploitation. Nevertheless, despite their situation, few of those interviewed had any realistic expectations of being able to return permanently to their rural homes in Transkei, but links with the rural home were maintained, and it was seen as a safetynet if all else failed. Most of the women indicated that they expected to remain self-reliant and that, although they themselves were supporting children and/or parents, they did not expect to be supported by kin in their turn. While men were present in their lives in a peripheral sense, as former husbands, boyfriends and fathers of their children, these women remained, in terms of survival, in a world of women.

References

Bay, E., 1982 *Women and Work in Africa*, Boulder, Westview Press

Beinart, W., 1982 *The Political Economy of Pondoland: 1860–1930*, Johannesburg: Ravan Press

Bozzoli, B., 1983 'Marxism, Feminism and South African Studies', *Journal of Southern African Studies*, vol.9, no.2

Cock, J., 1980 *Maids and Madams: A Study in the Politics of Exploitation*, Johannesburg: Ravan Press

Gulbrandsen, O., 1977 'A short note on migration, based on data from Ngwaketse tribal area', *Mimeo for Workshop on Migration*, NMS Gaborone

Hunter, M., 1979 *Reaction to Conquest: Effects of Contact with Europeans on the Pondo of South Africa* (abridged edition), Cape Town: David Philip (first published by Oxford University Press, 1936)

Izzard, W., 1985 'Migrants and Mothers: case-studies from Botswana', *Journal of Southern African Studies*, vol.11, no.2

Kimble, J., 1982 'Labour Migration in Basutoland, c.1870–1885', in S. Marks and R. Rathbone (eds), *Industrialisation and Social Change in South Africa*, London: Longman

Lesthaege, R., 1990 *Reproduction and Social Organisation in Sub-Saharan Africa*, California: Oxford University Press

Mayer, P., 1961 *Townsmen or Tribesmen: Conservatism and the Process of Urbanisation in a South Afrcan City*, Cape Town: Oxford University Press

—(ed.), 1980 *Black Villagers in an Industrial Society*, Cape Town: Oxford University Press

Moore, H., 1988 *Feminism and Anthropology*, Cambridge: Polity Press

Nattrass, J., 1983 *The Dynamics of Black Rural Poverty in South Africa*, Working Paper No.1, Development Studies Unit Durban: University of Natal

Peters, P., 1983 'Gender, Developmental Cycles and Historical Process: A Critique of Recent Research on Women in Botswana', *Journal of Southern African Studies*, vol.10, no.1

Preston-Whyte, E.M., 1978 'Families without Marriage', in W. J. Argyle and E. M. Preston-Whyte (eds), *Social System and Tradition in Southern Africa*, Cape Town: Oxford University Press

Sacks, K., 1979 *Sisters and Wives: The Past and Future of Sexual Equality*, Westport, Connecticut: Greenwood Press

Spiegel, A.D., 1986 'Hard Data or Bleeding Heart Data: The Value of Qualitative Data in Research in a Rural Village in Matatiele District', *Development Southern Africa*, vol.2, no.2, pp.253–64

Stichter, S., 1985 *Migrant Laborers*, Cambridge,: Cambridge University Press

Wakelin, P., 1986 'Migrant Labour in Transkei', *IMDS Statistical Series* 2-83, Umtata: University of Transkei

Notes on Contributors

Dima Abdulrahim received her PhD from the University of Exeter for work on Palestinian refugees in Lebanon and West Germany and concentrated on issues of gender, kinship and the construction of identity. In addition to a number of articles, this work is to be published in a forthcoming book. She is currently a research officer in 'ethnic health' for the North West and North East Thames Regional Health Authorities of the National Health Service in Britain. Her work involves the study of issues of health and race among ethnic minorities in Britain.

Parminder Bhachu is an urban anthropologist and currently the Henry R. Luce Professor of Cultural Identity and Global Processes Clark University, Massachusetts. She was based at the University of California, Los Angeles, when she wrote the chapter in this book. She is the author of *Twice Migrants: East African Sikh Settlers in Britain* (1985) and co-editor of *Enterprising Women: Ethnicity, Economy and Gender Relations* (1988) and of Immigration and *Entrepreneurship: Culture, Capital, and Ethnic Networks* (1992). Her current research focuses on the construction of cultural identities, especially those of 'minorities' in Britain and the United States.

Gina Buijs is currently a lecturer in anthropology at Rhodes University, Grahamstown, South Africa. She has co-edited a book on urbanisation in South Africa and published articles on labour relations, women and migration, as well as religion and social change. Her research interests include gender issues and medical anthropology.

Marita Eastmond is a lecturer in social anthropology at Gothenburg University, Sweden, and was a Visiting Research Fellow at the Refugee Studies Programme, Queen Elizabeth House, University of Oxford when she gave the paper at the CCCRW seminar included here. She has done fieldwork in Latin America, Sweden and the United States. Her PhD dissertation, *The Dilemmas of Exile,* is an interpretative account of the exile experiences of Chilean refugees in the United States. She has also written on the political symbolism of displaced groups. She is currently involved in research on forced migration and forms of collective expression and treatment of distress in refugee populations.

196 I   Notes on Contributors

Linda Hitchcox is attached to the Institute of Social Anthropology and St Antony's College, University of Oxford, where she obtained her DPhil. She is currently researching the migration of Vietnamese asylum seekers to Hong Kong. The research is focused on development and assistance issues in Vietnam.

Stella Mascarenhas-Keyes holds a doctorate in social anthropology from London University (1987), for a thesis entitled *Migration and the International Goan Community*. She has published several articles and is currently working as a freelance consultant. She is interested in migration, non-Western Christianity, gender issues and development.

Sarah Lund **Skar** is a lecturer in social anthropology at the University of Oslo, Norway. Her doctoral dissertation was concerned with indigenous understandings of migration in Andean Peru. She has published extensively on land tenure systems, kinship and gender in this region. Her current interests include hermaneutical approaches to ethnography and the indigenous use of texts among semi-literate people.

Hazel Summerfield has a degree in human sciences from Oxford University and studied law at the City University, London, and the College of Law. She currently works as an immigration and refugee legal advisor at a law centre in the East End of London, dealing mainly with Bangladeshi and Somali clients. She has previously worked with South American, Kurdish and Afghan refugees and her interests include development issues.

Cecillie Swaisland has lectured in sociology at the City of Birmingham Polytechnic and has been a visiting fellow at the University of Mauritius and at Rhodes University, South Africa. She has an MLitt from Oxford University and is the author of *Servants and Gentlewomen to the Golden Land: The Emigration of Single Women from Britain to Southern Africa, 1820–1939* (published by Berg in 1993). She is presently a research associate at the Centre for Cross-Cultural Research on Women at Queen Elizabeth House, University of Oxford.

Name Index

Abu-Lughod, J., 40
Afshar, H., 56
Allen, C., 25
Allen, S., 104
Allende, Salvador, 37, 45
Almeida, J.C., 121n, 134
Altorki, S., 113
Altorki, S. and El Sohl, C., 100, 112
Amos, O., 99
Angell, A. and Carstairs, S., 37n
Angelou, Maya, 102n
Anwar, M., 3
Ardener, E., 15
Ardener, S., 15
Azavedo, A.E., 121n

Bach, R.L., 150
Back, L.,100n, 110
Barnardo, S., 171
Ballard, R. and C., 70
Ballhatchet, K.A., 101
Bay, E., 189
Beinart, W., 181–182
Bhachu, P., 106, 113
Bhagavani, K.-K. and Coulson, M., 99
Bonner, P., 16
Boxer, C.R., 121, 122
Bozzoli, B., 180
Brah, A., 99
Brice, A.M., 175
Bristow, E.J., 170
Bryceson, D., 17
Burdett-Coutts, A., 164

Callaway, H., 151
Cama, B., 100n
Camus-Jacques, G., 148, 151
Caplan, P., 129

Carby, H., 99
Carey, S. and Shukor, A., 85
Castles, S. and Kossack, G., 119
Cecil, (Lady) A., 171
Chadda, G.K., 111–2, 112n
Clifton, L., 102n
Cock, J., 180
Colqhoun, E., 13n, 168
Colson, E., 4, 6
Connerton, P., 3
Cunha, T., 121, 122
D'Costa, A., 121
Da Costa, P.J., 123–124
Delamont, S. and Duffin, L., 162
Derrett, J.D.M., 123
de Souza, T.R., 121n, 122
Dhillon-Kashyap, P., 111n
Dhingra, L., 102n
Doughty, O., 170
D'Souza, B.G., 124, 125
Duff-Gordon, (Lady) L., 15, 170

El Sohl, C., 113
Espinoza Soriano, W., 21

Fairley, J., 41
Faithfull, G., 173
Fawcett, J.T., 119
Fernandes, A.C., 122
Foster-Carter, O., 99
Fuller Overton, J., 102, 115

Gandhy, B., 112
Ghai, Y., 105
Gifford, Z., 112
Gilroy, P., 100n, 110
Gomes, F.L., 122
Gonçalves, J.,122

Goodwin, G., 59
Gouramma, (Princess) V., 101
Gracias, J.B.A., 122
Greg, W.R., 172
Gulbrandsen, O., 180
Guy, J., 16

Hall, S., 111
Hammerton, A.J., 173
Harrell-Bond, B.E., 159
Harrison, J.B., 122
Hely-Hutchinson, (Lady), 14–15, 169,
    171, 175
Hewitt, R., 101n, 110
Higham, C. and Moseley, R., 102
Hobsbawm, E., 41
Hodgkin, T., 146
Hoft, D., 78
Ho Xuan Huong, 146
Hunter, M., 182, 186
Huynh Sanh Thong, 146

Ifeka, C., 124, 142
Inayat Khan, N.(Madeleine), 102
Izzard, W., 180, 188

Jackson, J.B., 1
Jacobson-Widding, A., 51
James, W., 100n
Jones, S., 100n, 110
Joseph, Saud, 58, 113

Kamm, J., 164, 173
Kapferer, B., 40
Karodia, F., 102n
Kaur, Maharanee J., 101
Kay, D., 44n
Kazi, H., 58
Khan, H.R., 124
Kimble, J., 180
King, D.K., 113
Knightley, (Lady), 169
Kuper, J., 124, 125

La Brack, B., 109, 110
Leonard, K., 109, 110
Leonardo, di, M. 103n, 111n, 113
Lesthaege, R., 189
Lewis, I., 85, 89, 93, 96

Login, (Lady), 101
Lowth, A., 175, 177

Mac an Ghaill, M., 106
Mandel, R., 72
Manuel, P. 111n
Martí, J., 38
Marx, R., 59
Mascarenhas-Keyes, S., 123–125, 133
Mayer, P., 179
Mehta, A.B., 125, 133
Menezes Braganza, L. de, 123
Metha, G., 111
Messick, B., 55
Monk, V., 174
Moore, H., 7, 15, 185
Morokvasic, M., 1, 10, 66, 113,
    116, 119, 142
Morrison, Toni, 103n
Moussa, H., 157
Munscher, A., 66
Murra, J., 21, 23, 28
Nattrass, J., 193
Nelson, D., 124, 142
Neruda, Pablo, 40
Nguyen Du, 146
Nguyen Khac Vien, 147, 160

Oberon, M., 102

Panandiker, V.A. and Chaudhuri, P.N.,
    123, 142
Parkes, B.R., 172
Parmar, P., 99
Pease, F., 21
Pelzer White, C., 147
Pereira, R.G., 121n, 122n
Peteet, J., 57, 58
Peters, P., 180, 192
Phizacklea, A., 5, 10
Philpott, A., 120
Pinochet, (General), 50
Pinto, J., 124, 125
Plant, G.F., 164, 177
Poulet, G., 3
Preston-Whyte, E., 192

Rampton, B.H., 100n
Rapp, R., 73

Riquelme, H., 39
Rodriques, L.A., 122
Ross, A., 165
Rubenberg, C., 71
Rye, M., 173

Sayigh, R., 58
Saxena, R.N., 123
Schapera, I., 17
  and Roberts, S., 189
Sengupta, P., 133
Shan, S., 102n
Sharma, U.M., 129
Shoemaker, R., 21
Showalter, G., 164
Simon, R.J. and Brettell, C.B., 10, 11
Singh, A.M., 119
Skar, H., 24
Sorabji, C., 101
Spiegel, A., 192
Spivak, C.G., 103n
Spring, A., 36
Srivastava, H., 123
Stearns, P.N., 162, 177
Stichter, S., 186

Tabori, P., 50
Trivedi, P.,100
Turner, S., 49
Turner, V., 39

Van Gennep, A., 39
Van Helten, J.J. and Williams, K., 13n
Van Onselen, C., 169n
Vassal, G.M., 147, 160
Vatuk, S., 133
Vicinus, M., 13, 15
Vidál, H., 44
Visram, R., 101, 102

Wagner, G.M.M., 171
Walker, C., 15–17
Watson, J.L., 119
Wilpert, C., 71
Wollheim, R., 3
Woodside, A., 146
Worsley, P., 40

Xavier, F.N., 121n

Youssef, N.H., 119

Subject Index

Aden, 7, 89–91
Agrupacion, 44, 48
ALAM ediciores, 39
amadikazi, 186, 187
ambiguity, 39, 50
Amora, 120–141 *passim*
ancestor worship, 146
Andes, 21
animal husbandry, 26, 31, 135
apartheid, 15
archipelago, 23, 28
asylum, 5, 38
  procedures, 65
  seekers, 5 8 –60, 63–66, 77, 80,
    145, 155, 158, 160
ayllu, 24–25, 27, 33

Bangladesh, 83–98 *passim*
barrio, 37, 45–47
Basotho, 16
Bechuanaland, 17
beer brewing, 191
Berlin, 5, 9, 12, 55–82 *passim*
Boers, 166
boundary, 1–25 *passim,* 59, 62, 67, 70
  as marker, 41
  ethnic, 109
Brahmins, 120
bridewealth (*see lobola*)
Britain, 87, 100, 106, 108, 162, 166, 169
bureaucracy, 46, 52, 122, 123

California, 35, 109
caste, 106
  and Brahmins, 120, 121n, 136
  and lower, 124–126
  and upper, 126, 128

  and Sudras, 120, 136
Catholic, 9, 120–141 *passim,* 149 (*see
  also* women)
Catholic church, 38
Chanchamayo, 23–31 *passim*
children, 4, 46, 51, 52, 125, 158, 182,
  183, 194
  care of, 127–131, 186, 187
  education of, 10, 49, 185
  socialisation of, 42
  and residence rights of, 87
Chinese, 149
  culture, 146
circumcision
  female, 96–97
civil war
  Somali, 92
class, 101, 105–106, 112, 167
  middle, 162, 172
  working, 103, 169
  (*see also* social class)
climate, 166
colonialism, 21–33 *passim,*
123, 128, 149
colonies (*see* colonisation, colonialism),
  162
  and colonial empire, 162
  and colonial life, 176
colonisation, 21–33 *passim*
colonos (*see* colonisers *mitmaquna*)
conflict, 69, 72
consumption
  patterns of, 105–108
contraception, 88
culture, 146
  Mexican, 109
dependency, 145

200

deportation, 59
detention centres *(see also* refugee camps),
  7, 8, 18, 154, 158
 and detainees, 157
 and High Island, 155
 and Whitehead, 155

discrimination, 153
divorce, 12, 60, 75–76, 83, 91, 92, 97–98
 and Muslim law, 96
domestic work, 65, 190, 191
 and definition of, 167
domicile, 86, 86n
dowry, 10–11, 73, 107
 and British Asian women, 101, 112
 daaj, 106–108
 and Muslim law, 93, 97
dress *(see also* dowry), 12, 132
 head scarves, 69, 71
 Punjabi suit, 107n
 western, 123

education, 9, 10, 18, 57–58, 68, 72, 74,
  77, 79, 140, 147, 172, 185, 190, 191
 higher, 88, 149
 inadequate, 173, 193
 religious, 87, 123
 western, 123, 130
electronics industry (California), 46–47
emigration *(see also* emigration
 societies, migration, migrants),13–15
Emigration Movement, 162
 and Colonial Training Home, 173
Emigration Societies (for women), 168
 and the British Ladies
 Female Emigration Society, 164
 and the British Women's
 Emigration Society (BWEA), 164,
  165n, 173, 176
 and the Colonial Land and
 Emigration Commission, 165
 and the Female Middle
 Class Emigration Society
 (FMCES), 164, 173–174, 174n
 and the Girls' Friendly Society, 165
 and the National Vigilance
 Association, 165
 and the Society for the
 Overseas Settlement of British

Women, 143
 and the Traveller's Aid Society, 165
 and the Society for the Propagation
 of the Gospel, 165
 and the Women's Overseas
 Migration and Appointments
 Society,164
 and the Young Women's
 Christian Association, 165
employer, 137–139, 151, 168, 170
 and employee, 138, 140
employment, 65–66, 79, 91, 130, 149
 absence of, 64, 73
 Employment Gazette, 104, 104n
 in government, 150
 of women, 173ff.
 of Asian women, 103–105
 possibility of, 78, 123
  and Law Copying Society, 173
  and Society for Promoting
  the Employment of women, 173
  and Victoria Printing Press, 173
 and attestation certificates, 181
endogamy, 107
ethnicity, 71, 100, 106, 110
 and ethnic minority, 149
ethnocentrism, 99
exile, 3–5, 35–52 *passim*

family, 9, 56–57, 60–61, 69, 73, 79
 in Goa, 135
 extended, 25
feminism, 58
 black, 100
Folk songs, 146
food, 28n, 60, 63, 65, 156
 Asian, 111
 in Goa, 122–123, 132
 and cooking, 133, 158
 and staple diet, 134

Gang activity, 155, 159
gender *(see also* gender relations), 1, 11,
  66, 120
 differences, 124
 equality, 47, 56
 specificity of, 4
 subordination, 55
gender relations *(see also* gender),

47, 56–58, 60–61, 63–64, 185
and conflict, 185
Germany, 55–80 *passim*
Goa, 9, 18, 119–141 *passim*
and coastal areas, 122n, 126
and 1897 Civil Code, 123
and Land Reforms Commission, 121n
and Pednem, 127
and Salsette, 126
and Techno. Economic Survey, 122

Heim, 60–61
highlands, 31–32
Hindu, 9, 119–141 *passim*
homestead, 185, 186, 192
Hong Kong, 7–8, 18, 151, 154
households, 16–17, 47–48, 87, 180, 189
conjugal, 75
in West Berlin, 62–64, 67, 69, 73–74, 78
in Goa, 129, 136–137
nuclear, 121, 134
produce of, 147
housewives, 120
and housework, 133
hypergamy, 108

identity, 36, 48, 71–72, 105, 109
and changes of, 127
and ethnic experience, 109–111
of women, 128, 141, 159
ideology, 4, 10, 15, 41, 92
and discourse, 35
ideological goals, 42
and orientation, 68
illegitimacy, 17
immigration (*see also* migrants,
migrancy, emigration), 83–84, 88–89,
92
Immigration Act
of 1971, 85, 86n
of 1988, 86
Inca, 21, 23
income, 192
India, 108, 122
Indochinese Communist Party, 148
informal sector, 191
Isaak nomads, 85, 91
Islam, 71–72
Islamic law (*Shari'a*), 71, 74, 80

Koran, 71
and marriage, 74

KwaZulu, 184
kin, 24, 43, 130, 186–188
relationships, 27

labour, 131, 135, 191
labourers(agricultural), 127, 131, 135–
136
casual, 139
and tied labour system, 138
land, 26, 149
and *communidades,* 121–122, 127,
135, 137
and ownership in Goa, 122, 134–135
and reform in Goa, 122
and Agricultural Tenancy Act, 1964,
135n
and Land to the Tiller Act 1976
and legislation, 138n
Länder, 60, 76
language
and linguistic skills, 93
Konkani, 124
Marati, 124
Portuguese, 116–141 *passim*
and environment, 128
Lebanon, 55–82 *passim*
legislation, 15, 193
Lima, 22–23, 26, 28, 30
liminality, 39
lineage, 146
and kin, 188
lobola, 186, 192
London, 83, 106, 108

marriage, 12–13, 17, 27–28, 72–75, 87,
98, 164, 172, 176, 185, 192
contract, 97
and East African, 106
and in Goa, 128
and Muslim law, 96
Mass, performance of, 43–44, 50
Matapuquio, 1, 2, 22–31 *passim*
media,
influence of the, 111, 112
men, 2
absence of, 13, 16, 17

as fathers, 64, 68, 131, 146, 172
as husbands, 27, 30–33 *passim,* 75–77,
    107, 125, 128, 130, 187–197 *passim*
interaction with women, 67, 145–160
    passim
male migrants, 84–98 *passim,* 119,
    124, 179–181
(*see also* migrants, migrancy and
migration)
as refugees, 35–52 *passim*
Merchant Navy, 84
mestizo, 25, 25n
metaphors, 43
Middle East, 9, 125
and the Gulf, 125
migrants (*see* also migration,
migrancy), 2, 7, 11–12, 17
Bangladeshi, 6–7, 85
economic, 18, 180, 182
international, 18
internal, 126
oscillating, 1
social, 6–7, 85
migration (*see also* migrants, migrancy),
    1, 8, 16, 23, 55, 58, 67, 72, 190
associational, 9, 125
International Migration Review, 56
internal in Goa, 119–141 *passim*
International, 119–141 *passim*
minka (see work exchange), 27
mitmaquna (colonisers), 1–2, 23, 25–26,
    29, 33
moieties, 24
montana, 23
mothers, 48, 64–65, 74, 130
and mothers-in-law, 87–88
and motherhood, progressive, 128–136
    passim
music, 41–42
musical groups, 42
Muslim (*see also* Islam), 7, 69–72, 83–84
and law (*see* Islamic law)
women (*see* women, Muslim)
myth of return, 3, 86

Nairobi, 108
networks
of women,62–63
Nguyen Du, 146

nurses, 167

Palestinians, 55–82 *passim*
and the *intifada,* 80
Palestinian Liberation
Organisation (PLO), 72, 80
passivity, 155, 159
patriarchal, 8, 16–17, 99, 145
Pednem, 120, 129–130, 134, 138, 140
Peru, 1, 21–33 *passim*
piecework, 91
Pondoland, 17, 179, 181, 186
polygamy, 74, 84
Popular Unity (movement of), 37, 40,
    42, 45
produce (agricultural),
    (*see also* household) 26, 28
prostitutes, 173
purdah, 90, 99, 112, 113

Quechua, 1, 21–33 *passim*
racism, 88, 100, 109
refugees, 1–3, 7–8
camps, 55–58, 64–66, 71, 73–74, 159
Chilean, 4, 36–52 *passim*
Palestinian, 5
Vietnamese 145, 157–158
regulations, (*see also* legislation)
and influx control, 179, 183, 190
remittances, 128, 135, 180
roles, 10, 145, 176
and gender (*see* gender)
of men, 47, 64 (*see* also men)
of women, 72–77 *passim*
and work, 47, 49
Royal Navy,84

seamen, 84–85, 89–90
servant, 14, 15
domestic, 125–139 *passim,* 161–176
    passim, 180, 181, 191
lady help, 174–176
and race, 175n
sexuality (*see also* sexual relations), 67
sexual relations, 12, 27, 96
access to sex, 97
in West Berlin, 74
in detention centres, 156
Sikhs

East African 2, 9–11, 12, 106–108
Jat, 109
London, 109
Punjabi, 109–110
Ramagarhia, 109
Silicon Valley (*see* electronics
industry, California)
social class, 13, 99–113 *passim,*
161–176 *passim*
and 'distressed gentlewomen', 173
(*see also* class)
Somalia, 83–98 *passim*
and Somali Community and
Cultural Association, 95
and Somali Education Project, 95
and Somali National Movement,
84n, 89–90, 95
and SOMREC, 95–96
South Africa, 161–176 *passim*
South African Colonisation Society
(*see also* Emigration Societies), 14,
176
status, 31, 157, 168
minority, 31
strikes, 100n
subordination, 55
sugar estates (plantations), 179, 181–182
and Sebenzi, 183
Sylhet, 85

Tong 'Three Submissions', 145, 147
torture, 38, 49
Tower Hamlets, 6, 83, 95
trade unions, 37, 49
Transkei, 17, 179–193 *passim*
tribal
and Gauddas, 120–121
and Kunbis, 120–121, 126–127
umzi (*see* homestead)
United Kingdom (*see also* Britain), 83–
98 *passim*
United Nations High Commission
for Refugees (UNHCR), 60–61, 154
United States
as host country, 35–52 *passim,* 99

values (cultural), 100
victims, 156
Vietnam, 8, 145–160 *passim*
and North Vietnam, 148
violence, 6–8, 38, 42, 70, 154, 158
in the family (domestic), 70, 75, 88,
96, 96n, 97
and physical abuse, 76

wage labour, 11, 182
casual work, 185
piece work, 184
togt, 183, 184, 191, 193
war, 149
civil, 92
women
Asian, 11, 99–117 *passim*
Bangladeshi, 12, 84
Catholic, 9–10, 119–141 *passim,* 149
demand for wives, 170
East African Sikh, 2, 9–11, 12, 99–117
passim
German, 67
Hindu, 9–10
images of, 146
as migrants, 193
(*see* also migrants, migrancy, migration)
Muslim, 83, 103
Palestinian, 12, 55–82 *passim*
Punjabi, 110
Somali, 83–84, 92
subordination of, 180
Vietnamese, 7–8, 157

work, 179 (*see also* roles)
and casual work, 185
workers, agricultural, 179, 181–182
and cane cutters, 184
work exchange (see *minka*), 27
working class (see class), 169
World Council of Churches, 35n

Zambia, 36n

Books about women by members of the Centre for Cross-Cultural Research on Women, Queen Elizabeth House, Oxford include:

Narrowing the Gender Gap
G. Somjee

Gender, Culture and Empire
H. Callaway

Images of Women in Peace and War
Edited by S. Macdonald, P. Holden and S. Ardener

Anthropology and Nursing
Edited by P. Holden and J. Littlewood

Roles and Rituals for Hindu Women
Edited by J. Leslie

Rules and Remedies in Classical Indian Law
J. Leslie

Visibility and Power
Edited by L. Dube, E. Leacock and S. Ardener

Wise Daughters from Foreign Lands
E. Croll

Arab Women in the Field
Edited by S. Altorki and C. Fawzi El-Sohl

Growing Up in a Divided Society
Edited by S. Burman and P. Reynolds

The Perfect Wife
J. Leslie

Women's Religious Experience
Edited by P. Holden

Food Insecurity and the Social Division of Labour in Tanzania
D. Bryceson

Caught Up in Conflict
Edited by R. Ridd and H. Callaway

Perceiving Women
Edited by S. Ardener

Margery Perham and British Rule in Africa
Edited by A. Smith and M. Bull

The Incorporated Wife
Edited by H. Callan and S. Ardener

Fit Work for Women
Edited by S. Burman

For a complete list of books in the Berg **Cross-Cultural
Perspectives on Women** series please see page ii.